By **Terry Trainor**

LuLu Edition

Copyright 2010 Terry Trainor

LuLu Edition, License Notes
This book is licensed for your personal enjoyment only. This book may not be re-sold or given away to other people. If you would like to share this book with another person, please purchase an additional copy for each recipient. If you're reading this book and did not purchase it, or it was not purchased for your use only, then please return to Lulu .com and purchase your own copy. Thank you for respecting the hard work of this author.

Chapter 1 Champagne or Gin

Chapter 2 Seven Dials of London

Chapter 3 Edward Pierce (1630 - 1695)
Chapter 4 Thomas Neale, Edward Pierce and Seven Dials
Chapter 5 Gin

Chapre 6 Gin Craze

Chapter 7 Beer Street

Chapter 8 Newgate Prison

Chapter 9 Executions and executioners at Newgate

Chapter 10 Analysis of executions between 1783 and 1902

Chapter 11 Low Lodging Houses

Chapter 12 Carpenders Park Manor
Chapter 13 Rising to Power

Chapter 14 Carpenders Park Manor
Chapter 15 The 1832 Reform Act

Chapter 16 The History of Manors in the County of Hertford

Chapter 17 London's History

Chapter 18 Railroads and Suburban Growth

Chapter 19 Victorians and Spiritualism

Preface

The book starts from around the 1650's into the end of Victorian London 1901. This started off as a pleasant little year book for the year 1864. The reason for that date was because the central part of the book was to going to be Carpenders Park Manor about sixteen miles north of London. I still do have the part about the manor but I am using it as a quintisential perception of Victorian life. There were poems, stanza's and prose to highlight the beautiful fields, meadows and meads that surrounded the Manor. It has a family the Carews who made their money from sugar crops across the globe.

Ironically the sugar they made their money from was used to make rum which was imported into England and allowed a picture of a family in the evening taking a glass of sweetened rum onto their patio on a summer evening and enjoying all they survay. I am a historian and understand what went on and when over time. What I did not expect was a smack in the mouth from the research it led me into. As soon as the layers were wrenched off the little poems and wonderful scenery seemed unimportant.

But as I sat down and reviewed everything over I found the the year book could be used as a yard stick. It enabled me to measure the different life styles of the diferent classes. As England became rulers of the world their own back garden was a disgrace. The people that helped to build this mighty Kingdom were thrown away when they were no longer needed. After they had been squeezed and used they were dispised for their poverty. The greed and the sociopathic upperclasses saw them as sewerage something to get rid of on the first opportunity. As millions of working class people were living in slums the dispare and utter disgust at the way they lived turned towards drink. Drunkeness was the only way they could get away from the filth and the diseases that plagued their daily lives. I have already touched on the London slums in an other book,' From the Slums of London to South Oxhey in the 1940's and 1950's. While writing that book my mind set was, at first, if they had money to spend on drink they could have afforded better living conditions. What a fool I am!

Chapter 1 Champagne or Gin?

Since the dawn of man alcahol has caused wars, poverty, crime, murder and eventually death by excess. It has always been a comodity that everybody wanted there was always a ready market. One market was for people who could afford to drink. This sort of social drinking was seen as polite and being invited to party's was a level of your standing in polite society. It seems odd on one hand it was a measure of how popular a person was. Not to be invited to a party was a snub at a persons status or they had fallen out of fashion. The other was to give anything to get the money for a drink and in the late 1700's onwards it was gin. Because of its popularity Backroom distilleries soon sprang up everywhere, dripping out various noxious liquors at a feverish pace. Paramount among these homegrown spirits was gin, or, as she was commonly known, "Madam Geneva." Flavored with juniper berries and packing a wallop, Madam Geneva seamlessly supplanted brandy in the public memory, and gin drinking soon became the favorite pastime of the damned and downtrodden. Lower-class English life in the early 18th century was nasty, brutish, and short. Dubious sanitation, stifling debt laws, and a general sense of squalor combined to make the prospect of getting "drunk for a penny, dead drunk for tuppence" remarkably attractive. In a world where the conspicuous disparity between rich and poor was inescapable, people welcomed every chance they had to forget their problems. Dillon ably describes the speed with which inexpensive and widely available gin became "the avenging angel of the slums, and the comforter of the poor; she was the curse of London and the friend of market-women." This dichotomy between aristocratic and lower-class London is central to Dillon's thesis: that London's gin craze, viewed through the woozy lens of alcohol abuse, was really about class struggle. "The thing conservatives hated most about drink," he argues, "was the transformation it offered; the way it broke down traditional barriers. That was what they hated most about the entire age." So it's not altogether surprising that, soon after its arrival, conservatives began working to outlaw gin, arguing that its evils were "so many, so great, so destructive to the lower, poorer sort of people" Dillon presents his case well, seamlessly integrating his extensive research into the broader narrative. But the volume of evidence he marshals occasionally works against him. As the accounts of gin-induced crimes and deaths pile up, it's hard not to suspect that Madam Geneva's well-heeled opponents may have been motivated as much by the reasonable wish not to have to step over dead bodies in London's gutters as by any desire to oppress the lower classes. The lower classes of Londen mainly lived in the Seven Dials areas, some say the nearest thing to a village Central London had.

Chapter 2 Seven Dials of London

The Seven Dials refers to the layout of the cobbled streets in this London 'village,' which includes Monmouth Street, Earlham Street and Mercer Street. The seven streets radiate out from the central sundial Looking closely you'll see the dial only has only six faces; this is due to an earlier urban planning drawn up by Thomas Neale in the 17th century who devised the characteristic seven dials street layout to maximize the number of houses that could be built on the site so maximizing his profit. His aim was to create an affluent, upper class area similar to Covent Garden Piazza. He didn't exactly succeed. By the 1700s it was home to shops selling second and third hand goods, Charles Dickens Junior noted the shops stocking "every rarity of pigeon, fowl and rabbit, together with rare Birds such as hawks, owls and parrots, love birds and other species native and foreign". In 1690, William III granted Thomas Neale, 'the Street Proprietor', freehold of the land known as 'Marshland' or 'Cock and Pye Fields' (named after a public house on the site) in return for his raising large sums of money for the Crown. However, Neale had to purchase the remainder of the lease (which expired in 1731), for £4000, and continue to pay ground rents of £800 per annum for buildings on the land. These were very substantial financial commitments and Neale's problem was how to lay out a development which would show a profit. His solution was imaginative, financially ingenious, and still stands today in the unique street layout of Seven Dials. By adopting a star shaped plan with six radiating streets (subsequently seven were laid out), he dramatically increased the number of houses which could be built on the site; plans submitted in 1692 to Sir Christopher Wren, the Surveyor-General, for a building license showed at least 311 houses and an estate church. Construction began in March 1693 and most of the surviving building leases are dated 1694. As soon as the streets had been laid out, sewers installed and the initial corners developed, the Sundial Pillar was designed; the Pillar was topped by six sundial faces (the seventh "style" being the column itself). Neale chose Edward Pierce to build the Sundial Pillar because he was the greatest carver of his generation, working in stone, wood and marble. The first inhabitants were respectable, if not aristocratic, comprising of gentlemen, lawyers and prosperous tradesmen. However, in 1695, Neale disposed of his interest in the site and the rest of the development was carried out by individual builders over the next 15 years. Today, his involvement is recorded only by two street names - Neal Street and Neal's Yard. In the 1730's, the then owner, James Joyce, broke up the freehold, selling off the triangular sections separately. In the absence of a single freeholder, there was no-one to enforce Neale's restrictive covenants. The area became increasingly commercialized as the houses were sub-divided and converted into shops, lodgings and factories.

The Woodyard Brewery was started in 1740 and during the next hundred years spread over most of the southern part of Seven Dials. Comyn Ching, the architectural ironmongers, were in business in Shelton Street from before 1723, and elsewhere there were woodcarvers, straw hat manufacturers, pork butchers, watch repairers, wigmakers and booksellers, as well as several public houses. Though not as notorious as the St. Giles 'rookery' (slum) to the north, there were numerous incidents of mob violence in Seven Dials. In the 1790s, there was considerable re-facing or reconstruction as leases were renewed, and the façades of many of the older houses are now of that date, as are several of the painted timber shop fronts installed at the same time. The area was particularly favored by printers of ballads, political tracts and pamphlets, who occupied many of the buildings in and around Monmouth Street. By the middle of the 18th century, the area had 'declined' to the extent that 39 night-watchmen were needed to keep the peace. By the early 19th century the area became famous, together with St. Giles to the north, as the most notorious rookery in London. Shaftsbury Avenue was cut through along the north-west side of Seven Dials in 1889 as a combined work of traffic improvement and slum clearance. The Woodyard Brewery closed in 1905 and its old premises were converted into box, fruit and vegetable warehouses serving Covent Garden Market. Covent Garden Market moved out in the 1970s, which led to many changes of ownership and uses and dereliction. Seven Dials was declared a Conservation Area in 1974 and since the mid-1970s much restoration has been carried out within the parameters of the former GLC Covent Garden Action Area Plan, one aim of which was to safeguard and improve the existing physical character and fabric of the area. The reconstruction of the Sundial Pillar is a symbol of the regeneration of this area. The earliest known sundial is an Egyptian one of around 1500 BC and they were also well known in Roman times, as demonstrated in the writings of Plautus and Vitrivius. Such dials would have divided the hours of daylight into 12 'temporal' hours. The length of each hour would have changed seasonally, being longer in summer than in winter. It was an Arabian astronomer, Muhammad Ibn Jabir Al-Battani, around the middle of the ninth century, who first solved a spherical triangle, given two sides and the included angle. It was another Arabian, Ali Ibn Omar Abul-Hassan al-Marrakushi, who lived at the beginning of the 13th century, who introduced the idea of "equal hours", making all the hours of equal length. This idea did not become well established until the 14th century. After the time of the Crusades, sundials with gnomons parallel to the Earth's axis were to be found all over Europe. The mathematical knowledge necessary to construct accurate sundials, whether trigonometrical or the geometry of projection was part of the rediscovery in Renaissance Europe of ancient mathematics. This coincided with an upsurge of interest in recreational mathematics, and an everyday need for reliable public timepieces. Sundials were often erected in public places to regulate the growing number of clocks, which though popular were unreliable and inaccurate. This piece in the Athenian Mercury of 1692/3 the year before the erection of the Sundial Pillar, provides a graphic illustration of the need for sundials:

"I was walking in Covent Garden where the clock struck two, when I cam to Somerset-house by that it wanted a quarter of two, when I came to St Clements it was half past two, when I came to St Dunstans it wanted a quarter of two, by Mr. Knib's Dyal in Fleet-street is was just two, when I cam to Ludgate it was half an hour past one, when I came to Bow Church it wanted a quarter of two, by the Dyal near Stocks Market it was a quarter part two, and when I came to the Royal Exchange it wanted a quarter of two: This I aver for a Truth, and desire to know how long I was walking from Covent Garden to the Royal Exchange?" The Sundial at Seven Dials is illustrative of a common phenomenon of the time. A visitor to London in the late 17th century might have walked from Whitehall up to Seven Dials and would have passed approximately twenty sundials.

Neale was an MP for 30 years, Master of the Mint and the Transfer Office, Groom Porter, gambler and entrepreneur. His projects ranged from the development of Seven Dials, Shadwell, East Smithfield and Tunbridge Wells, to land drainage, steel and papermaking, mining in Maryland and Virginia, raising shipwrecks, to developing a dice to check on cheating at gaming. He was also the author of numerous tracts on coinage and fund-raising, and was involved in the idea of a National Land Bank, the precursor of the Bank of England. He was one of the most influential figures of late Stuart England and one of the least chronicled. He used his many contacts garnered via family, court and county connections, to act as middleman between men of money, the Court, other parties, fellow MPs and the general public. His Venetian Lottery in 1694 became the talk of the town, as did his marriage to England's richest widow and he became known as 'Golden Neal'. From 1688, Neale developed his interests as a Member of Parliament, sitting on 62 committees. In February 1678, he was appointed Groom Porter to Charles II, a post which he also held under James II and William III. In July 1678, Neale was granted the office of Master of the Mint for life but didn't take up the appointment until July 1686.

Chapter 3 Edward Pierce (1630 - 1695)

Pierce was a leading sculptor, architect and stonemason of his generation. He became well known as a sculptor and was 'much employed by Sir Christopher Wren in his carvings and designs' after the Great Fire of London in 1666. Pierce's best known works, as a sculptor, are the carved busts of Oliver Cromwell and Christopher Wren - both in the Ashmoleum Museum in Oxford. He was also employed by Wren for masonry work and design for many of the City churches and St. Paul's Cathedral. He executed wooden carving at various churches, including the wooden model for the copper dragon weathervane on the steeple of St Mary-le-Bow. His greatest work as an architect was the Bishop's Palace at Lichfield, built under his supervision and to his designs 1686-7. He died in 1695 at Surrey Street near the Thames and was buried at St Clement Danes. He left behind him an important collection of books, prints and drawings, and the original drawing of the Seven Dials Monument, now held in the British Museum, may have come from this collection.

Chapter 4 Thomas Neale, Edward Pierce and Seven Dials

Neale's development at Seven Dials arose from his connections at Court and his services to the Crown. In return for raising large sums of money through the Venetian Lottery, William III granted Neale freehold of the land knows as 'Marshland' or 'Cock and Pye Fields' (named after a public house on the site) in 1690. However, he had to purchase the remainder of the lease, which expired in 1731, for £4000, and continue to pay ground rents of £800 per annum for buildings on the land. These were very substantial financial commitments and Neale's problem was how to lay out a development which would show a profit. His solution was imaginative, financially ingenious, and still stands today in the unique street layout of Seven Dials. By adopting a star shaped plan with six radiating streets (subsequently seven were laid out), he dramatically increased the number of houses (and thus frontages) which could be built on the site. Plans showing no less that 311 houses and an estate church were submitted. In 1692 to Sir Christopher Wren, Surveyor-General applied for a building license. At that time rental values were based on the frontage, and not on the square footage. As soon as the streets had been laid out, sewers installed and the initial corners developed, the Sundial Pillar was designed. Neale chose Pierce to build the Sundial Pillar because he was the greatest carver of his generation, working in stone, wood and marble. In 1695, Neale disposed of his interest in the site and the rest of the development was carried out by individual builders over the next 15 years. Today, his involvement is recorded only by two street names - Neal Street and Neal's Yard.

Chapter 5 Gin

Backroom distilleries soon sprang up everywhere, dripping out various noxious liquors at a feverish pace. Paramount among these homegrown spirits was gin, or, as she was commonly known, "Madam Geneva." Flavored with juniper berries and packing a wallop, Madam Geneva seamlessly supplanted brandy in the public memory, and gin drinking soon became the favorite pastime of the damned and downtrodden. Lower-class English life in the early 18th century was nasty, brutish, and short. Dubious sanitation, stifling debt laws, and a general sense of squalor combined to make the prospect of getting "drunk for a penny, dead drunk for tuppence" remarkably attractive. In a world where the conspicuous disparity between rich and poor was inescapable, people welcomed every chance they had to forget their problems. Dillon ably describes the speed with which inexpensive and widely available gin became "the avenging angel of the slums, and the comforter of the poor; she was the curse of London and the friend of market-women." This dichotomy between aristocratic and lower-class London is central to Dillon's thesis: that London's gin craze, viewed through the woozy lens of alcohol abuse, was really about class struggle. "The thing conservatives hated most about drink," he argues, "was the transformation it offered; the way it broke down traditional barriers. That was what they hated most about the entire age." So it's not altogether surprising that, soon after its arrival, conservatives began working to outlaw gin, arguing that its evils were "so many, so great, so destructive to the lower, poorer sort of people" Dillon presents his case well, seamlessly integrating his extensive research into the broader narrative. But the volume of evidence he marshals occasionally works against him. As the accounts of gin-induced crimes and deaths pile up, it's hard not to suspect that Madam Geneva's well-heeled opponents may have been motivated as much by the reasonable wish not to have to step over dead bodies in London's gutters as by any desire to oppress the lower classes. Even so, when public drunkenness reached epidemic proportions, the laws passed treated the common man much more harshly than the country-estate tippler. Certainly gin advocates recognized this disparity, claiming that the laws specifically targeted the poor and dirty, while Sir Drink-A-Lot and Lord Sousebury went unpunished. When personal rights are abridged in the name of the public good, conflict usually ensues, and gin-soaked London was no exception. Every time the government attempted to regulate the gin trade, plebeians rioted in the streets, preachers thundered in pulpits and pamphlets, and, in back-alley dram shops, things continued much as they had before. Eventually, though, all crazes end. By the late 1750s, Londoners had apparently had enough, and gin drinking ceased to be a public menace. Dillon attributes this to wiser governmental policies (read: supply-side taxation), and the rise of the middle class. A spate of public reforms had unexpectedly rendered London livable, giving rise to a new class of people who saved their money rather than spent it and preferred sober entertainments, such as prayer. With the decline of the vice-addled populace, writes Dillon, Madam Geneva became the benign lady we know and enjoy today. So was the gin craze a function of urban decay? Dillon suggests that it was, and that it has implications for modern times. He draws a largely convincing parallel with the war on drugs. After all, both crazes featured rampant substance abuse and impotent governmental attempts at curtailing it. But Dillon's analysis is hobbled by a few unresolved issues. Gin drinking was much more unabashedly mainstream than drug use is, as were its proponents, which rendered gin advocacy more socially acceptable than, say, marijuana advocacy. Madam Geneva boasted Daniel Defoe and several powerful lobbying groups among her supporters, respected voices that Parliament could not ignore and that could speak freely without fear of being marginalized. The best that drug war opponents can muster up, however, is Snoop Dogg--one reason why their cause has not been embraced by the mainstream. But that debate may be academic. Dillon makes the point that, once the genie is out of the bottle, so to speak, it can't be legislated back in--though that hasn't stopped people from trying throughout the centuries. As long as pedants and public moralists feel compelled to impose behavioral standards on the poor and disenfranchised, there will be gin laws, well-intentioned but ineffective; and as long as people require an escape from the toil of everyday life, there will be gin. Drawn from the past, applied to the present, this is the lesson of Dillon's fine book. It is history as it should be: entertaining without being glib, informative without being didactic. Gin might not be as harmful as its spirituous namesake, but it is certainly just as addictive.

Chapre 6 Gin Craze

The gin crisis was genuinely severe. From 1689 onward, the English government had encouraged the industry of distilling, as it helped prop up grain prices, which were then low, and increase trade, particularly with colonial possessions. Imports of French wine and spirits were banned to encourage the industry at home. Indeed, Daniel Defoe and Charles Davenant, among others, particularly Whig economists, had seen distilling as one of the pillars of British prosperity in the balance of trade.[1] (Both later changed their minds—by 1703 Davenant was warning that, "Tis a growing fad among the common people and may in time prevail as much as opium with the Turks",[2] while by 1727 Defoe was arguing in support of anti-gin legislation.[3]) In the heyday of the industry there was no quality control whatsoever (gin was frequently mixed with turpentine), and licences for distilling required only the application. When it became apparent that copious gin consumption was causing social problems, efforts were made to control the production of the spirit. The Gin Act 1736 imposed high taxes on sales of gin, forbade the sale of the spirit in quantities of less than two gallons, and required an annual payment of £50 for a retail licence. It had little effect beyond increasing smuggling and driving the distilling trade underground.[4] Various loopholes were exploited to avoid the taxes, including selling gin under pseudonyms such as "Ladies' Delight", "Bob", "Cuckold's Delight" and the none-too-subtle "Parliament gin".[5] The prohibitive duty was gradually reduced and finally abolished in 1743. Francis Place later wrote that enjoyments for the poor of this time were limited: they had often had only two, "sexual intercourse and drinking", and that "drunkenness is by far the most desired" as it was cheaper and its effects more enduring.[6] By 1750, over a quarter of all residences in St Giles parish in London were gin shops, and most of these also operated as receivers of stolen goods and coordinating spots for prostitution. Set in the parish of St Giles, a notorious slum district which Hogarth used in several of his works around this time, *Gin Lane* depicts the squalor and despair of a community raised on gin. Desperation, death and decay pervade the scene. The only businesses that flourish are those which serve the gin industry: gin sellers; distillers (the aptly named Kilman); the pawnbroker where the avaricious Mr. Gripe greedily takes the vital possessions (the carpenter offers his saw and the housewife her cooking utensils) of the alcoholic residents of the street in return for a few pennies to feed their habit; and the undertaker, for whom Hogarth implies at least a handful of new customers from this scene alone. Most shockingly, the focus of the picture is a woman in the foreground, who, addled by gin and driven to prostitution by her habit —as evidenced by the syphilitic sores on her legs— lets her baby slip unheeded from her arms and plunge to its death in the stairwell of the gin cellar below. Half-naked, she has no concern for anything other than a pinch of snuff.[a] This mother was not such an exaggeration as she might appear: in 1734, Judith Dufour reclaimed her two-year-old child from the workhouse where it had been given a new set of clothes; she then strangled it and left the infant's body in a ditch so that she could sell the clothes (for 1s. 4d.) to buy gin.[10] In another case, an elderly woman, Mary Estwick, let a toddler burn to death while she slept in a gin-induced stupor.[11] Such cases provided a focus for anti-gin campaigners such as the indefatigable Thomas Wilson and the image of the neglectful mother became increasingly central to anti-gin propaganda.[11] Sir John Gonson, whom Hogarth featured in his earlier *A Harlot's Progress,* turned his attention from prostitution to gin and began prosecuting gin-related crimes with severity.

The gin cellar, "Gin Royal", below advertises its wares with the slogan:

Drunk for a penny
Dead drunk for twopence
Clean straw for nothing

Other images of despair and madness fill the scene: a lunatic cavorts in the street beating himself over the head with a pair of bellows while holding a baby impaled on a spike the dead child's frantic mother rushes from the house screaming in horror; a barber has taken his own life in the dilapidated attic of his barber-shop, ruined because nobody can afford a haircut or shave; on the steps, below the woman who has let her baby fall, a skeletal pamphlet-seller rests, perhaps dead of starvation, as the unsold moralising pamphlet on the evils of gin-drinking, *The Downfall of Mrs Gin*, slips from his basket. An ex-soldier, he has pawned most of his clothes to buy the gin which shares space in his basket with the pamphlet which denounces it. Next to him sits a black dog, a symbol of despair and depression. Outside the distiller's a fight has broken out, and a crazed cripple raises his crutch to strike his blind compatriot. Images of children on the path to destruction also litter the scene: aside from the dead baby on the spike and the child falling to its death, a baby is quieted by its mother with a cup of gin, and in the background of the scene an orphaned infant bawls naked on the floor as the body of its mother is loaded into a coffin on orders of the beadle.[13] Two young girls who are wards of the parish of St Giles indicated by the badge on the arm of one of the girls each take a glass. Hogarth also chose the slum of St Giles as setting for the first scene of *The Four Stages of Cruelty* which he issued almost simultaneously with *Beer Street* and *Gin Lane*. Tom Nero, the central character of the *Cruelty* series wears an identical arm badge. In front of the pawnbroker's door, a starving boy and a dog fight over a bone, while next to them a girl has fallen asleep; approaching her is a snail, emblematic of the sin of sloth. In the rear of the picture the church of St. George's Church, Bloomsbury can be seen, but it is a faint and distant image, and the picture is composed so it is the pawnbroker's sign which forms a huge corrupted cross for the steeple: the people of Gin Lane have chosen to worship elsewhere.

Chapter 7 Beer Street

The first and second states of *Beer Street* featured the blacksmith lifting a Frenchman with one hand. The 1759 reissue replaced him with a joint of meat and added the pavior and housemaid. In comparison to the sickly hopeless denizens of Gin Lane, the happy people of Beer Street sparkle with robust health and bonhomie. "Here is all is joyous and thriving. Industry and jollity go hand in hand".[15] The only business that is in trouble is the pawnbroker: Mr Pinch lives in the one poorly-maintained, crumbling building in the picture. In contrast his Gin Lane counterpart, the prosperous Gripe, who displays expensive-looking cups in his upper window (a sign of his flourishing business), Pinch displays only a wooden contraption, perhaps a mousetrap, in his upper window, while he is forced to take his beer through a window in the door, which suggests his business is so unprofitable as to put the man in fear of being seized for debt. The sign-painter is also shown in rags, but his role in the image is unclear. The rest of the scene is populated with doughty and good-humoured English workers. It is George II's birthday (30 October) (indicated by the flag flying on the church of St Martin-in-the-Fields in the background) and the inhabitants of the scene are no doubt toasting his health. Under the sign of the "Barley Mow", a blacksmith or cooper sits with a foaming tankard in one hand and a leg of ham in the other. Together with a butcher-his steel hangs at his side-they laugh with the pavior (sometimes identified as a drayman) as he distracts a housemaid from her errand. Ronald Paulson suggests a parallel between the trinity of signs of ill-omen in *Gin Lane*, the pawnbroker, distiller, and undertaker, and the trinity of English "worthies" here, the blacksmith, pavior, and butcher. Close by a pair of fish-sellers rest with a pint and a porter sets down his load to refresh himself. In the background, two men carrying a sedan chair pause for drink, while the passenger remains wedged inside, her large hoop skirt pinning her in place.[b] On the roof, the builders, who are working on the publican's house above the "Sun" tavern share a toast with the master of a tailor's workshop. In this image it is a barrel of beer that hangs from a rope above the street, in contrast to the body of the barber in *Gin Lane*. The inhabitants of both Beer Street and Gin Lane are drinking rather than working, but in Beer Street the workers are resting after their labours—all those depicted are in their place of work or have their wares or the tools of their trade about them-while in Gin Lane the people drink instead of working.[17] Exceptions to this rule come, most obviously, in the form of those who profit from the vice in *Gin Lane*, but in *Beer Street* Hogarth takes the opportunity to make another satirical statement. Aside from the enigmatic sign-painter, the only others engaged in work in the scene are the tailors in an attic. The wages of journeyman tailors was the subject of an ongoing dispute, which was finally settled by arbitration at the 1751 July Quarter sessions (in the journeymen's favour). Here Hogarth shows them continuing to toil while all the other inhabitants of the street, including their master, pause to refresh themselves. Hogarth also takes the opportunity to comment on artistic pretensions. Tied up together in a basket and destined for use as scrap at the trunk-maker are George Turnbull's *On Ancient Painting*, *Hill on Royal Societies*, *Modern Tragedies*, *Polticks vol. 9999* and William Lauder's *Essay on Milton's Use and Imitation of the Moderns in His "Paradise Lost"*, all examples, real and imagined, of the type of literature that in Hogarth's opinion fabricated connections between art and politics and sought out aesthetic connections that did not exist. Lauder's work was an outright hoax which painted Milton as a plagiarist. Hogarth intended *Beer Street* to be viewed first to make *Gin Lane* more shocking but it is also a celebration of Englishness and depicts of the benefits of being nourished by the native beer. No foreign influences pollute what is a fiercely nationalistic image. An early impression showed a scrawny Frenchman being ejected from the scene by the burly blacksmith who in later prints holds aloft a leg of mutton or ham (Paulson suggests the Frenchman was removed to prevent confusion with the ragged sign-painter).[19] There is a celebration of English industriousness in the midst of the jollity: the two fish-sellers sing the *New Ballad on the Herring Fishery* (by Hogarth's friend, the poet John Lockman), while their overflowing baskets bear witness to the success of the revived industry; the King's speech displayed on the table makes reference to the "Advancement of Our Commerce and the cultivating Art of Peace"; and although the workers have paused for a break, it is clear they are not idle. The builders have not left their workplace to drink; the master tailor toasts them from his window but does not leave the attic; the men gathered around the table in the foreground have not laid their tools aside. Townley's patriotic verses make further reference to the contrast between England and France: Paulson sees the images as working on different levels for different classes. The middle classes would have seen the pictures as a straight comparison of "good" and "evil" while the lower classes would have seen the connection between the prosperity of Beer Street and the poverty of Gin Lane. He focuses on the well-fed woman wedged into the sedan chair at the rear of *Beer Street* as a cause of the ruin of the gin-addled woman who is the principal focus of *Gin Lane*. The free-market economy espoused in the King's address and practised in Beer Street leaves the exponents prosperous and corpulent but at the same time makes the poor poorer. For Paulson the two prints are a depiction of the results of a move away from a paternalistic state towards an unregulated market economy. Further, more direct, contrasts are made with the woman in the sedan chair and those in *Gin Lane*: the woman fed gin as she is wheeled home in a barrow and the dead woman being lifted into her coffin are both mirror images of the hoop-skirted woman reduced to madness and death.

Sign-painter

Paulson suggests that sign-painter's stance forms what Hogarth called the "Line of Beauty"

The sign-painter is the most difficult figure of the two images to characterise. In preliminary sketches he appeared as another jolly fat archetype of Beer Street, but by the time of the first print Hogarth had transformed him into a threadbare, scrawny, and somewhat dreamy character who has more in common with the inhabitants of Gin Lane than those who populate the scene below him.[9] Most simply he may be a subtle aside on the artist's status in society he carries the palette that Hogarth had made his trademark and which can be seen in several of his self-portraits. However he is painting a sign advertising gin, so his ragged appearance could equally reflect the rejection of the spirit by the people of Beer Street. He may be also be a resident of Gin Lane, and Hogarth includes him as a connection to the other scene, and as a suggestion that the government's initial policy of encouraging the distillation of gin may be the cause of both Gin Lane's ruin and Beer Street's prosperity. He is ignored by the inhabitants of Beer Street as they ignore the misery of Gin Lane itself.[21] Paulson suggests that he is the lone "beautiful" figure in the scene. The corpulent types that populate *Beer Street* would later feature as representations of ugliness in Hogarth's *The Analysis of Beauty*, while the painter, as he leans back to admire his work, forms the serpentine shape that Hogarth identified as the "Line of Beauty". Thomas Clerk, in his 1812 *The Works of William Hogarth*, writes that the sign-painter has been suggested as a satire on Jean-Étienne Liotard (called John Stephen by Clerk), a Swiss portrait painter and enameller whom Horace Walpole praised for his attention to detail and realism, mentioning he was "Devoid of imagination, and one would think memory, he could render nothing but what he saw before his eyes".[22] In his notes in Walpole's *Anecdotes of painting in England*, James Dallaway adds a footnote to this statement about Liotard claiming "Hogarth has introduced him, in several instances, alluding to this want of genius".

Influences

Beer Street and *Gin Lane* with their depictions of the deprivation of the wasted gin-drinkers and the corpulent good health of the beer-drinkers, owe a debt to Pieter Bruegel the Elder's *La Maigre Cuisine* and *La Grasse Cuisine* engraved by Pieter van der Heyden in 1563, which shows two meals, one of which overflows with food and is populated by fat diners, while in the other the emaciated guests squabble over a few meagre scraps. Brueghel's compositions are also mirrored in the layers of detail in Hogarth's two images.[24][25] Inspiration for these two prints and *The Four Stages of Cruelty* probably came from his friend Fielding: Hogarth turned from the satirical wit of

Marriage à-la-mode in favour of a more cutting examination of crime and punishment with these prints and Industry and Idleness at the same time that Fielding was approaching the subject in literature.[26] Paulson thinks it likely that they planned the literature and the imagery together as a campaign.

Reception

Charles Lamb picked out this detail of a funeral procession in Gin Lane as a mark of Hogarth's skill: "extending of the interest beyond the bounds of the subject could only have been conceived by a great genius". Charles Knight said that in Beer Street Hogarth had been "rapt beyond himself' and given the characters depicted in the scene an air of "tipsy jollity". Charles Lamb considered Gin Lane to be "sublime", and focused on the almost invisible funeral procession that Hogarth had added beyond the broken-down wall at the rear of the scene as mark of his genius. His comments on Gin Lane formed the centre of his argument to rebut those who considered Hogarth a vulgar artist because of his choice of vulgar subjects: There is more of imagination in it-that power which draws all things to one,-which makes things animate and inanimate, beings with their attributes, subjects and their accessories, take one colour, and serve to one effect. Every thing in the print, to use a vulgar expression. Every part is full of "strange images of death." It is perfectly amazing and astounding to look at. Both John Nichols and Samuel Felton felt that the inclusion of Turnbull's work in the pile of scrap books was harsh, Felton going as far as to suggest Hogarth should have read it before condemning it. After the Tate Britain's 2007 exhibition of Hogarth's works, the art critic Brian Sewell commented that "Hogarth saw it all and saw it straight, without Rowlandson's gloss of puerile humour and without Gainsborough's gloss of sentimentality", but in a piece entitled "Hogarth the Ham-fisted" condemned his heavy-handedness and lack of subtlety which made every of his images an "over-emphatic rant in his crude insistence on excessive and repetitive detail to reinforce a point". The reception by the general public is difficult to gauge. Certainly one shilling put the prints out of reach for the poorest people, and those who were pawning their clothes for gin money would not be tempted to buy a print, but there is evidence that Hogarth's prints were in wide circulation even among those that would have regarded them as a luxury, and there are records from the 18th century indicating that his works were used for moral instruction by schoolmasters.[32] At any rate, the Gin Act passed in no small measure as the result of Fielding and Hogarth's propaganda was considered a success: gin production fell from 7 million imperial gallons (32,000,000 L) in 1751 to 4.25 million imperial gallons (19,300,000 L) in 1752, the lowest level for twenty years. By 1757, George Burrington reported, "We do not see the hundreth part of poor wretches drunk in the street". Social changes, quite apart from the Gin Act (among them the increase in the price of grain after a series of bad harvests) were reducing the dependence of the poor on gin, but the problem did not disappear completely: in 1836, Charles Dickens still felt it an important enough issue to echo Hogarth's observations in *Sketches by Boz*. Like Hogarth, Dickens noted that poverty rather than gin itself was the cause of the misery: A later engraving of *Beer Street* by Samuel Davenport (probably for Trusler's *Hogarth Moralized*) had slight variations from all of the Hogarth states. Gin-drinking is a great vice in England, but wretchedness and dirt are a greater; and until you improve the homes of the poor, or persuade a half-famished wretch not to seek relief in the temporary oblivion of his own misery, with the pittance which, divided among his family, would furnish a morsel of bread for each, gin-shops will increase in number and splendour. The vast numbers of prints of *Beer Street* and *Gin Lane* and *The Four Stages of Cruelty* may have generated profits for Hogarth, but the wide availability of the prints meant that individual examples did not generally command high prices. While there were no paintings of the two images to sell, and Hogarth did not sell the plates in his lifetime, variations and rare impressions existed and fetched decent prices when offered at auction. The first (proof) and second states of *Beer Street* were issued with the image of the Frenchman being lifted by the blacksmith, this was substituted in 1759 by the more commonly seen third state in which the Frenchman was replaced by the pavior or drayman fondling the housemaid, and a wall added behind the sign-painter. Prints in the first state sold at George Baker's sale in 1825 for £2.10s, but a unique proof of *Gin Lane* with many variations, particularly a blank area under the roof of Kilman's, sold for £15.15s. at the same sale.[e] Other minor variations on *Gin Lane* exist - the second state gives the falling child an older face, perhaps in an attempt to diminish the horror,[35] but these too were widely available and thus inexpensive. Copies of the originals by other engravers, such as Ernst Ludwig Riepenhausen, Samuel Davenport and Henry Adlard were also in wide circulation in the 19th century.

Chapter 8 Newgate Prison

The Gaol by Kelly Grovier

"Hell itself, in comparison, cannot be such a place" suggested an unfortunate resident of Newgate Prison in 1662. Kelly Grovier's pacy account of the institution from its founding in 1188 by Henry II through its renovation by Richard Whittington in the 15th century, its various reconstructions following fires, to demolition in 1902 examines the horror of the place with relish: "The mingled stench of disease and faeces and the cacophonous din of wailing and screeching in the maze of unventilated wards was unutterably horrifying."

The prison was attacked and burnt down during the Gordon riots in 1780 and, while it did not loom so large in the minds of the locals as did the Bastille for Parisians sacked only a few years later - it was a potent symbol. It would be possible to write its history by simply looking at the novels, plays, pamphlets, images and ballads that it has inspired. Ben Jonson spent time there, as did Christopher Marlowe, who included the prison into his later plays; Daniel Defoe wrote biographies of two celebrated inmates, before fictionalising the prison in Moll Flanders; John Gay's savagely satirical The Beggar's Opera was initially called "The Newgate Opera"; William Hogarth and Gustave Doré illustrated the miserable place; and Dickens returned to the scene near-obsessively, including it almost as an extra character in Nicholas Nickleby and Oliver Twist. Yet, as Grovier makes clear, Newgate was also a place of performance and self-fashioning, where prisoners could become celebrities for a brief time. Those who spent time in Newgate's various manifestations (the jail was rebuilt at least three times) include Jack Shephard, a serial absconder, who received more than a thousand visitors when he was rearrested after his fourth escape, and Claude Duval, whose execution in 1670 was, according to a contemporary account, attended by "a great company of ladies...their cheeks blubber'd with tears". These examples are far from unusual. Plunkett and MacLaine, Anne Askew, Captain Kidd, James Hind, Wat Tyler and Elizabeth Brownrigg all spent time in Newgate. The accounts of their deeds - in pamphlet form, in pulp biographies, and in the massively popular Newgate Calendar - took hold in the public imagination and created a demand that stirred the writings of Defoe and Dickens. The prison also contributed to the developing cultural importance and visibility of crime, with ballads, woodcuts and songs representing the famed criminals to the populace. The prison is a repository of hundreds of stories and Grovier retells them with some vim. The source materials allow him to encompass all manner of subjects: from the reforming work of Samuel Johnson, Elizabeth Fry and Jeremy Bentham, to accounts of the prison as an institution, with its own economy, vocabulary ("Newgate Cant") and social organisation. Grovier's treatment of the material organisation of the place is excellent, ranging from its physical layout to the design of the gallows, from the class implications of the renovations, to the role of the various corrupt officers in administering "justice" ("Garnish, Captain, garnish" shouts Gay's keeper Lockit, asking for a fee to make Macheath's stay more comfortable). These stories are not new - Stephen Halliday's Newgate: London's Prototype of Hell (2006) mined a similar seam of sensation and social history - but they remain gripping. Newgate's role in the evolution of London, in the creation of crime in the public imagination, in the development of the concept of the prison, is unmatched, and Grovier relates it compellingly.

Newgate

It is not possible to determine when Newgate first became a prison or when exactly the new gatehouse itself was originally built. Newgate was to be London's 5th gate into the city. There are reliable records going back to 1218 of it being used to house criminals. It was finally demolished in 1904 having been rebuilt at least

twice along the way.
A new prison at Newgate was begun in 1770 and proceeded slowly. Before it could be finished, the building was badly damaged by fire during the Gordon riots of 1780 and it was not finally completed until 1785. This building was then used in that form until 1856 when it was remodelled internally to reflect the new perceptions of what a prison should be like. London's Millbank and Pentonville prisons had been designed to be the first modern prison and to practice the new "penitentiary system." This rebuild was very short lived as the building was very badly damaged, again by fire in 1877, and had to be largely rebuilt. As a result of the Prisons Act of 1877, Newgate ceased to be an ordinary prison in 1882 and was used only for those awaiting trial and prisoners sentenced to death awaiting execution. Newgate had the great advantage, from the authorities' point of view at least, of being next door to the Central Criminal Court (Old Bailey) which was the trial venue for all of London's most serious criminals. It saved the cost and security risk of transporting prisoners by horse drawn van from other prisons for their trial. The Central Criminal Court Act of 1856 permitted prisoners from anywhere in the country accused of a very serious offence to be tried at the Old Bailey. The Act was passed to allow for poisoner, William Palmer (from Rugeley in Staffordshire), to get a fair trial free from local prejudice. The advent of an efficient railway system had made it possible to transport prisoners over considerable distances. Palmer was returned to Stafford prison for his execution. Similarly, Maria and Frederick Manning and Kate Webster were kept at Newgate during their trials and then returned to the Surrey county gaol at Horsemonger Lane for execution. Newgate closed for good in late May 1902 so that the new Central Criminal Court which opened in 1907 (always known as the Old Bailey) could be built on the site. Here is a picture of Newgate just before demolition. The Debtor's door through which the condemned prisoners exited in the days of public hangings and the site of the gallows at that time are marked. Up to 1877, in its several incarnations, Newgate was the principal prison for London and Middlesex and housed all manner of prisoners of both sexes, including those remanded in custody and prisoners awaiting transportation or

execution and those imprisoned for debt. When Newgate closed, its male prisoners and indeed its gallows were transferred to Pentonville while the female prisoners were moved to Holloway prison, which had been recently renovated and turned into London's first women's prison. Conditions in Newgate in the early part of the 19th century were appalling and led to great efforts by early prison reformers such as John Howard and Elizabeth Fry to improve things. Elizabeth Fry was deeply shocked by the conditions that women were detained under, in the Female Quarter as the women's area was known, when she visited the prison in 1816. She found the place crowded with half naked women and their children. The women were typically waiting for transfer to the prison ships that would take them to the Colonies. Women were brought to Newgate from county prisons in the south of England to await transportation and kept there for weeks or months until a ship was available. Many of the ordinary women prisoners were drunk, due to the availability of cheap gin, and some were clearly deranged. They were kept in leg irons if they could not afford to pay the Keeper of Newgate for "easement." Fry formed an "Association for the improvement of the female prisoners in Newgate" and as part of that, set up a school within the prison for the younger children in 1817. The following year, she gave evidence to Parliamentary Committee on her findings. She was able to get a proper Matron appointed to look after the women in 1817 and conditions slowly improved. Prisoners under sentence of death were kept shackled and apart from other prisoners and in the case of murderers, fed on bread and water for the final 2-3 days of their miserable lives before meeting the hangman. Their only permitted visitors were prison staff and the Ordinary (prison chaplain). Conditions improved after 1834, condemned prisoners spending around 2-3 weeks awaiting execution after the law was changed to allow three clear Sundays to pass before they were hanged. They were no longer kept in irons and were given better food than the ordinary prisoners. They were also permitted visits by their families and friends. As London was the crime capital of England, so it was that Newgate was the execution capital and between 1783 and 1902, a total of 1,169 people were put to death there or nearby (12 or 13 hangings being carried out at other locations prior to 1834). The total comprised 1,120 men and 49 women. The last remnants of the "Bloody Code" as it was known remained in force up to 1836. Over 200 felonies were punishable by death in 1800, although in practice people were only executed for about 20 of them. See analysis below. Those convicted of the more minor ones, although sentenced to death, typically had their punishment reduced to transportation. The concept of imprisonment as a punishment only really came in after 1840. Transportation ended around 1888. Public executions were carried outside Newgate in the lane known as the Old Bailey from the 9th of December 1783 (following the ending of hangings at Tyburn). It is unclear where the gallows was erected before 1809 - contemporary reports talking of "outside Newgate" and "in the Old Bailey." After 1809, almost all hangings took place on the portable gallows in front of the Debtors' Door and continued here up to the 25th of May 1868, when Michael Barrett became the last to hang for the Clerkenwell bomb outrage that killed seven people. Three women were burned at the stake in the Old Bailey, for the crime of coining which was deemed to be high treason. They were Phoebe Harris, Margaret Sullivan and Catherine Murphy. In all three cases, they were first hanged until they were dead and then their bodies burnt. Similarly, the Cato Street conspirators who had also been convicted of high treason were sentenced to be hanged, drawn and quartered there (the male punishment for high treason), but in fact were hanged and then beheaded. There were to be 567 public hangings, including those of 25 women, between January 1800 and May 1868. These drew huge crowds, especially if one of the prisoners was notorious. From 1752 to 1832, the bodies of those executed for murder were taken to Surgeon's Hall in the Old Bailey where they were publicly anatomised. Up to 1834, the bodies of persons executed for crimes other than murder could be returned to relatives for a fee. There were only two confirmed executions at Newgate in the years 1834-1836, those of John Smith and James Pratt, who were hanged for buggery on the 27th of November 1835. After 1836, only murderers were to be hanged at Newgate and their bodies were buried in unmarked graves within the walls. Ninety nine men and eight women were to suffer for this crime between 1837 and 1902. Of this total, 58 men and five women were executed in private between the 8th of September 1868 and the 6th of May 1902 when George Wolfe became the last person to be executed here. There were four double hangings, a treble and a quadruple hanging during this period.

Chapter 9 Executions and executioners at Newgate

From around 1771 to September 1786, when he died, Edward Dennis was the official executioner and carried out 201 hangings and the three burnings at Newgate. He had previously officiated at Tyburn from 1771. On Tuesday, the 9th of December 1783, he and William Brunskill hanged nine men and one woman (Frances Warren) side by side on the "New Drop" at Newgate's first execution (see picture). Note that they all have white nightcaps drawn over their heads. Sessions, as trials at the Old Bailey were known at that time, were held eight times a year by then and it was normal to sentence those found guilty of crimes other than murder in groups at the end of the trial day. Murderers were sentenced at the end of their individual trials. Those sentenced to death for felony and not "respited" (commuted to transportation) were also hanged in groups - men and women together. Multiple executions were the norm at this time and took place normally around six weeks after the Sessions finished and the Recorder of the Old Bailey had prepared and presented his report indicating which prisoners were recommended for reprieve and which were to be executed. From July 1752 onwards, murderers had to be hanged within two days of their sentence, unless this would have been a Sunday, which meant that they were typically hanged on a Monday and therefore usually separately from ordinary felons, this day continuing to be used at Newgate for murderers up to 1880. Ordinary criminals could be hanged on any day of the week, Wednesdays being the most common one. Prisoners were led from the "Condemned hold" into the Press yard where their leg irons were removed and their wrists and arms tied. They were attended by the Ordinary and when they had all been prepared, were led across the yard to the Lodge and out through the Debtor's Door and up a short flight of steps onto the gallows. Dennis hanged 95 men and one woman

(Elizabeth Taylor for burglary) between February and December of 1785 at Newgate, with 20 men being hanged on one day alone (Wednesday, the 2nd of February). Dennis was often assisted at these marathons by the man who was to become his successor, William Brunskill, who went on to hang an amazing 537 people outside Newgate as principal hangman. He also executed a further 68 at Horsemonger Lane Gaol in the County of Surrey between 1800 (when it opened) and 1814. John Langley took over from him in 1814 and hanged 37 men and three women in his three years in office, including Eliza Fenning. Click here for her story. He died in April 1817 and was succeeded by James Botting who was known as "Jemmy". Botting hanged 42 men and two women during his two year tenure, during which in 1818, shoplifting was removed from the list of capital crimes at the instigation of Sir Samuel Romilly. The gallows used by Dennis, Brunskill and Botting had two parallel beams from which a maximum of a dozen criminals could be hanged at once. (see picture) The platform was 10 feet long by 8 feet wide and was released by moving the lever or "pin" acting on a drawbar under the drop. The condemned were given a drop of between one and two feet so death was hardly ever "instantaneous." On one occasion, presumably because the mechanism had failed a simple beam and cart was used to get the prisoners suspended, as had been done at Tyburn. This was for the execution of Ann Hurle and Methuselah Spalding in February 1804. This lapse attracted severe criticism in the press. In July 1819, James Foxen assumed the position having previously assisted Botting, and hanged 207 men and six women over the next 11 years. The five Cato Street conspirators became the last to suffer hanging and beheading on Monday, May 1st, 1820, for conspiring to murder several members of the Cabinet. Foxen was assisted by Thomas Cheshire for this high profile execution and an unnamed and secret person who actually cut off the traitor's heads. (see picture). In view of their crime, their bodies were the property of the Crown and were buried within Newgate.

Thomas Cheshire, or Old Cheese as he was known, officiated as principal at a quadruple hanging on the 24th of March 1829 of three highway robbers and one man convicted of stealing in a dwelling house. These were Cheshire's only executions as principal at Newgate. The gallows was now modified, from then on, having only one beam with capacity for six persons. In 1820, there were 42 executions on seven "hanging days" at Newgate, all carried out by James Foxen. Not one of these was for murder. Twelve were for "uttering" forged notes, 12 for robbery or burglary, and five for highway robbery. At this time, murderers, rapists, arsonists, forgers, coiners and highwaymen were virtually always executed and were seldom offered transportation. The largest multiple execution in 1820 was that of eight men on the 11th of December and the smallest was of three men on the 24th of October. Sarah Price was the only woman to suffer in 1820, alongside six men, for "uttering" forged bank notes or coins on the 5th of December.

On the eve of a hanging, the portable New Drop gallows was brought out by a team of horses and placed in front of the Debtor's Door of Newgate. Large crowds gathered around it and it would be guarded by soldiers with pikes. Wealthy people could pay as much as £10 for a seat in a window overlooking the gallows at the hanging of a notorious criminal. At around 7.30 a.m., the condemned prisoners were led from their cells into the Press Yard where the Sheriff and the Ordinary (prison chaplain) would meet them. Their leg irons were removed by the prison blacksmith and Foxen and his assistant would bind their wrists in front of them with cord and also place a cord round their body and arms at the elbows. White nightcaps were placed on their heads. The prisoners would now be led across the Yard to the Lodge and then out through the Debtor's Door where they would climb the steps up to the gallows. There would be shouts of "hats off" in the crowd. This was not out of respect for those about to die, but rather because the people further back demanded those at the front remove their hats so as not to obscure their view. Once assembled on the drop, Foxen would put the nooses round their necks while they prayed with the Ordinary. Female prisoners might have their dress bound around their legs for the sake of decency but the men's legs were left free. When the prayers had finished, the Under Sheriff gave the signal and the hangman moved the lever, which was connected to a drawbar under the trap, and caused it to fall with a loud crash, the prisoners dropping 12-18 inches and usually writhing and struggling for some seconds before relaxing and becoming still. If their bodies continued to struggle, the hangman, unseen by the crowd within the box below the drop, would grasp their legs and swing on them so adding his weight to theirs and thus ending their sufferings sooner. The dangling bodies would be left hanging for an hour before being either returned to their relatives or, in the case of murderers, sent for dissection. Execution Broadsides were usually sold among the crowd, purporting to give the last confessions of the condemned. These were like tabloid newspapers of the day and were often total fabrication. As they were printed prior to the execution, they were quite often unused if a reprieve was granted after printing, not an uncommon occurrence at that time. They would show a stylised woodcut picture of the hanging and had details of the crime. Ordinary newspapers were very few in number at this time and relatively very expensive so were only read by the wealthy. William Calcraft took over from Foxen in March of 1829 and carried out 86 executions here, his first job being the hanging of the hated child murderer, Ester Hibner, on the 13th of that month. Prior to taking up the position, he had sold pies at hangings and had got to know Foxen and Cheshire. Calcraft was to go on to hang a total of 86 people, including six women at Newgate, before he was retired in 1872. One of his most famous cases was Francis Courvoisier, who had murdered his master, Lord William Russell. Another was Britain's first railway murderer, Franz Muller, who he publicly hanged on the 14th of November 1864 for killing Mr. Thomas Briggs. Calcraft carried out both the last public hanging at Newgate (Michael Barrett) and the first private one four months later, that of Alexander Mackay on the 8th of September 1868. Mackay was 18 years old and had been convicted of the murder of Emma Goldsmith, his employer. The gallows had been erected in an enclosed yard near the Chapel, and the execution was attended by representatives of the Press. A little before 9.00 a.m., Mackay was led into the yard supported by the Chaplain, the Rev. Mr. Jones, and ascended the steps onto the platform where he joined in with Mr. Jones' prayers. Calcraft pulled the lever and Mackay dropped a few inches and took several minutes to become still, according to contemporary reports. George Smith assisted Calcraft at this hanging. The black flag was raised over the prison after the trap had opened. His body was left hanging for an hour before being taken down and prepared for the formal inquest, which took place that afternoon. Mackay was then buried within the prison in an unmarked grave.

Like his predecessors, Calcraft was also responsible for carrying out floggings at Newgate and was paid a salary with additional monies for hangings and floggings. With the advent of a comprehensive railway network, he was able to work over most of the country in his later years and became Britain's principal hangman. During Calcraft's time, the number of executions fell dramatically (see below). Proper condemned cells had been constructed in Newgate during the early 1830's, created by knocking two ordinary cells into one thus ending the use of the appalling "Condemned Hold" which was little more than a dark, feted dungeon. From 1848, condemned prisoners were guarded round the clock by two or three warders to prevent suicide. They took their exercise in a covered walkway known as Birdcage Walk or Dead Man's Walk, their cell being at the far end of this William Marwood was Britain's next hangman and officiated at 17 executions, including that of 45 year old Francis Stewart, for killing her grandson. Assisted by George Incher, he hanged the four Lennie Mutineers for murder and mutiny on the 23rd of May 1876 in Newgate's only quadruple private execution. This hanging was widely reported in the press. In 1881, a purpose built execution shed pictured here, containing a new gallows, was erected in one of the yards. This picture shows the view that witnesses had of an execution. The lower half doors were closed once the prisoner and other officials had entered and all witnesses saw was the prisoner disappear from site and the taught rope. This facility remained in use until closure in 1902, the gallows being then moved to Pentonville prison and first used there for the execution of John MacDonald on the 30th of September 1902. My friend, Aaron Bougourd, has kindly lent me this rare picture of the gallows and interior of the execution shed, one of the very few photos of a British gallows. This picture is copyright and may not be copied or reproduced without permission. You can see the metal bracket and chain hanging from the centre of the beam. Up to four brackets could be set up for multiple hangings. The lever is behind the right hand upright and there are pulleys for raising the trapdoors on each upright. A ladder is in the foreground leaning against the wall. Bartholomew Bins carried out one hanging after Marwood, that of Patrick O'Donnell, before handing it over to James Berry who performed 12 executions here between 1884 and 1890. Berry was to hang Mary Eleanor Wheeler in 1890. He was replaced by James Billington who hanged 24 men and three women up to 1901, including Louisa Masset, the first person to be executed in Britain in the 20th century. He also executed the infamous baby farmer, Amelia Dyer who at 57, became the oldest woman to be hanged in modern times. Click here for more on baby farmers. Another of his famous customers was Thomas Neill Cream who, in December 1892, standing hooded and noosed on the trap said, "I am Jack the...." just as the drop fell. In reality, he could not have been Jack the Ripper. Billington carried out the last triple execution at Newgate when he hanged Henry Fowler, Albert Milsom and William Seaman (for two different murders) on the 9th of June 1896. The last hanging at Newgate was carried out by Billington's son, William, on the 6th of May 1902. The prisoner was 21 year old George Wolfe, who had beaten and stabbed his girlfriend, Charlotte Cheeseman, to death.

Chapter 10 Analysis of executions between 1783 and 1902 and the crimes for which people were put to death

1783-1799
559 people were put to death in this short period of just over 16 years, an average of 35 per year. 539 men and 17 women were hanged for a wide variety of crimes and 3 women were burnt for coining. (Women accounting for 3.6% of the executions) (A small number of these executions took place at or near where the crime was committed.)

1800-1899
There were 621 hangings at Newgate of which 30 were of women (4.8%), 543 were in public including

those of 24 women. During this period in London, a further 23 men were hanged at Execution Dock at Wapping under Admiralty jurisdiction between 1802 and 1830.

1800-1833
There were 521 executions, all by hanging in public, comprising of 499 men and 22 women. Only 44 of these executions were for murder, the rest being for various other felonies, particularly burglary and forgery. See analysis below.

1835 – Just two executions took place at Newgate when John Smith and John Pratt became the last to hang for sodomy in England on the 27th of November of this year.

1834, 1836 & 1838
No executions at all at Newgate, possibly for political reasons, as the laws had changed dramatically in the previous two to three years.

1837-1868 (public hangings)
A further 42 men and three women were hanged in public up to the 25th of May 1868, all for murder (including five men who were executed for murder and piracy – "The Flowery Land" pirates.)

1868-1899 (private hangings)
51 men and three women were executed for murder, including 4 men for murder and mutiny on a ship called the "Lennie" (the Lennie Mutineers).

1900-1902. Seven men and two women were hanged for murder in the 20th century prior to the closure of Newgate.

Chapter 11 Low Lodging Houses

Is chiefly to be found in Whitechapel, in Westminster, and in Drury Lane. It is in such places the majority of our working men live, especially when they are out of work or given to drink; and the drinking that goes on in these places is often truly frightful, especially where the sexes are mixed, and married people, or men and women supposed to be such, abound. In some of these lodging- houses as many as two or three hundred people live ; and if anything can keep a man down in the world, and render him hopeless as to the future, it is the society and the general tone of such places. Yet in them are to be met women who were expected to shine in society- students from the universities - ministers of the Gospel - all herding in these filthy dens like so many swine. It is rarely a man rises from the low surroundings of a low lodging-house. He must be a very strong man if he does. Such a place as a Workman's City has no charms for the class of whom I write. Some of them would not care to live there. It is no attraction to them that there is no public-house on the estate, that the houses are clean, that the people are orderly, that the air is pure and bracing. They have no taste or capacity for the enjoyment of that kind of life. They have lived in slums, they have been accustomed to filth, they have no objection to overcrowding, they must have a public-house next door. This is why they live in St. Giles's or in Whitechapel, where the sight of their numbers is appalling, or why they crowd into such low neighbourhoods as abound in Drury Lane. Drury Lane is not at all times handy for their work. On the contrary, some of its inhabitants come a long way. One Saturday night I met a man there who told me he worked at Aldershot. Of course to many it is convenient. It is near Covent Garden, where many go to work as early as 4 A.M.; and it is close to the Strand, where its juvenile population earn their daily food. Ten to one the boy who offers you "the Hevening Hecho," the lass who would fain sell you cigar-lights and flowers, the woman who thrusts the opera programme into your carriage as you drive down Bow Street, the questionable gentleman who, if chance occurs, eases you of your pocket-handkerchief or your purse, the poor girl who, in tawdry finery, walks her weary way backwards and forwards in the Strand, whether the weather be wet or dry, long after her virtuous sisters are asleep- all hail from Drury Lane. It has ever been a spot to be shunned. Upwards of a hundred years ago, Gay wrote in his "Trivia"-

> Oh, may thy virtue guard thee through the roads
> Of Drury's mazy courts and dark abodes.

It is not of Drury Lane itself, but of its mazy courts that I write. Drury Lane is a shabby but industrious street. It is inhabited chiefly by tradespeople, who, like all of us, have to work hard for their living; but at the back of Drury Lane - on the left as you come from New Oxford Street - there run courts and streets as densely inhabited as any of the most crowded and filthy parts of the metropolis, and compared with which Drury Lane is respectability itself. A few days since I wanted to hear Happy William in a fine new chapel they have got in Little Wild Street. As I went my way, past rag-shops and cow-houses, I found myself in an exclusively Irish population, some of whom were kneeling and crossing themselves at the old Roman Catholic chapel close by, but the larger number of whom were drinking at one or other of the public-houses of the district. At the newspaper-shop at the corner, the only bills I saw were those of The Flag of Ireland, or The Irishman, or The Universe. In about half an hour there were three fights, one of them between women, which was watched with breathless interest by a swarming crowd, and which ended in one of the combatants, a yellow-haired female, being led to the neighbouring hospital. On his native heather an Irishman cares little about cleanliness. As I have seen his rude hut, in which the pigs and potatoes and the children are mixed up in inextricable confusion, I have felt how pressing is the question in Ireland, not of Home Rule, but of Home Reform. I admit his children are fat and numerous, but it is because they live on the hill-side, where no pestilent breath from the city ever comes.

In the neighbourhood of Drury Lane it is different; there is no fresh air there, and the only flowers one sees are those bought at Covent Garden. Everywhere on a summer night (she "has no smile of light" in Drury Lane), you are surrounded by men, women, and children, so that you can scarce pick your way. In Parker Street and Charles Street, and such-like places, the houses seem as if they never had been cleaned since they were built, yet each house is full of people - the number of families is according to the number of rooms. I should say four-and- sixpence a week is the average rent for these tumble-down and truly repulsive apartments. Children play in the middle of the street, amidst the dirt and refuse; costermongers, who are the capitalists of the district, live here with their donkeys; across the courts is hung the family linen to dry. You sicken at every step. Men stand leaning gloomily against the sides of the houses; women, with unlovely faces, glare at you sullenly as you pass by. The City Missionary is, perhaps, the only one who comes here with a friendly word, and a drop of comfort and hope for all. Of course the inhabitants are as little indoors as possible. It may be that the streets are dull and dirty, but the interiors are worse. Only think of a family, with grown- up sons and daughters, all living and sleeping in one room! The conditions of the place are as had morally as they are physically. It is but natural that the people drink more than they eat, that the women soon grow old and haggard, and that the little babes, stupefied with gin and beer, die off, happily, almost as fast as they are born. Here you see men and women so foul and scarred and degraded that it is mockery to say that they were made in the image of the Maker, and that the inspiration of the Almighty gave them understanding; and you ask is this a civilised land, and are we a Christian people? No wonder that from such haunts the girl gladly rushes to put on the harlot's livery of shame, and comes here after her short career of gaiety to die of disease and gin. In some of the streets are forty or fifty lodging-houses for women or men, as the case may be. In some of these lodging-houses there are men who make their thirty shillings or two pounds a week. In others are the broken-down mendicants who live on soup-kitchens and begging. You can see no greater wretchedness in the human form than what you see here. And, as some of these lodging-houses will hold ninety people, you may get some idea of their number. When I say that the sitting-room is common to all, that it has always a roaring fire, and that all day, and almost all night long, each lodger is cooking his victuals, you can get a fair idea of the intolerable atmosphere, in spite of the door being ever open. It seemed to me that a large number of the people could live in better apartments if they were so disposed, and if their only enjoyment was not a public-house debauch. The keepers of these houses seemed very fair-spoken men. I met with only one rebuff, and that was at a model house in Charles Street. As I airily tapped at the window, and asked the old woman if I could have a bed, at first she was civil enough, but when I ventured to question her a bit she angrily took herself off, remarking that she did not know who I was, and that she was not going to let a stranger get information out of her. As to myself, I can only say that I had rather lodge in any gaol than in the slums of Drury Lane. The sight of sights in this district is that of the public-houses and the crowds who fill them. On Saturday every bar was crammed; at some you could not get in at the door. The women were as numerous as the men; in the daytime they are far more so; and as almost every woman has a child in her arms, and another or two tugging at her gown, and as they are all formed into gossiping knots, one can imagine the noise of such places.

City readers will know whom I refer to- has opened a branch establishment in Drury Lane, and his place was the only one that was not crowded. I can easily understand the reason - one of the regulations of D.D.'s establishment is that no intoxicated person should be served. I have reason to conclude, from a conversation I had some time ago with one of D.D.'s barmen, that the rule is not very strictly enforced; but if it were carried out at all by the other publicans in Drury Lane I am sure there would be a great falling off of business. Almost every woman had a basket; in that basket was a bottle, which, in the course of the evening, was filled with gin for private consumption; and it was quite appalling to see the number of little pale-faced ragged girls who came with similar bottles on a similar errand. When the liquor takes effect, the women are the most troublesome, and use the worst language. On my remarking to a policeman that the neighbourhood was, comparatively speaking, quiet, he said there had been three or four rows already, and pointed to a pool of blood as confirmation of his statement. The men seemed all more or less stupidly drunk, and stood up one against another like a certain Scotch regiment, of which the officer, when complimented on their sobriety, remarked that they resembled a pack of cards - if one falls, down go all the rest. Late hours are the fashion in the neighbourhood of Drury Lane. It is never before two on a Sunday morning that there is quiet there. Death, says Horace, strikes with equal foot the home of the poor and the palace of the prince. This is not true as regards low lodging-houses. Even in Bethnal Green the Sanitary Commission found that the mean age at death among the families of the gentry, professionalists, and richer classes of that part of London was forty-four, whilst that of the families of the artisan class was about twenty- two. Everyone, for surely everyone has read Mr. Plimsoll's appeal on behalf of the poor sailors must remember the description of his experiences in a lodging-house of the better sort, established by the efforts of Lord Shaftesbury in Fetter Lane and Hatton Garden. "It is astonishing," says Mr. Plimsoll, "how little you can live on when you divest yourselves of all fancied needs. I had plenty of good wheat bread to eat all the week, and the half of a herring for a relish (less will do, if you can't afford half, for it is a splendid fish), and good coffee to drink, and I know how much - or, rather how little - roast shoulder of mutton you can get for twopence for your Sunday's dinner." I propose to write of other lodging- houses- houses of a lower character, and filled, I imagine, with men of a lower class. Mr. Plimsoll speaks in tones of admiration of the honest hard-working men whom he met in his lodging- house. They were certainly gifted with manly virtues, and deserved all his praise. In answer to the question, What did I see there? He replies: "I found the workmen considerate for each other. I found that they would go out (those who were out of employment) day after day, and patiently trudge miles and miles seeking employment; returning night after night unsuccessful and dispirited, only, however, to sally out the following morning with renewed determination. They would walk incredibly long distances to places where they heard of a job of work; and this, not for a few days, but for many, many days. And I have seen such a man sit down wearily by the fire (we had a common room for sitting, and cooking, and everything), with a hungry, despondent look - he had not tasted food all day and accosted by another, scarcely less poor than himself, with 'Here, mate, get this into thee,' handing him at the same time a piece of bread and some cold meat, and afterwards some coffee, and adding, 'Better luck to-morrow; keep up your pecker.' And all this without any idea that they were practising the most splendid patience, fortitude, courage, and generosity I had ever seen. Perhaps the eulogy is a little overstrained. Men, even if they are not working men, do learn to help each other, unless they are very bad indeed; and it does not seem so surprising to me as it does to Mr. Plimsoll that even such men "talk of absent wife and children." Certainly it is the least a husband and the father of a family can do.

The British working man has his fair share of faults, but just now he has been so belaboured on all sides with praise that he. is getting to be rather a nuisance. In our day it is to be feared he is rapidly degenerating. He does not work so well as he did, nor so long, and he gets higher wages. One natural result of this state of things is that the class just above him [-132-] - the class who, perhaps, are the worst off in the land - have to pay an increased price for everything that they cat and drink or wear, or need in any way for the use of their persons or the comfort and protection of their homes. Another result, and this is much worse, is that the workman spends his extra time and wages in the public-houses, and that we have an increase of paupers to keep and crime to punish. There is no gainsaying admitted facts; there is no use in boasting of the increased intelligence of the working man, when the facts are the other way. As he gets more money and power, he becomes less amenable to rule and reason. Last year, according to Colonel Henderson's report, drunk and disorderly cases had increased from 23,007 to 33,867. It is to be expected the returns of the City police will be equally unsatisfactory. As I write, I take the following from The Echo: In a certain district in London, facing each other, are two corner- houses in which the business of a publican and a chemist are respectively carried on. In the course of twenty-five years the houses have changed hands three times, and at the last change the purchase money of the public-house amounted to £14,300, and that of the chemist's business to only £1,000. Of course the publican drives his carriage and pair, while the druggist has to use Shanks's pony. But this is a digression. It is of lodging-houses I write. It seems that there are lodging-houses of many kinds. Perhaps some of the best were those of which Mr. Plimsoll had experience. The Peabody buildings are, I believe, not inhabited by poor people at all. The worst, perhaps, are those in Flower and Dean Street, Spitalfields, and the adjacent district. One naturally assumes that no good can come out of Flower and Dean Street, just as it was [-134-] assumed of old that no good could come out of

Nazareth. This was illustrated in a curious way the other day. One of the earnest philanthropists connected with Miss Macpherson's Home of Industry at the corner, was talking with an old woman on the way of salvation. She pleaded that on that head she had nothing to learn. She had led a good life, she had never done anybody any harm, she never used bad language, and, in short, she had lived in the village of Morality, to quote John Bunyan, of which Mr. Worldly Wiseman had so much to say when he met poor Christian, just as he had escaped with his heavy burden on his shoulder out of the Slough of Despond, and that would not do for our young evangelist. "My good woman," said he sadly, "that is not enough. You may have been all you say, and yet not be a true Christian after .all." "Of course it ain't," said a man who had been listening to the conversation. "You'll never get to heaven that way. You must believe on the Lord Jesus Christ, and then you will be saved." "Ah," said the evangelist, "you know that, do you? I hope you live accordingly." "Oh yes; I know it well enough," was the reply; "but of course I can't practice it. I am one of the light-fingered gentry, I am, and I live in Flower and Dean Street ;" and away he hurried as if he saw a policeman, and as if he knew that he was wanted.

The above anecdote, the truth of which I can vouch for, indicates the sort of place Flower and Dean Street is, and the kind of company one meets there. It is a place that always gives the police a great deal of trouble. Close by is a court, even lower in the world than Flower and Dean Street, and it is to me a wonder how such a place can be suffered to exist. What with Keane's Court and Flower and Dean Street the police have their hands pretty full day and night, especially the hatter. Robbery and drunkenness and fighting and midnight brawls are the regular and normal state of affairs, and are expected as a matter of course. When I was there last a woman had been taken out of Keane's Court on a charge of stabbing a man she had inveigled into one of the houses, or rather hovels- you can scarcely call them houses in the court. She was let off as the man refused to appear against her, and the chances arc that she will again be at her little tricks. They have rough ways, the men and women of this district; they are not given to stand much upon ceremony; they have little faith in moral suasion, but have unbounded confidence in physical force. A few miles of such a place, and London were a Sodom and Gomorrah.

But I have not yet described the street. We will walk down it, if you please. It is not a long street, nor is it a very new one; but is it a very striking one, nevertheless. Every house almost you come to is a lodging- house, and some of them are very large ones, holding as many as four hundred beds. Men unshaven and unwashed are standing loafing about, though in reality this is the hour when, all over London, honest men are too glad to be at work earning their daily bread. A few lads and men are engaged in the intellectual and fashionable amusement known as pitch and toss. Well, if they play fairly, I do not know that City people can find much fault with them for doing so. They cannot get rid of their money more quickly than they would were they to gamble on the Stock Exchange, or to invest in limited liability companies or mines which promise cent. per cent. and never yield a rap but to the promoters who get up the bubble, or to the agent who, as a friend, begs and persuades you to go into them, as he has a lot of shares which he means to keep for himself, but of which, as you are a friend, and as a mark of special favour, he would kindly accommodate you with a few.

But your presence is not welcomed in the street. You are not a lodger, that is clear. Curious and angry eyes follow you all the way. Of course your presence there- the apparition of anything respectable- is an event which creates alarm rather than surprise.

In the square mile of which this street is the centre, it is computed are crowded one hundred and twenty thousand of our poorest population- men and women who have sunk exhausted in the battle of life, and who come here to hide their wretchedness and shame, and in too many cases to train their little ones to follow in their steps. The children have neither shoes nor stockings. They are covered with filth, they are innocent of all the social virtues, and here is their happy hunting- ground; they are a people by themselves.

All round are planted Jews and Germans. In Commercial Street the chances are you may hear as much German as if you were in Deutschland itself. Nor is this all; the place is a perfect Babel. It is a pity that Flower and Dean Street should be, as it were, representative of England and her institutions. It must give the intelligent foreigner rather a shock.

But *place aux dames* is my motto, and even in the slums let woman take the position which is her due. In the streets the ladies are not in any sense particular, and can scream long and loudly, particularly when under the influence of liquor. They are especially well developed as to their arms, and can defend themselves, if that be necessary, against the rudeness or insolence or the too- gushing affection of the other sex. As to their manners and morals, perhaps the less said about them the better.

Let us step into one of the lodging-houses which is set apart exclusively for their use. The charge for admission is threepence or fourpence a night, or a little less by the week. You can have no idea of the size of one of these places unless you enter. We will pay a visit in the afternoon, when most of the bedrooms are empty. At the door is a box- office, as it were, for the sale of tickets of admission. Behind extends a large room, provided at one end with cooking apparatus and well supplied with tables and chairs, at which arc seated a few old helpless females, who have nothing to do, and don't seem to care much about getting out into the sun. Let us ascend under the guidance of the female who has charge of the place, and who has to sit up till 3 A.M. to admit her fair friends, some of whom evidently keep bad hours and are given rather too much to the habit of what we call making a night of it. Of course most of the rooms are unoccupied, but they are full of beds, which are placed as close together as possible; and this is all the furniture in the room, with the exception of the glass, without which no one, male or female, can properly perform the duties of the toilette. One woman is already thus occupied. In another room, we catch sight of a few still in bed, or sitting listlessly on their beds. They are mostly youthful, and regard us from afar with natural curiosity - some actually seeming inclined to giggle at our intrusion. As it is, we feel thankful that we need not [-142-] remain a moment in such company, and we leave them to their terrible fate.

A few hours later they will be out in the streets, seeking whom they may devour. Go down

Whitechapel way, and you will see them. in shoals haunting the public-houses of the district, or promenading the pavement, or talking to men as sunk in the social scale as themselves. They are fond of light dresses; they eschew bonnets or hats. Some are half- starved; others seem in good condition; and they need be so to stand the life they have to lead. Let us hope Heaven will have more mercy on such as they than man. It cannot be that decent respectable women live in Flower and Dean Street.

But what of the men? Well, I answer at the first glance, you see that they are a rough lot. Some are simply unfortunate and friendless and poor; others do really work honestly for their living as dock-[-143-]labourers, or as porters in some of the surrounding markets, or at any chance job that may come in their way; many, alas, are of the light- fingered fraternity. The police have but a poor opinion of the honesty of the entire district - but then the police are so uncharitable! The members of the Christian community and others who come here on a Sunday and preach in more than one of the lodging- houses in the street have a better opinion, and certainly can point to men and women reclaimed by their labours, and now leading decent godly lives. It requires some firmness and Christian love to go preaching in these huge lodging- houses, in which one, it seemed to me, might easily be made away with. Even in the daytime they have an ugly look, filled as they are with idle men, who are asleep now, but who will be busy enough by-and-by - when honesty has done its work and respectability is gone to bed. As commercial speculations I suppose money is made by these places. The proprietor has but little expense to incur in the way of providing furniture or attendance, and in some cases he supplies refreshments, on which of course he makes a profit. But each lodger is at liberty to cater for himself, or to leave it alone if times are bad and money is scarce. At any rate there is the fire always burning, and the locker in which each lodger may stow away what epicurean delicacy or worldly treasure lie may possess. I have been in prisons and workhouses, and I can say the inmates of such places are much better lodged, and have better care taken of them, and are better off than the poor people of Flower and Dean Street. The best thing that could happen for them would be the destruction of the whole place by fire. Circumstances have much to do with the formation of character, and in a more respectable neighbourhood they would become a little more respectable themselves.

In the lodging- houses at Westminster the inhabitants are of a much more industrious character. In Lant Street, Borough, they are quite the reverse. A man should have his wits about him who attempts to penetrate into the mysteries or to understand the life of a low lodging-house there.

For ages the Mint in the Borough has gained an unenviable name, not only as the happy hunting-ground of the disreputable, the prostitute, the thief the outcast, the most wretched and the lowest of the poor, yet there was a time when it was great and famous. There that brave and accomplished courtier, the Duke of Suffolk, brought his royal bride, the handsome sister of our Henry VIII. It was there poor Edward VI. came on a visit all the way from Hampton Court. It was the goodly gift of Mary the unhappy and ill- fated to the [-146-] Archbishop of York. Somehow or other Church property seems to be detrimental to the respectability of a neighbourhood, hence the truth of the old adage, "The nearer the church, the farther from God." At any rate this was the case as regards the Mint in the Borough, which in Gay's time had sunk so low that he made it the scene of his "Beggar's Opera," and there still law may be said to be powerless, and there still they point out the house in which lived Jonathan Wild. In the reign of William, our Protestant hero, and George I., our Hanoverian deliverer, a desperate attempt was made to clear the place of the rogues an d vagabonds to whom it afforded shelter and sanctuary; but somehow or other in vain, though all debtors under fifty pounds had their liabilities wiped off by royal liberality. The place was past mending, and so it has ever since remained. It is not a neighbourhood for a lady at any time, but to inhabit it all that is that, by fair means or foul (in the Mint they are as little particular as to the way in which money is made as they are in the City or on the stock Exchange), you have fourpence to pay for a night's lodging. All round the place prices may be described as low, to suit the convenience of the customer. You are shaved for a penny. Your hair is cut and curled for twopence. The literature for sale may be termed sensational, and the chandlers' shops, which are of the truest character if I may judge by the contents, do a trade which may be described as miscellaneous.

It is sad to see the successive waves of pauperism rise and burst and disappear. On they come, one after another, as fast as the eye can catch them, and far faster than the mind can realise all the hidden and complex causes of which they are the painful result. One asks, Is this always to be so? Is there to be no end to this supply, of which we see only the surface, as it were? Are all the lessons of the past in vain? Cannot Science, with all its boasted arts, remove the causes, be they what they may, and effect a cure? Is the task too appalling for philanthropy? Some such thoughts came into my head as I looked upon the dense mass of men and women, destitute of work and food, who, at an early hour on the first Sunday in the New Year were collected from all the lodging-houses in the unpretentious but well-known building known as the Gray's Yard Ragged Church and Schools, in a part of London not supposed, like the Seven Dials, to be the home of the wretched, and close by the mansions of the rich and the great. When I entered, as many as seven hundred had been got together, and there was a crowd three hundred strong, equally hungry, equally destitute, and equally worthy of Christian benevolence. On entering, each person, as soon as he or she had taken his or her seat, [-149-] was treated to two thick slices of bread-and-butter and a cup of coffee, and at the close of the service there was the usual distribution of a pound meat- pie and a piece of cake to each individual, and coffee *ad libitum*. It may be added that the cost of this breakfast does not come out of the funds of the institution, but is defrayed by special subscriptions, and that Mr. John Morley had sent, as he always does, a parcel of one thousand Gospels for distribution. But what has this got to do, asks the reader, with the thought which, as I say, the sight suggested to me? Why, everything. In the course of the morning, Mr. F. Bevan, the chairman, asked those who had been there before to hold up their hands, and there was not one hand held up in answer to the question. There was a similar negative response when it was asked of that able-bodied mass before me- for there were no very old men in the crowd - as to whether any of them were in regular work. This year's pauperism is, then, but the crop of the year. Relieved to-day, next year another crowd will follow; and so the dark and sullen waves, mournfully moaning and wailing, of the measureless ocean of human sorrow and suffering, and want and despair, ever come and ever go. The Christian Church is the lifeboat sailing across this. ocean in answer to the cry for help, and rescuing them that are ready to perish. There are cynics who say even all this Christmas feasting does no good. It is a fact that on Christmas week there is a sudden and wonderful exodus from the workhouses around London.

 We cannot get improved men and women till we have improved lodging-houses. Recently it was calculated that in St. Giles's parish (once it was St. Giles's-in-the-Fields), there were no less than 3,000 families living in single rooms. Again, in the parish of Holborn, there were quite 12,000, out of a population of 44,000, living in single rooms. Under such circumstances, what can we expect but physical and moral degradation? Healthy life is impossible for man or woman, boy or girl. A Divine Authority tells us, men do not gather grapes of thorns or figs of thistles. As I write, however, a ray of light reaches me. It appears nearly 10,000 persons are now reaping the benefit of the Peabody Fund. In the far east there are buildings at Shadwell and Spitalfields; in the far west at Chelsea, in Westminster, and at Grosvenor Road, Pimlico - the latter perfectly appointed edifice alone accommodating 1,952 persons. As many as 768 are lodged in the Islington block, and on the south side of the Thames there are Peabody buildings at Bermondsey, in the Blackfriars Road, Stamford Street, and Southwark Street. One room in the Peabody buildings is never let to two persons. A writer in The Daily News says: Advantage has been taken by the Peabody trustees to purchase land brought into the market by the operation of the Artisans and Labourers' Dwellings Act. At the present moment nineteen blocks of building are in course of removal either by the City or the Metropolitan Board of Works. They are situate at Peartree Court Clerkenwell; Goulston Street, Whitechapel; St. George the Martyr, Southwark; Bedfordbury; Whitechapel and Limehouse, near the London Docks; High Street, Islington Essex Road, Islington; Whitecross Street; Old Pye Street, Westminster; Great Wild Street, Drury

Lane; Marylebone, hard by the Edgware Road; Wells Street, Poplar; Little Coram Street; and Great Peter Street, Westminster. All these are under the control of the Metropolitan Board of Works. The remaining three - at Petticoat Square, at Golden Lane, and at Barbican -.

are being removed by the Corporation of the City of London. It is estimated that forty-one acres of land will be laid bare by this clearance - a space capable of lodging properly at least as many thousand people. There are of course other helpers in the same direction as the Peabody trustees, without being quite in the same sense public bodies administering a large fund for a special purpose, with the single object of extending its sphere of usefulness in accordance with public policy. Some of the companies, however, work for five per cent. return, and their efforts to construct suitable dwellings for workpeople and labourers are very valuable. The Improved Industrial Dwellings Company has buildings at Bethnal Green Road, at Shoreditch, at Willow Street, and close to the goods station of the Great Northern Railway, besides two blocks near the City Road. The Metropolitan Association has blocks buildings in Whitechapel, and in many spots farther west, as have the Marylebone Association, the London Labourers' Dwellings Society, and other bodies of similar kind. The success of Miss Octavia Hill in encouraging the construction of dwellings of the class required is well known, as are the buildings erected by Sir Sydney Waterlow, Mr. G. Cutt, and Mr. Newson. It is almost needless to add that the Baroness Burdett-Coutts has taken a warm interest in this important movement, as a building at Shoreditch now accommodating seven hundred persons will testify.

Chapter 12 Carpenders Park Manor

As the London prisons punished poverty with hard and brutal sentences and the Gin houses dealt with the addicts and drowned the drinkers as long as they could pay. The people from the London slums along the Seven Dials sank further into misery, the more unhappy they got the more gin they would drink. The more drink they drank the deeper into debt they got. It was a merry-go-round of hell and most people could not get off. For the wealthy it was not a devastating problem. Fifteen miles north of the slums in London a manor had just been restored to house an upper class family called Carew. The large house was called Carpenders Park Manor, locally it was called Carpenders Park Mansion.

This estate took its name from the family of Carpenter, who were in possession of it during the seventeenth and eighteenth centuries. To whom there are various inscriptions in the church. It was formerly included in the manors of More and Wiggenhall. After the Carpenders ceased to possess it, it has been divided into a number of smallholdings. During the reign of George II the house and about 150 acres of land adjoining were in the possession of Hatch Moody of St. Margaret's county Middlesex. By his will dated 1747 he left the estate to his son Samuel, with an entail on his heir's male and contingent remainder to his daughters Ann and Letitia. Samuel rebuilt the house at Carpenders, and died in 1823, William Longmore died before the testator, and Matthew died in 1825, when Mary Anne Longmore came into possession. She, with her sons and grandsons, conveyed it in 1846 to Jonah Smith Wells of Islington, and he in 1862 sold it to Robert Russell Carew, from whom it has come to Mrs. Carew. The large house created a little work for the surrounding area for the family. There were Mr. and Mrs. Carew one son and two daughters. There was a full house of staff to look after them.

Lady's Maid

To correctly manage a large Victorian Manor a full team of dedicated staff were needed to ensure each process is carried out correctly. Mrs. Carew had a lady's maid and she was hired by and reported directly to the mistress of the house, rather than the Housekeeper. Because her position necessitated a close proximity to her mistress, the lady's maid was often mistrusted and generally disliked by the lower servants, who possibly felt that she was haughty, or might "tattle" on them. Often, this treatment of the lady's maid caused her to feel isolated, as if she didn't quite fit into either world: her position allowed privileges of comfort and luxury not enjoyed by the lower servants, yet no matter how high-ranking her position was, her station remained among the "poor domestic servants". To qualify for the position, the lady's maid was to be neat in appearance; have stronger verbal skills; be pleasant; be able to read and write well; be proficient with her needle and handwork; and was expected to tell the truth, without gossiping. Honesty was an absolute necessity, as the lady's maid would be handling her mistress' clothing, jewels and personal items. The daily duties of the Lady's Maid included helping her mistress dress and undress, and maintaining her mistress' wardrobe, including laundering the most delicate items and using her dressmaking skills to create new articles of clothing for any and all occasions. In addition, the lady's maid prepared beauty lotions for her mistress' delicate skin, and she styled her mistress' hair.

Housemaids

Under the supervision of the Housekeeper, there were several house maid positions, including parlour maids, chambermaids, laundry maids, still-room maids, "between maids"- these maids performed double-duty as both kitchen and housemaid, and maids-of-all-work. These were the employees who really maintained the house. Each had their own set of duties and responsibilities, which included lighting fires and keeping them stoked, bringing up clean hot water for washing and bathing, and removing the dirty water after (four times a day—before breakfast, at noon, before dinner, and at bedtime); emptying and cleaning chamber pots; thoroughly cleaning all the public rooms of the house, making beds, sweeping, dusting and cleaning the bedrooms, as well as all the other rooms and areas of the house, scrubbing floors on their hands and knees, sweeping ashes, cleaning and polishing grates, candlesticks, marble floors and all the furniture,, brushing carpets and beating rugs, washing loads of laundry, which needed to be soaked, blued, washed, rinsed, rinsed again, wrung out, hung to dry and then ironed. The housemaid's work was back-breaking and exhausting, more so than we can truly imagine. There were lamps to clean and fill, each and every day, and because the working area was in the basement, maids frequently had to lug hot water up to the third floor of the house where the bedrooms were. In addition, in order to tend the fires in the house and keep them lit, a maid also had to carry loads of coal up each flight of stairs to all the fireplaces in the house.

Indeed, the housemaid's day was long, intensive and painfully strenuous, beginning at 6:00 a.m. when she rose and dressed, then made tea for the Lady's Maid and Housekeeper and served them by 6:30 a.m. on until 10:30 p.m. or later, when she could finally retire for the night with the house completely in order and ready for her to start all over again the following day.

Groom

"The Groom's first duties are to keep his horses in condition; but he is sometimes expected to perform as a valet to ride out with his master, on occasions, to wait at table, and otherwise assist in the house: in these cases, he should have the means of dressing himself, and keeping his clothes entirely away from the stables. "In the morning, about six o'clock, or rather before, the stables should be opened and cleaned out, and the horses fed, first by cleaning the rack and throwing in fresh hay, putting it lightly in the rack, that the horses may get it out easily; a short time afterwards their usual morning feed of oats should be put into the manger. While this is going on, the stable-boy has been removing the stable-dung, and sweeping and washing out the stables, both of which should be done every day, and every corner carefully swept, in order to keep the stable sweet and clean.The real duties of the groom follow: where the horses are not taken out for early exercise, the work of grooming immediately commences. "Having tied up the head," to use the excellent description of the process given by old Barrett, "take a currycomb and curry him all over the body, to raise the dust, beginning first at the neck, holding the left cheek of the headstall in the left hand, and curry him from the setting-on of his head all over the body to the buttocks, down to the point of the hock; then change your hands, and curry him before, on his breast, and, laying your right arm over his back, join your right side to his left, and curry him all under the belly near the fore-bowels, and so all over from the knees and back upwards; after that, go to the far side and do that likewise. Then take a dead horse's tail, or, failing that, a cotton dusting-cloth, and strike that away which the currycomb hath raised. Then take a round brush made of bristles, with a leathern handle, and dress him all over, head, body, and legs, to the very fetlocks, always cleansing the brush from the dust by rubbing it with the currycomb. In the curry-combing process, as well as brushing, it must be applied with mildness, especially with fine-skinned horses; otherwise the tickling irritates them much. The brushing is succeeded by a hair-cloth, with which rub him all over again very hard, both to take away loose hairs and lay his coat; then wash your hands in fair water, and rub him all over while they are wet, as well over the head as the body. Lastly, take a clean cloth, and rub him all over again till he be dry; then take another hair-cloth, and rub all his legs exceeding well from the knees and hocks downwards to his hoofs, picking and dressing them very carefully about the fetlocks, so as to remove all gravel and dust which will sometimes lie in the bending of the joints." In addition to the practice of this old writer, modern grooms add wisping, which usually follows brushing. The best wisp is made from a hay band, untwisted, and again doubled up after being moistened with water: this is applied to every part of the body, as the brushing had been, by changing the hands, taking care in all these operations to carry the hand in the direction of the coat. Stains on the hair are removed by sponging, or, when the coat is very dirty, by the water-brush; the whole being finished off by a linen or flannel cloth. The horsecloth should now be put on by taking the cloth in both hands, with the outside next you, and, with your right hand to the off side, throw it over his back, placing it no farther back than will leave it straight and level, which will be about a foot from the tail. Put the roller round, and the pad-piece under it, about six or eight inches from the fore legs. The horse's head is now loosened; he is turned about in his stall to have his head and ears rubbed and brushed over every part, including throat, with the dusting-cloth, finishing by "pulling his ears," which all horses seem to enjoy very much. This done, the mane and foretop should be combed out, passing a wet sponge over them, sponging the mane on both sides, by throwing it back to the midriff, to make it lie smooth. The horse is now returned to his headstall, his tail combed out, cleaning it of stains with a wet brush or sponge, trimming both tail and mane, and forelock when necessary, smoothing them down with a brush on which a little oil has been dropped.

The Footman

Directly below the butler was the footman. The footman's position was multifarious, and included a wide veriety of duties that ranged from accompanying the mistress in her carriage as she paid calls or went shopping, to polishing the household copper and plate; or from waiting at table, to cleaning knives, cutlery, shoes and boots. Other duties of the footman (who was frequently referred to as "James" or "John", no matter what his real name might have been), would have included acting as the Lady's personal footman. That is, among his other duties, he would have prepared her early morning or breakfast tray; cleaned her shoes; brushed any mud off her dress hems and riding habits; paid small charges of her travelling expenses such as toll gates and handsome cabs (he could reclaim these expenses from the Housekeeper); and if she owned a dog, he would be the one to take it for a walk. He would also accompany her when she went out in the carriage, sitting on the box with the coachman (then in later days, with the chauffer), and would open and close for her the carriage door, as well as the door to any stores she entered, unless there was already a doorman. He waited for her return, carried any packages for her, and once he helped her back into the carriage, he covered her knees with a blanket or fur rug. When the mistress went calling and no one was at home, she waited in the carriage while the footman left her visiting card at the front door. The footman also acted as valet to the eldest son, and sometimes to the master, himself. He was responsible for laying the luncheon table; he cleaned all the mirrors in the household; he carried coal and wood, and similar tasks. Other general duties of the footman included trimming lamps; running all errands; carrying coal; lighting the house at dusk; cleaning silver and gold; answering the drawing room and/or parlour bells; announcing visitors; waiting at dinner; attending the gentlemen in the smoking room following dinner; and attending in the front hall as dinner guests were leaving. Because of their public exposure at dinner and to guests, footmen were expected to be the most presentable of the male servants. In addition to there being an "ideal height" requirement for footmen, they were also assessed on their appearance in "full livery"

(Uniform), which for outdoors consisted of an ornate tail coat, knee breeches, stockings, white gloves, buckled shoes and powered hair with cocked hat. For inside the manor their livery was sometimes a bit less formal. Instead of a tail coat and buckled shoes, they usually wore a dress coat and pumps. Later in the century it was more common to see a uniform of white tie and tails with brass buttons that were stamped with the family crest.

The laundry-maid

"The laundry-maid is charged with the duty of washing and getting-up the family linen, a situation of great importance where the washing is all done at home; but in large towns, where there is little convenience for bleaching and drying, it is chiefly done by professional laundresses and companies, who apply mechanical and chemical processes to the purpose. These processes, however, are supposed to injure the fabric of the linen; and in many families the fine linen, cottons, and muslins, are washed and got-up at home, even where the bulk of the washing is given out. In country and suburban houses, where greater conveniences exist, washing at home is more common, in country places universal. The laundry establishment consists of a washing-house, an ironing and drying-room, and sometimes a drying-closet heated by furnaces. The washing-house will probably be attached to the kitchen; but it is better that it should be completely detached from it, and of one story, with a funnel or shaft to carry off the steam. Adjoining the bleaching-house, a second room, about the same size, is required for ironing, drying, and mangling. The contents of this room should comprise an ironing-board, opposite to the light; a strong white deal table, about twelve or fourteen feet long, and about three and a half feet broad, with drawers for ironing-blankets; a mangle in one corner, and clothes-horses for drying and airing; cupboards for holding the various irons, starch, and other articles used in ironing; a hot-plate built in the chimney, with furnace beneath it for heating the irons; sometimes arranged with a flue for carrying the hot air round the room for drying. The laundry-maid should commence her labours on Monday morning by a careful examination of the articles committed to her care, and enter them in the washing-book; separating the white linen and collars, sheets and body-linen, into one heap, fine muslins into another, coloured cotton and linen fabrics into a third, woollens into a fourth, and the coarser kitchen and other greasy cloths into a fifth. Every article should be examined for ink or grease-spots, or for fruit or wine-stains. Every article having been examined and assorted, the sheets and fine linen should be placed in one of the tubs and just covered with lukewarm water, in which a little soda has been dissolved and mixed, and left there to soak till the morning. Early on the following morning the fires should be lighted, and as soon as hot water can be procured, washing commenced; the sheets and body-linen being wanted to whiten in the morning, should be taken first; each article being removed in succession from the lye in which it has been soaking, rinsed, rubbed, and wrung, and laid aside until the tub is empty, when the foul water is drawn off. After this first washing, the linen should be put into a second water as hot as the hand can bear, and again rubbed over in every part, examining every part for spots not yet moved, which require to be again soaped over and rubbed till thoroughly clean; then rinsed and wrung, the larger and stronger articles by two of the women; the smaller and more delicate articles requiring gentler treatment. The operations should be concluded by rinsing the tubs, cleaning the coppers, scrubbing the floors of the washing-house, and restoring everything to order and cleanliness. Thursday and Friday, in a laundry in full employ, are usually devoted to mangling, starching, and ironing.

The Housekeeper

Always referred to as "Mrs." by the other servants, whether she was married or not, the housekeeper was second in command of the household, and was the immediate representative of her mistress. It was necessary for the housekeeper to have an understanding of accounts. She was expected to keep an account book where she accurately and precisely noted all sums paid for any and every purpose, the current expenses of the house, tradesmen's bills, etc. These accounts were balanced and examined by the Mistress. The housekeeper was responsible for maintaining order in the house and directing the female staff. She allocated duties and made sure that they were satisfactorily completed. In addition to overseeing the female staff, the housekeeper was also in charge of the household linens. She kept inventory, and made sure that the family and staff always had a clean supply of linens and bedding. The housekeeper was responsible for the inventory of other household necessities, such as soap and candles, sugar, flour and spices. As well, she supervised the china closet and the stillroom department, where cordials and preserves were made and stored. In addition, she was to see that all the furniture in the house was cleaned and polished, and she attended to all the necessary marketing details, and ordering goods from the tradesmen.

The Parlour Maid

The Parlour Maid would have risen at 6.00 am to begin their duties which would have included sweeping and dusting the drawing room, dining room, front hall and other sitting rooms, as well as tidying the grates and light the fires. They would also have had to clean the lamps and polish the candlesticks, carry up the cans of hot water to the bedrooms, make the other servants beds, sweep, and dust, arrange the rooms and clean the front staircases and front hall. They would then make the beds of rest of the household, dust under the beds; shake the curtains, wash paintwork and light the fires. Each bedroom would need to be supplied with soap, candles, clean towels, writing paper and the Parlour Maid would have to answer the bell at all times. On special days their work might also include. Clean knives; rub up table sliver and tidy pantry. Dress for luncheon. Clean away luncheon, wash up table silver. Fill coal scuttles as needed. Prepare guest bedrooms, turn down the beds, and fill the jugs with water. Close curtains, put in order and take up hot water.

Kitchen Maid

In larger homes, where there was a "Professed Cook", she was assisted by both kitchen maids and scullery-maids, whose duties included lighting the kitchen fires early in the morning, and cleaning the kitchen for Cook's use during the day. In some households, it was the responsibility of the senior kitchen maid to cook meals for other servants, while Cook focused her attention on provisions for the household "above stairs".

Cook

A professed cook would not do any general housecleaning, nor any 'plain cooking', and her ingredients would be prepared for her by the kitchen staff. The busiest times of the day for the cook were the morning and the early evening. In the morning hours, Cook would first meet with the mistress of the house for her to review and approve menus, then she would prepare soup for the following day, as soup was "not usually meant to be eaten the same day it was made". Next, Cook would prepare the jellies, pastries, creams and entrées required for the evening meal, and then luncheon was prepared for those "above stairs". The afternoon hours allowed Cook a little bit of down time, unless guests were staying in the house, or if a dinner party was to be held. Then, on such occasions as these servants found no time for rest from morning to late evening. The hours between 5:00 p.m. and 10:00 p.m. were extremely hectic for Cook. Once dinner had been served, Cook's work for the day was finished, and the remainder of the clean up and chores fell to the kitchen maids and scullery maids. These remaining chores in and of themselves, were extremely laborious, as a full dinner for 18 people could easily produce some 500 separate items of china, glassware, kitchenware and cutlery that needed to be cleaned. The "Plain Cook", unlike the aforementioned "professed cook", would have general housekeeping duties to perform, many which were not related to cooking at all, especially in households where there were no kitchen or scullery maids. She might be expected to dust and sweep the dining room or parlour; light the fires, sweep the front hall and/or door-step, and even clean the grates—all in addition to maintaining the work of the kitchen. She would need to rise early, 6:00 in the summer months, and 6:30 in the winter, to light the kitchen fire, and then complete all her work upstairs before cooking breakfast. Plain Cooks were usually expected to only cook simple meals. For example, for luncheon, she might serve a joint of meat, vegetables and pudding. For dinner, she would prepare much the same meal, or she might vary it by serving fish, vegetables, potatoes and tarts. Following dinner, the plain cook would need to clean the dishes, and scour tables and kitchen counters, and perhaps mop the kitchen floor so that it would be clean for the next morning. These were all tasks that the scullery maid would typically perform, but in a household where there was no scullery maid, these chores were left to the plain cook. She was to see to it that all these duties were completed before going to bed, and finally, it was her responsibility to see that the kitchen fires had burnt low; that the gas (in homes that had gas) in the kitchen and passages was turned off; and that the basement doors and windows were securely fastened. At last, she could retire for the night.

The Butler

The butler wore gentlemen's period-fashions. He was often a distinguished figure of a man with an imposing presence, which demanded respect from his subordinates. The list of duties required by the butler varied with the list of duties required by the butler varied with the position and status of his employer. In smaller households, the butler's work was fairly difficult. He hired and dismissed the lower staff (male), and he was personally responsible for their conduct. He was to be certain that all the work of the staff ran smoothly, and that any issues were quickly handled. If the house contained a plate room, it was usually located near the butler's pantry. Each night the butler would need to be sure it was securely locked. Either the butler or the footman was expected to sleep nearby, as guard. In the morning the butler passed out the pieces of plate that needed to be cleaned, and occasionally he cleaned them himself, at the same time he cleaned the household's ornamental items of silver. The butler was responsible for the arrangement of the dining table and the announcing of dinner. Together with the footmen, he waited at table. It was the butler's job to carve the joint of meat, and to remove the covers from other dishes. He served wine and set out each additional course. While dessert was being enjoyed, the butler made sure that the drawing room where the family would soon retreat for coffee or tea was in order. He made sure that lamps or candles were in proper working order, and that the fire was warmly glowing. He then returned to his pantry and awaited the ring of the bell, which signaled he may return to the company. He would then announce that the drawing room was ready. Once the family had settled into the drawing room, the butler would hand around cups and saucers, while the footman followed behind, carrying a pot of tea or coffee. The butler's final tasks of the day were to see that all doors and windows were locked; that the plate was safely secured; and that all the fires in the house were safe.

Upper Class Victorians Create Work

Rich Victorians always had servants. Cooks, butlers, gardeners, housemaids, nannies and governesses were employed by this social class. The middle class families did not usually have as many servants as the upper class families. Many of the servants had moved from the country, where many of the farming jobs had been eliminated by the invention of machines. Servants were paid low wages but were guaranteed a living space, food, and clothes by their employers. Middle and upper class Victrian families lived in large, comfortable houses. These houses had ample space for the family, which averaged between four to six children, and the servants. This was a sharp contrast to the overcrowded and unhealthy conditions of the working and poor classes of this time. Victorian houses of wealthy owners had features such as bay windows, stained glass in the windows and doorways, patterned brickwork and slate roofs. The success of the middle-classes in the Victorian period can be seen in their ability to universalise a set of principles based on individuality and progress. In moving from a society based on rank and privilege to one based on free exchange, the very idea that an individual, through hard work, thrift and self reliance, could achieve social and economic success provided an equalising principle. But, whilst the idea of social mobility was, and still is, central to legitimising the idea of a market economy, many critics of industrialisation, such as Thomas Carlyle, feared that the community was threatened by the aggressive individualism of some or the frustrated aspirations of others. A sense of social order was formulated in the mixing of political economy, paternalism and evangelical religion which ascribed specific roles to groups of people. The working classes were encouraged to improve but they were also reminded they should be content with their lot as labourers. Whilst women's work, either for wages or to ensure the success of the family business, might be essential, the idealised wife and mother was prescribed the responsibility for cultivating morality and spirituality in the home as a corrective to the worst excesses of competitive industry. These perspectives were popularised in a range of books and articles in the nineteenth century but are perhaps best demonstrated by Samuel Smiles and his best seller Self Help published in 1859. Smiles argued, along with others of his time, that individuals were responsible for their own future: men had the same characteristics and potentialities that could be maximised through hard work, perseverance, thrift, prudence and self-reliance. These ideas emphasised individuals rather than classes, morals rather than economic realities, and talked of the deserving and undeserving, the rough and the respectable, thus reducing persistent inequalities to moral rather than economic causes. The children of rich Victorians spent the majority of their day with their nanny. The nanny was responsible for the children's daily activities. Nannies also taught children proper behavior, disciplined the children, and took care of them when they were ill. For the most part, children of wealthy parents did not attend school outside of the home. Governesses and tutors taught these children in the children's homes. Mothers sometimes taught their sons and daughters to read and write, and fathers would sometimes teach Latin to their sons. Only sons were sent to boarding schools such as Eton and Rugby. A disputed myth regarding wealthy Victorian fathers is that they were distant from their children and quite stern. Although this may have been the case for some families, there are indications that many Victorian fathers cherished their children and enjoyed spending time with them. Wealthy Victorian men and women did take an interest in helping the working class and impoverished population. Ragged Schools, which were a type of charity school, were started by upper class Victorians for the education of the lower class children.

Chapter 13 Rising to Power

Such economic and financial divergences were compounded by differences of religion, background and politics. But, whilst it is difficult to talk of the Victorian middle-class as a group with a coherent outlook, they nevertheless gained coherence out of the political and social changes of the period. Giving voice to urbanisation and industrialisation this emerging middle-class emphasised competition, thrift, prudence, self-reliance and personal achievement as opposed to privilege and inheritance. The moral terms of this outlook enabled the middle-class to accommodate diversity. Being middle class was defined by taking responsibility for one's self, one's family and the community but the precise terms of this were open to individual interpretation. In practice however, most middle-class Victorians acknowledged that the environment had an influence on men's behaviour. In fact, the rise of the middle-classes in the Victorian period has as much to do with this recognition as the promotion of political economy. Improvement was a key part of middle-class culture. The persistence of poverty and the tendency of the working classes not to emulate middle-class behaviour provided the impetus for a host of reform movements. The Victorian middle-class defined their own values in these attempts to make the poor 'see' their own interests. Policy proposals and reform strategies promoted middle-class values and helped to cement middle-class leadership and authority.

Holding on to Power

Education reform, factory reform and the New Poor Law emphasised progress and civility through work, thrift and rationality. But, perhaps more significantly, local voluntary societies such as Mechanics Institutes and temperance societies promoted improvement cross class communication and rational recreation. Personal narratives of success were an important part of this culture. Records of achievement were popularised and promoted in books like Self Help as examples of how all individuals could and should improve. Individualised narratives of great men building fortunes from nothing became a staple part of Victorian middle-class culture. However, they need to be read with a certain scepticism. A close reading of these stories often reveals that personal contacts and supportive connections were important in establishing a business or in gaining entry to a profession. Having access to networks of support in the Manchester business community was central to the success of the engineer and industrialist James Nasymth. Nasmyth gained legal advise, credit and customers through a network of professionals and businessmen in the area. Like many successful Victorian businessmen, Nasmyth was introduced to these networks through his family relations and family friends. Despite the expansion of the economy and the growth of towns and cities, reputation and personal contact remained significant factors in business arrangements and recruitment in the Victorian period. The working class could and did enter the ranks of the lower middle-class through small capital accumulation and the ownership of a small business but such concerns were often in a very precarious market position. Booth's inquiries into London in the late nineteenth century show the fragility of small businesses. They often yielded modest incomes for hard work. With little access to credit, they were not well equipped to withstand competition or slack periods of trade. The white-collar salaried professions, such as public administration and banking, did however, provide the potential for mobility.

Privileged

In many such professions, promotion up the ranks was structured into the job. But, even here personal contact was a crucial element in filling posts. White-collar workers were largely recruited from within the ranks of the middle-classes. Clerk positions would more generally provide opportunities for the working class to move into the ranks of the middle-class. However, many of these posts were very poorly paid and of quite uncertain status. This uncertain status grew towards the end of the century as they became associated with women's work. Thrift, responsibility and self-reliance were important aspects of Victorian middle-class culture. These middle class 'virtues' could be used to define a society in which success was contingent on individual perseverance and energy. In practice, middle-class society was not as open as this rhetoric implied. For a start, the categories of class were uncertain and shifting. The relationship between affluence and attitude was certainly not clear to contemporaries. Categories such as, 'respectability' and 'deserving' were often used rather than class labels in describing communities of like-minded individuals.According to the Railway Times, Bushey Station was opened on December 4th, 1841. There were three trains a day to London, at 8. 21 Am., 9.36 am. and 12.07 pm. The times of the two returning trains were 3 pm. and 6 pm. People employed by the L.N.W.R. had to be housed not too far from access to their work and this caused the development of the roads to the east of the railway line. In 1873 the passage under the line was lengthened to allow access from the West Side.

The Train Service at Bushey

According to an old map, which may not be accurate, this passageway joined a footpath, which crossed what was, until a few years ago, a coal yard into Pinner Road. In 1878 goods were accepted at the station. In 1913 the electric line, which necessitated the widening of the track and additions to the station, was opened. In the 1920's the station was the busiest between London and Watford, and on several occasions won the prize for the prettiest and tidiest. The weathervane on Bushey Station clock is of special merit, a steam engine. All these different places seem to be written as singular subjects. I have tried to bring these subjects together to form a community. The areas of Carpenders Park, Oxhey, South Oxhey and Watford are all interlinked and cantered around Carpenders Park Manor

January 1864

Chapter 14 Carpenders Park Manor

The manor was built on the foundations of an earlier mansion belonging to Samuel Moody in the latter part of the 1700's It is the year 1864 and a new version of a manor on Oxhey Lane has been finished and is beginning to work very well. The work has been finished for just over a year and everything is on schedule for the first guest season. Visitors will start to arrive in May. Mrs. Carew looks to the sky, it was anvil grey with a huge black swathe in it center. It is going to be a bad storm she can feel it in her bones. All households except the very poorest had servants to do their day to day work. The cook and the butler were the most important. The butler answered the front door and waited on the family. The cook was responsible for shopping for food and running the kitchen, she would often be helped by kitchen and scullery maids. Housemaids cleaned the rooms and footmen did the heavy work. People would come from the country to work as servants in the town houses. These jobs were popular because they gave them somewhere to live and clothes. On average they earned about £50 a year. Often they spent their working lives with the same household.

Winter Storms

As the New Year begins storms it also brought people outside their dwellings staring at a black sky. Wind lashed the trees and front doors, a big storm was about to happen, very soon Small ice flakes whipped in the wind stinging uncovered skin and eyes watered. After some time the black sky stayed but the winds calmed down, snow began to fall. Like a roaring bear, gusts of winds blew the nearby sea shore sending spray to join snow. The wind swept across the land with ferociousness, blowing loose objects about the roads. An old man curled up against his small fire, snow blowing under his door, and eaves, cold. Snow started to fall, harder, the flakes were huge, and swirled in the blustery winds. All night long snow fell, in the morning villagers went outside to see the damage caused. All night long snow fell, in the morning villagers went outside to see the damage caused. The sun shone with such brightness, the blue sky and the carpets of snow hurt their eyes. The snow was deep, and big white chunks of frozen snow stuck to the bottoms of shoes. A tall tree stood in the middle of the estate, and heavy lines of snow bent its boughs. That night was so cold every one went to collect logs for a fire, smoke rose out of chimneys. Dark figures were seen in silhouette behind icy windows, the doors were bolted the eaves blocked. Friends gathered in each others houses, sipping strong wine and singing, muffled by the snow. It was the worst storm that many could recall, elders told of storms, and how bad they were back in the old days. Listeners listened tongue in cheek. In the wintry world without, the coming year bursts out of the frost. Amid the piles of snow buds our future summer one of the blow flowers. A very rare beauty, it is one of the finest miracles of our winter. Robert Carew, the owner of Carpenders Park Mansion looked out of the huge library window and wondered how local people might be coping in the first freezing weather of the New Year. He asked the Lady of the house to get a servant and look through the wardrobes to see what warm clothing they could give to the laborers that lived near by. Robert Carew walked to the stables and asked the stable hands to ready a coach with the strongest of horses for a trip to the local cottages and old hovels. He explained to Mrs. Carew what his plans for the day were. In these difficult winter days we must open our hearts to old fashioned hospitality and sympathy with the suffering. We need to reflect that though a kind of providence generally tempers the cold winds to the shorn lamb. But today there is a conjunction of circumstances so peculiar as to require sharp agencies at the moment when humanity seems least prepared for them. It has to be people like us to put forth energies and virtues befitting the occasion. It is for us to open our hearts, our hands our store rooms and wardrobes and emulate each other in sheltering and strengthening our less fortunate brothers and sisters. Let us pay down cheerfully our part of the price to assist our poorer niegbours. The coach filled with things people will need. Robert Carew and Mrs. Carew, with some of the servants went out on this freezing morning knocking on cottage doors offering help to anybody who needed help. An old traveler walk unsteadily along the white road and the coach pulled up along side him. He was poorly dressed but did not seem to feel the cold. Mrs. Carew got down and handed the old man some warm clothes. The traveler had brilliant white hair and the deepest blue eyes she had ever seen and he talked with a voice, and knowledge that was so very interesting and so very kind the offered him some food to go with his warm clothes. He changed clothes behind a tree and his warm clothes were covered by a large thick coat that Robert still wore when it was cold. The white haired old man thanked them and told them that their generosity would be rewarded in many ways. The coach made its way slowly down Oxhey Lane and stopped by the cottages at Watford Heath. Men were out clearing the snow and The Carews with their servants discussed with families of their needs and addressed their needs from the piles of clothes and food from the coach. They carried on all day until the coach was empty so they made their way back to the mansion. When they finally got home the head house keeper ushered them in and said there will be hot drinks and warm food served in the dinning room after they had changed. Mrs. Carew asked the house keeper, Sally, about the servants that helped them today. Sally said, "They will be looked after in the kitchen." Mrs. Carew explained to Sally that they had all had a long day and she suggested that the staff on the coach should dine with them in the dining room. Sally looked as if she might fall over and mentioned how unusual this was. They all began to warm up and the food was very welcome it had been a good day, the sort of day that will never be forgotten. Earlier on when the sun came out the skies as blue as lapis lazuli. The wind still strong tossed the light surface of the snow in a fine spray. The cold bonded the whole down in hardness that allowed people to walk a little easier. Standing still and looking around on this severe day a new and wonderful feeling to be at the same level as the hedge-tops and across valleys are now all even. Frozen snow under your feet, to find only the rivers showing themselves by their winery hues, amid the trees and rocks. Staff for the estate has been hand picked. The laundry and kitchen gardens are ready for spring and the fruit trees will be thick with blossom. There are two entrances to the estate, one opposite Braiziers Dairy Farm and the other a few hundred yards down the hill. Both entrances have lodges to protect the grounds. The lodge down the hill is by the Heartsbourne River. Which is a beautiful addition to the already splendid estate grounds? This river runs through the estate and can be seen on many excursions.

Chapter 15 The 1832 Reform Act

The image of the nineteenth century as a period of great opportunity for men of energy and skill is one that has been long established. In the past, historians have argued that an industrious middle-class made great fortunes in the early days of the industrial revolution and converted economic success into political power in the 1832 Reform Act. This political power was then used to ensure policy reflected the middle-class interests. Such arguments present the middle-class as a coherent body mobilising their economic and political power to forge society in their image. Challenging landed privilege and aristocratic corruption, this industrial and urban middle-class can be seen as striving to establish a society based on merit rather than on one's birth. Through education reform, schemes of civic improvement and the growth of the market the Victorian middle class saw themselves as facilitating equality of opportunity by enabling the working classes to realise their abilities. These reforms mean that today we live in an open society in which we all have the potential to become middle-class...doesn't it? The Victorian middle-class is largely associated with the growth of cities and the expansion of the economy. The term was used from around the mid-eighteenth century to describe those people below the aristocracy but above the workers. As a social category, the 'middling sort' always referred to a broad band of the population, but this diversity increased in the nineteenth century. Alongside the businessmen associated with the growth of manufacturing, the period saw the increased numbers of small entrepreneurs. Shopkeepers and merchants who undertook to transport and retail the fruits of industry and empire. The increased scale of industry and oversees trade, together with the expansion of empire fuelled the proliferation of commerce and finance such as banks, insurance companies, shipping and railways. This system needed administrating by clerks, managers and salaried professionals. The expansion of cities, towns and the economy produced new spaces that needing regulating and running. The Victorian period witnessed the massive expansion of local government and the centralised state, providing occupations for a vast strata of civil servants, teachers, doctors, lawyers and government officials as well as the clerks and assistants which helped these institutions and services to operate. Such diversity makes a satisfactory definition of the middle-class impossible. There is no clear relationship to the means of production. Although there were some individuals that accumulated spectacular wealth in the nineteenth century through entrepreneurial activity, there were many more businessmen who scraped a living and many who worked for wages as public servants, managers or clerks. The economic boundary of the 'middle-class' was not clear. Some members of the middle-class used their wealth to buy land and stately homes, becoming as rich, if not richer than the aristocracy. At the same time, many members of the skilled working class could earn as much if not more than some members of the lower middle-class.

Winter and the Poor

Rising from his bed, he scraped the frost on the inside of a window. The village was covered in deep snow, drifting up hedges and walls. Walking from the bedroom he shivered, a draught came through the eaves. His freezing hands snapped twigs and thin wood for a fire, to keep warm. Snow brought misery to the peasants in their hovelled, white villages. Nobody could work as most worked on the land, in the fields or roads. No work no pay was the way things are for the urchins and the poor. Drifts and freezing winds chilled their bones, extra rags put on. In bitter winter we must open ours hearts with sympathy for the poor. Providence, kindness, caring, tempers the wind to the shorn lambs. The shepherd wanders out with stick, to help sheep in hollows of hills. Prodding the drifts looking for lost sheep and the snow burns his hands. It is now the iron depth of winter, harsh unforgiving weather, bitterly cold. The old dare not venture out, as a slip might break there brittle old bones. The sick are wrapped up, inches from a tiny fire, rubbing and blowing into hands. As the wind finds its way under doors, cracked windows, and threadbare roofs it was freezing.

Walking over Watford Heath

The history of the Watford Heath seems to reflect quite closely that of the history of nearby Oxhey Lane. It was built on manorial waste and the first recorded landlord (in 1861), T. Bates, he was also the first landlord of the Load of Hay some ten years earlier. The House was one of the first beerhouses in the Watford area to obtain a beer license, presumably suggesting that it was reasonably well thought of. The house was known locally earlier this century as the Crocked Chimney. When we enjoyed Heavy SnowThe frost of a cold January continues through till March, A proverb was, as the day lengthened the cold strengthened. In spite of cold, people in the countryside, enjoy the freeze. Sliding, skating, shooting and snowballing and just walking. Sliding, skating, shooting and snowballing and just walking. Boys fly down frozen, snow covered hills on all sorts of sledges. Faster than birds running with wonderful delight, falling and rolling. The grown up people enjoy the snow, in their sledges bells ringing. Drawn by horse's sledges sliding effortlessly over road and path. Ladies and gentlemen wrapped in furs, full of joy and seasonal laughter. Cracking their leather whips astounding clamour parading through towns. Returning later attended by torch-bearers, what a pleasurable day? Dancing, and sport, places to go, followed by evening balls, masquerades. In towns walking by day is a bracing and delightful form of exercise. But in the closing evening towns and cities a reign of enjoyment begins. Arriving home, there blazes out bright fire from the English hearth. And all congregate around it in groups, from business, sons and brothers. Husband returns bringing the news of the day, and his wife opens the piano. Songs sung, good conversation fills the measures of domestic bliss and harmony. Later the theatre and concerts unfold their charms, wonders and delight. Enjoy the cage of Bajazet and the conquests of Tamerlane, with a fine old port.

There were strict codes of practice for a mid Victorian wife.

A wife may learn how to form her husband's happiness; in what direction the secret of his comfort lies; she must not cherish his weaknesses by working upon them; she must not rashly run counter to his prejudices. Her motto must be, never to irritate. She must study never to draw largely upon the small stock of patience in man's nature, nor to increase his obstinacy by trying to drive him; never if possible, to have scenes. I doubt much if a real quarrel, even if made up, does not loosen the bond between man and wife, and sometimes, unless the affection of both be very sincere, lastingly. If irritation should occur, a woman must expect to hear from most men strength and vehemence of language far more than the occasion requires. Mild as well as stern men are prone to this exaggeration of language; let not a woman be tempted ever to say anything sarcastic or violent in retaliation. The bitterest repentance must needs follow such an indulgence. Men frequently forget what they have themselves said, but seldom what is uttered by their wives. They are grateful, too, for forbearance in such cases; for, whilst asserting most loudly that they are right, they are often conscious that they are wrong. Give a little time, as the greatest boon you can bestow, to irritated feelings of your husband.

The markets are crowded with all sorts of seasonal game and flowers. Here we have a shopping list from the butcher. There are wild ducks, hares, plovers, woodcocks, and snipes at low prices. In the London markets, hares cost a shilling each, ducks for two bob. The brace and snipes are fourpence, but in Devon snipes are a penny each. On a cool brisk sunny day upper class Victorian families went for long walks. Some of their servants may go with them and they would take a packed lunch. If the walk was very long the Groom would bring the coach along.

Turning right outside the manor towards Harrow is Grim's Dyke

Mr and Mrs Carew went for a long walk on a bright March day. The turned right from the manor and walked for about two miles along Oxhey Lane. They came to a road on their left hand side called Old Reddings. The made their way up the hill to the common and explored the common and walked the lengnth of Grim's Dyke. It was a long day and Mrs. Carew was tired after her excursion but she enjoyed herself emmensely and could not wait to put a date in her diary for a return trip. Harrow Weald Common is a remnant of the once extensive woodland of the Forest of Middlesex. Following the Enclosure Acts, gravel extraction was granted as one of the common rights of Harrow parishioners, and this industry was carried on until the late C19th. Adjacent to the common is an area known as The City Open Space, once the site of cottages built for employees of the brick and tile works. Grim's Dyke Open Space is named after the ancient earthwork that runs for 3 miles between Harrow Weald Common and Pinner Green, its original purpose unknown. Harrow Weald Common is one of the remnants of the extensive woodland of the Forest of Middlesex once covering the area, Weald being an old word for 'forest'. Weald was the second largest settlement in Harrow after Pinner in the Middle Ages, although not referred to as Harrow Weald until 1553. By 1759 the extent of the common land was reduced to 300 hectares since when it has shrunk still further to its present size. In the C18th it was a haunt of highwaymen and the steep hill and wildness made it perilous for coach travelers. Following the Enclosure

Acts, gravel extraction had been granted as one of the common rights of Harrow parishioners here, as well as pannage: the right to pasture pigs, and turbary: the right to cut peat for fuel. Gravel extraction took place in the C19th on a large scale for construction and road building, and the undulating floor of the woods is the result of this industry. In 1886 there had been an attempt to get government agreement to sell what remained of this common land since it was considered no longer of use for gravel extraction, but the movement opposing this was successful. One of the supporters of the campaign was W S Gilbert who was then living at Grim's Dyke. Gravel extraction carried on until 1899 when, as a means of conserving the common, the Metropolitan Commons (Harrow Weald) Supplemental Act was passed, revoking most of the commoners' rights, following which a Board of Conservators was set up to manage the site. Within the wider area of the common is 2ha of oak and hornbeam coppice remaining from the ancient woodland of Weald Wood. Adjacent to Harrow Weald Common is an area known as The City Open Space, once the site of cottages built for employees of the brick and tile works run by the Blackwell family, and within the overall site is Grim's Dyke Open Space. Grim's Dyke ('Grimm's Ditch', Grim in Old English meaning devil or goblin) is an ancient earthwork that runs for 3 miles between Harrow Weald Common and Pinner Green, whose original purpose is not known. The date of its construction is debated: it may be C5th or C6th, or may have Celtic or Roman origins. Similarly its purpose has caused much speculation: it may be have been built by the Catuvellauni tribe as defense against the Romans; a boundary ditch during the reign of Offa the King of Mercia; to keep out cattle raiders; for agricultural purposes; to drive animals towards during hunting chases. It is the remains of a massive ditch which was originally said to be much larger. It used to be marked as 'Grimesdich' 1289, 'Grymesdich' 1541. The name has been used for many years and it has changed a little over time. Grim may mean Woden or is Grim a goblin? It is said it was dug by the devil in one day. From Warren Lane cross the road and continue ahead along Priory Drive. Follow the road as it bends sharply to the right but, 50yds (43m) further on, go through a kissing gate on your left, signposted

'Bentley Way'. Continue along the track, with Bentley Priory to your right, and go through another kissing gate. Where another path joins at right angles, carry on ahead (note that this is the path this circular walk returns along). The fenced area on the left is the deer park. At the end of the fencing ignore the path to the left but continue ahead as the track veers to the left, crosses a brook, and then reaches another kissing gate before emerging on to the common. Continue ahead and, at a crossing of paths, turn sharp right across the common, along a beaten down path. This passes through a wood and then crosses a footbridge. Bear right and follow this meandering, tree-lined track. When it joins a path leading to a farm continue towards a road ahead. Turn right. Ignore the first footpath sign on the left and take the one along an enclosed path a few paces further on, just before Honeysuckle House. Follow this path. Turn right and take the first left into Brookshill Drive. At the end of Brookshill Drive turn right towards Copse Farm. Follow this track then, at the end turn right. A few paces further on, go through the wooden gate on the left-hand side and continue walking ahead along this footpath through the wood. It swerves to the right of a gate and later runs along the side of Harrow Weald Common. From there it is a few minutes walk from Grim's Dyke. When the footpath reaches the end of the common turn right. When you get to the road turn left. After about Aquater of a mile cross over and pass through a large wooden gate. Go through a kissing gate and then along a footpath that bisects the common, with the grounds to Bentley Priory on your left-hand side, and Heriot's Wood down the hill to your right. Follow this footpath as it gently descends, before joining the outward path Retrace your steps back to Warren Lane.

April 1864

Mr. And Mrs Carew were very fond of music and the classics. As the weather improved they would regulary get the train from Bushey station and go to Iondon for many Grand Balls with the aristocracy. As a household that could afford a piano, Mr Carew's daughters would learn to play and sing, to entertain themselves and the family and company. Reading was another pastime that was enjoyed by the Carew fanily. Of course, the upper class and upper middle class had the most money to spend on books, newspapers, and magazines. The poorer had to make do with the plenty of cheap publications. The 'penny dreadfuls' and 'shilling shockers' were lurid stories of murder, crimes, and supernatural happenings, which were extremely popular with many of the lower classes. And the Victorian era was when the first public libraries opened, putting books within the reach of the poor to a greater extent. Mr. Carew was a skilful card player, and among the upper classes it was most seriously. Large sums of money might be played for, and to be caught cheating at cards was considered extremely scandalous, a man caught cheating might be ostracised by society. The family enjoyed various kinds of theatrical entertainment and would enjoy going to the theatre, opera, and concerts. Sometimes the servants went to a music hall as it was very was very popular with the working class. Music halls showed a variety of different turns - singers, comedians, jugglers, acrobats. There were other forms of public entertainment, like circuses, fairs, waxwork shows etc. Some of these might not be regarded as quite respectable by the upper and middle classes, but they were enjoyed by many people. The Carew family blended in with their own class of people and enjoyed a rich social life. Boating was all the rage in the late Victorian era, and people of all classes enjoyed taking a boat out on the Thames. With cheap railway fares, even a poor family might be able to hire a boat for the day. The wealthy often stayed on the river in houseboats, which were more like floating houses, and some of them had steam launches. See Jerome K. Jerome's book Three Men In A Boat for example, which is an account of a boating trip taken by three middle class young men from Kingston up to Oxford. The seaside was very fashionable in the Victorian era. A middle class family might spend a holiday at a boarding house or hotel. A working class family might have to make do with a day trip. An upper class family might stay at a fashionable seaside resort, like Torquay in Devon for example, or even stay on the French Riviera, Cannes and Nice were very popular resorts for the upper class English. Sports were played by all classes, but again there would be differences. For example, county cricket teams were normally made up of 'amateurs' (men who could afford to play simply for fun, and didn't have to worry about taking time off work etc), and 'professionals' who played for a living and were usually from working class backgrounds. Tennis, archery, and croquet were all popular games with the upper and middle classes, as they could be played on a lawn by both sexes, and so gave opportunities for socialising. Horse riding was a popular activity with the upper classes, as was hunting. Upper class gentlemen enjoyed going shooting, ladies did not normally shoot, but often followed the shooting party to watch the men, and they would all have lunch together.

We often hear about the lifestyles of Victorian men and women endless parties, social occasions and formal outings. But it is less clear what Victorian children did throughout their childhoods. In fact, Victorian children lived as their parents did in luxury homes with nannies to look after them and many toys to play with. They would often be taken for walks in the park as well as to music festivals and fun carnivals. It is certain their lives were completely different to the lives poor Victorian children lived, which consisted of working in factories and chimney sweeping. Rich Victorian girls and boys also had very different childhoods, particularly from the age of around 11 or 12. Young Victorian boys would most often be sent to prestigious schools such as Eton as soon as they were old enough, where they would be highly educated in order for them to follow suitable professions in adulthood. They would be encouraged to participate in sports such as cricket and shooting. Victorian girls, on the other hand, would receive much less education (particularly before the 1870 Education act, which required all children from five to 13 to attend school). Instead, they would be kept in the home and taught to become good wives. They would be encouraged to present themselves beautifully and practice good social etiquette. This was done in order for them to secure rich husbands in their later teen years. Up until the age of around eight to ten, Victorian children would usually be looked after by nannies, perhaps only seeing their parents at mealtimes. They would have daily schedules that included walks in the park, piano lessons and reading, in addition to many changes of clothes. It was considered important to teach the children good manners and for them to be well presented at all times.

The Rich Victorian Children

They had easy, luxurious lives for the most part. Their families would of course have no trouble for money, so they would dine well, wear nice clothes and have plenty of toys such as skipping ropes spinning tops, rocking horses, hobby horses, wooden dolls and such. However they were expected to show great respect for their parents and show good manners. Most were home educated by a governess; for boys it was until ten or twelve years old, when he would go on to a fancy school like Eton. He would be taught things like reading, arithmetic, writing religion, Greek, Latin, history, and maybe even some business skills. Music and art were things practiced more at home. Girls on the other hand, until later on, were taught more only to sew and to be good housewives and mothers. Few knew how to write unless they were the very Upper class.

Boys might also have been taught in the fields of archery, shooting, riding, hunting and other popular rich passtimes; girls too were fond of their ponies and all. Every now and again could fancy a little trip on a boat on their pond.

Offa

A doubtful charter of Offa granted thirty-four 'mansions' at Cassio also granted to the abbey of St. Albans. Having done some researching the Hertfordshire history and the many manors in the Oxhey and Watford area the whole picture begins to emerge. At the time of the Doomsday Survey Cassio was assessed at twenty hides, and contained woodland to feed a thousand swine. This holding, which probably included the whole manor of Watford, belonged to the abbey of St. Albans. It had belonged to the abbey in the time of King Edward. Alwin had formerly held one hide in Cassio, which Turold held of Geoffrey de Mandeville, the huntsman, one of Queen Edith's men. Geoffrey attached this hide to Bushey, one of his principal manors in this part of Hertfordshire, to which it did not belong in the time of King Edward. Abbot John in 1255–6 leased the capital message of Cassio and a fulling mill to Petronilla de Ameneville in exchange for land in Micklefield and elsewhere reserving to himself all perquisites of court, tallages, and escheats. Henry III confirmed the grant in order that Petronilla might not be ejected during a vacancy of the abbey, and was to endure as long as she should wear the religious habit. This manor provided twenty-four hens at Christmas, six hundred eggs at Easter, and twenty-four cheeses at the Passion of St. Alban, to the abbey kitchen. Abbot John de la Moote built a new barn, and under Abbot John of Wheathampstead a new cow-house was built there. In 1428 Thomas Lavenham, up to the Dissolution farmed the manor. William Dauncey held it under a lease of 1532 for thirty-one years. The manor of Cassiobury, with the woods called Cashio Grove and Whependen Grove, was granted in 1545 to Sir Richard Morrison, who began a mansion at Cassiobury, which was completed by his son Charles, who succeeded his father in 1556. Bridget relict of Sir Richard, who had married Francis earl of Bedford as her third husband, held the manor for life. On her marriage with John de Grava, she discarded the religious habit when this lease became void. In 1271 she and her husband released to the abbot their entire claim in the manor, saving to themselves the right to fish and hunt in the demesne and the use of a house at St. Albans near the tannery of the monastery. Bridget outlived her son, who died in 1599 seised of the reversion, leaving Charles his son and heir, a minor, whose ward ship was committed to Bridget his grandmother, Henry earl of Kent, and Thomas lord Grey of Wilton. Bridget died in 1600, and the property passed to her grandson Sir Charles, who died in 1628, leaving an only daughter Elizabeth, who married Arthur Capell, created Lord Capell of Hadham in 1641. As a loyal adherent of Charles I he forfeited all his estates under the Commonwealth, Cassiobury and the rectory of Watford being granted in 1645 to Robert Devereux earl of Essex, leader of the Parliamentary forces. Lord Capell was beheaded in 1648–9, but at the Restoration his lands were given back to his son Arthur, created Viscount Malden and earl of Essex in 1661. He had in the previous year been made custos rotulorum and lord lieutenant of Hertfordshire. In 1668 was made lord lieutenant of Wiltshire also. He became lord lieutenant of Ireland in 1672, and the purity of his administration there, which lasted five years, was in striking contrast to the general corruption prevailing at the time. He was imprisoned in the Tower for complicity in the Rye House Plot, and died there before his trial, whether by murder or suicide has never been satisfactorily determined. Carpenders Park Mansion is included in many of the historic details but they were quite hard to find, hidden amongst all the other Manors.

Robert Carew was a magistrate and an avid Christian. He used to donate large sums of money to his local church. It is ironic that such a respected man in his community and his business in the City of London made fortunes in producing rum which caused most of the problems in the Seven Dials in central London. He would sit on the bench and punish the wretched paupers after drinking his rum.

Heartsbourne River

Back at Carew's estate in Carpenders Park Mansion the Estate was nearly ready to receive visitors. The river today is just a stream running through what was his estate. The stream has walkways following it along its passage and as it is the beginning of May 1864 the extensive work over the last two years is expected to create a spectacular estate opening this year. Tennis courts and areas for sport are up and running. For the beginning of May we have some friends staying for a few weeks so everything must work perfectly. The daily routines of the mansion have been put in place. The grounds of this grand building are about 250 acres and beautiful walkways designed to thrill any of the guests that have had been invited for 1864. The menu was quite grand as was all the Victorian upper class land owners. A sample of what a guest might expect staying at a friends Manor. Breakfast might be: bacon, eggs, ham, haddock, pork, beef, lamb a few vegetables and plenty of fruit. Port, beer, tea and coffee would be on the side table to drink. After breakfast it was time to have the first explore of the grounds and to go to the start of the estate down the hill to where the Heartsbourne River entered Carpenders Park Mansion Estate, just to the left of one of the lodges. There the guests could spend some time on the banks of the river and get an idea of what they would like to do on the rest of their holiday. It had been decided sometime ago that Robert would oversee the entire visit to prepare for future visits. Also Robert felt as the party might include children it would be better all round if he looked after them. The grounds of the Manor are beautiful. They run along this bank and there are bushes covered in bloom, lilacs, quinces, roses and honeysuckle. In the shrubberies, and hawthorns, blue bells grow along fields and woods. Sedges, with dark brown heads, beautiful planted with the rough-leafed comfrey. A water hen sits on her nest by the stump of a partly hidden tree. And a kingfisher flits with tawny-red breast with green back, near his nest. Deeper into the woods along warm banks greenery is bursting through. The sweet flowers of the woods nodded to their old pals and to the sun. Coltsfoot and cardamine embellish the old fallow green, moist meadows grow into the mead further down stream. The star of Bethlehem gleams in the woods and from shady places. The celandine and kingcup glow in a golden luster and the daisy once more greets the beautiful day. With the crocus spreading a purple blaze flooded over the lea's and meadows. It's a sight you have to see to take it in. Above all the favorites of the field, the violet takes front stage, white and purple diffuse sweetness under the hedges. How many scenes of happy childhood dreams do the first sight recall? Back at the manor Robert showed his kitchen gardens. There were many fruit trees in the kitchen garden and Robert took the time to explain and show the beauty of a pear tree in bloom and the plants that lived with the pear. The bursting blossom of a pear tree stands out with rich blossom, promising plenty of fruit for the year buds along each twisted branch and bough. Rosebushes have sent forth leaves and fresh long crimson shoots, and the syringa is perfectly clothed with pale green, newly formed leaves. The taccamahac is studded with yellow, sweet scented gummy leaves and catkins, they grin, as you walk down old lanes, forgotten fields and secret places. The chestnut pale sticky leaves brightening woods with every sun beam and the mighty oak whispers to the sun, "Let us have one day's warmth." The hedges are impatient showing bits of green here and there; it is neither winter nor summer but lovely spring in Old England. The cuckoo will have to sing on a bare branch, besides buds. Then greenness will steal along the sheltered hedge-sides and fields. It will be a great summer. The butler stepped out through the glass garden doors and motioned to Mr. Carew that afternoon tea was now being served. They all made their way to a day room where cream cakes, home made biscuits and warm scones were available. Mr. Carew stated that it might be an idea not to eat too much as a formal dinner would be served this evening. What a fantastic day? After a light lunch Robert took his guests around the home farm and explained to his guests how it worked. The children of his guests gave names to all the animals and now they were treated like pets. On entering their rooms their clothes had been very neatly laundered and put into dressers and the rooms began to look like they had been lived in and everyone prepared for dinner. At seven o'clock a gong was sounded and that was a ten-minute call to let everyone know it would soon be dinnertime. Well-dressed friends made their way towards the dinning room to a big table where nametags were at each place setting. There was a menu at each place, it was a huge affair. The dinner menu was lavish and laid out on a huge dinning table. There was Mulligatawny Soup, Roast Haunch of Mutton, Boiled Turkey, forcemeat for Veal, Boiled Tongue, Roast Pheasant, Almond Cheese Cakes, great big hocks of ham, beef, pork, chicken and many sweet meats. Dinner lasted well into the night and everyone seemed to enjoy the evening. The menu for each meal changed slightly every day but the same meal was served on the same day on each week. There where changes to include seasonal meals and enjoy seasonal produce. The days outing was to start at ten o'clock but the guests were ready well before that and walked around the house and gardens. Wallflowers in the mansion garden were rich and plentiful, masses of gold from the deep ruddy to the pale with a delicious spicy odour. The first part of the day was to visit the management of the house which would include the laundry room and the other departments needed to run the house.

A Beautiful Day

As Roberts plantations were in far away places he spent as much time with his children as he could as he used to be away for many months at a time, some times years. In a normal upper class Victorian family the children were looked after by nannies, they were seen but not heard. Today was a beautiful sunny day and May once again nature opened her secrets to all her friends, from the boy who ran errands, to the nobility and royalty of the country. She has hung fourth her richest draperies, she has repainted, reburnished, reguilded and she has drawn the veil from her most magnificent pictures, and all earth was her studio. The trees in the English countryside are white with thick blossom and the ground is carpeted with a myriad of flowers. Soft breezes diffuse the most delicious odours, and the sun, spreading from meadow to mead looks into the smallest places and the densest clefts of hills and thickets of the forests, rushing rivers and serene lakes. It bids the lowliest creatures awake from their long slumbers to come forth to the festival of May. The nightingale has come from the south; the voice of the turtle is heard far and wide. The swallows come from the shores and gardens of China on whose sea cliffs she has built her nest of the purest foam. Or has hung it beneath the flapping ornament of a tall pagoda's eaves above the scent of tea trees. All this over the heads of visitors admiring the plum blossoms and the vernal willows. Bird beast and man at the head of all revel in this glorious season of flowers, greenness and freshness. The aging primrose looks out from their woodland homes, their dim eyes closing with the joy of beauty. Cowslips star in the deep and delicate grass on mead's and uplands dazzling all with their precious beauty. Mr. Carew had five children, three girls and two boys. It was the youngest two Katherine and Jessica who had invited friends to stay for the holiday. There was Philip whose family came from Hendon, Mary from Watford, Charles from Cassiobury, Millie from Bushey, and finally Stuart from Hampermill. There were seven children, a handful for one person. This morning the group walked down to a lake about two hundred yards from the lower lodge entrance. It was a beautiful May morning and they all had questions to ask before they even got to the lake. Robert suggested they sit down on the lake bank and draw some pictures of the things they liked the best. There are plenty of things around the small lake. The day was glorious; it was a day for poets. It was warm, bright and the landscape growing visibly richer every hour. Plum bloom fell in showers in the light breeze and another pear tree with brilliant white blossom. Chestnut trees and sycamore trees made green swards in the woods and hedges. The larches were beautiful with delicate and delicious spring green. Wild cherries were in flower, rockets purple and white in full bloom around the lake. There was also a grape hyacinth in bloom a rich beautiful blue. Plus tulips and anemones like gems in a glass case of many rich hues and colours. Also in May 1864 the factory act about children working in the textile industries was added to all factories for working children. Minimum age for working in factories reduced to 8 years old. Eight to thirteen years old to work a maximum of six and a half hours on weekdays and only six hours on Saturday. Thirteen to eighteen year olds to work a maximum of 12 hours a day and the same applied to women. Safety guards had to be fitted to all machines. Finally three hour's solid education for children.

Robert suggested that the children should play some games down by the lake so they sat down and tried to think of some. The game they all agreed on was a game called Roses wedding each person asked a question and the answer must be the name of a flower.

What was she at her first dance? *Answer a Wallflower.*

How could she be described on her best behavior? *Primrose*

What was the motive of an impecunious suitor? *Marigold*

What did he therefore slyly whisper to a friend of Rose? *Anemone*

What was the rank and surname of her fiancé? *Marechal Neil*

What was his characteristic and Christian name? *Sweet William*

What was his birthplace and another of his characteristics? *London Pride*

What request did he make when he left her? *Forget-me-not*

Robert asked the children to listen while he asked a question. Why are Forget-me-nots called this? The children tried all sorts of guesswork. Some of the answers were really funny. But nobody knew the answer. Robert asked the children if they have given up? The group loudly shouted," Yes" "Well" said Robert, "In days of old and knights were bold; a brave knight took his betrothed out for an evening walk. True Forget-me-nots usually grow in damp places like where we are now be lakes or rivers. The river they walked along was a raging torrent and the brave knight saw some Forget-me-nots growing right by the side of the river on a steep bank. He carefully made his way down the bank picked a handful of the flowers and handed them up to his fiancé. As she grabbed them the brave knight slipped and fell into the river. As the current carried him away he shouted forget-me-not, and that was how the flower got its name. Now I have told you the story you must promise me to stay away from the waters edge." The children seemed sad about this story so Robert insisted they carry on playing their previous game.

What was the message when he went on a journey? *Speedwell*

With what did she greet him on his return? *Tulips*

Robert gave Patrick a stern look for that one but he let it pass.

What did he wear for the last time before the wedding? *Bachelor's Buttons*

How far did he travel to the wedding? *Chamomile*

What was the colour of the brides dress? *Lavender*

What did the wedding cause in the town? *Aster*

How many people where there? *Phlox*

In what was the bridegroom's money invested? *Stocks*

What did she use when making sauce his pudding? *Cornflower*

What was the keynote of their confidences? *Honesty*

By the side of the lake is a beautifully build water feature. It allows the water to slowly run over the top and is very pretty indeed Heartsbourne stream, which originates from a few springs near Bushey, and finishes up in the Colne, near Watford. Pelham the famous stone mason who is one of the best known in the country built this feature.

The children enjoyed this game and asked if they could play the same game but this time using the name of birds.

What a coward does in the hour of danger? *Quail*

An action performed when eating? *Swallow*

Portion of a whole, and range of hills? *Partridge*

A famous English architect? *Wren*

Equality and a state of decay? *Parrot*

To dodge the head? *Duck*

Expressing beauty? *Crow*

A monarch and a toiler on the sea? *Kingfisher*

To sell goods? *Hawk*

Something bright and a woodland plant? *Starling*

A vegetable and the name of a male bird? *Peacock*

A schoolboy frolic? *Lark*

The name of a disease? *Thrush*

Abbreviated periodical, and a popular dish? *Magpie*

Cockney term for a certain animal, to perform an act of devotion? *Osprey*

After the game it was time again to walk to the house to have a light lunch. Today it will be freshly cooked bread and some pots of various pastes, followed by a selection of fine sugared fruit. After the break all meet back at the lake for more games.

The games they had played earlier proved to be very popular, so popular in fact that they wanted to play the Birds Wedding.

Brides name? *Jenny Wren*

Bridegroom's name? *Jackdaw*

Best man's name? *Albatross*

Coachman's name? *Martin*

How they rode to church? *Swift*

When and under what circumstances they met? *Nightingale*

Brides present to bridegroom? *Signet*

Colour of bride's dress? *Dove*

Colour of bridesmaids' dress? *Canary*

Where was the honeymoon spent? *Turkey*

What caused the first quarrel? *He woodpecker*

What did she do then? *Grouse*

What did he do with the money? *Played ducks and drakes*

Of what did her father accuse him? *Robin*

What did she call herself when this happened? *Gull*

With what did her father hit him? *Hammer*

What did she do? *Howled*

What did he call her? *Goose*

What did he find it difficult to do when ill? *Swallow*

Of what did he die? *Thrush*

What did she wear? *Black cap*

A trip to Hampton Court

The glorious weather continues. A very early start this morning as they were going on a trip to Hampton Court. The meant a coach ride to Bushey station and a train into London. The group walked over the meadows from Esher by Moulsey. They were struck with the wonderful progress of vegetation. The wild cherries in the woods were like masses of snow. The woods were richly variegated with the trees in different stages of o leafiness. The hedges luxuriantly green throwing out the delicate odour peculiar to the hawthorn in spring. Everything was beautiful, and the beauty of the very ditches with calthas and kingcups of the richest green and golden blossoms. The cardamines pink and white each with lovely flowers. The earth in its fresh greenness, cheerful sunshine, and the air full of delicate smells make every field a paradise and brings back youth to everyone. The cowslips sprinkled in millions over the meadows, not yet in full blow, and the orchids already displaying its sweet purple. So beautiful was everything it was a perfect day. They walked by the vale of the Thames. It is a noble river with its bank full, clear, careering stream with its willowy islands and swans gliding along near the brink, or basking on the islands where an old mother swan sits on its high piled nest of rushes. What is finer than the banks of the Thames? The lordly trees overhanging rivers in the parks grounds and gardens. A rich colour of green, meadow seen on all sides. Fishermen were in punts and skiffs with happy rowing to and fro in the vicinity of the great metropolis of England. They walked in Palace Gardens; saw the hemophilia insignis in flower, a low purple iris, the star of Bethlehem with its pure white flowers blooming about the feet of the tall limes in the avenues where they had been planted with great taste. The abundance of wallflowers gave great richness to the boarders and breathed forth their spiciness through the whole scene. On several of the flower beds, long borders of about a yard wide, of mixed cowslips, red and yellow, and oxlips, yellow and purple, presented a piece of the richest of all mosaic. It exceeded in beautiful effect anything they could have imagined from simple little English flowers. It is worth while for all that have gardens of any extent to have such boarders. It shows how fine, tall and bold these flowers can become by cultivation. It is true that they are all spring flowers and when their blow was over would leave a blank space. But if they were planted in rows, leaving a few inches of space between each row, when one flower died off annuals planted between the rows would soon fill the space with their beauty. As they returned the nightingales were singing, both merrily and sadly. It has the sound of a mountain stream running and leaping on in its beauty and riotous gladness when the bird is in full power and spirit. While it sings it seems to feel all the felicity of the vernal seasons and to express it as no other voice can express it. They all had lunch in a lovely little restaurant and made their way back to the station and got the returning train to Bushey and a coach ride back to the manor. It had been a beautiful day out and all were tired when they arrived back. After a change of clothes and a rest it was time for dinner. They all ate more than usual and played a game of Famous Names for an hour, then they all went to bed and dreamed of the lovely day out they all had.

Chapter 16 The History of Manors in the County of Hertford

The manor of WATFORD according to a monastic writer of the fifteenth century was granted by Offa, king of Mercia. No mention is made of it in any of Offa's charters it may have been covered by the grant of Cassio. There is still extant the will of Ethelgiva or Ethelgifu in which she leaves the 'land of Watford' to Leofrune. This land appears afterwards to have passed to Edwin of Caddington, who left it to the abbey of St. Albans by a will earlier than 1066. Watford is not mentioned in the Domesday Survey, but was probably again included in Cassio.

In the civil wars in the reign of John a sum of £100 and a palfrey worth 10 marks were exacted from the abbot for this manor, and a little later a further sum of 100 marks was demanded. Land in Watford, and various rents and services there, were acquired by Abbot Roger. William Blaket, and at about the same time various tenements and rents in the parish were bought from William Atehale, Reginald de Ponte, William Chalfhunte and Edith his wife, John Dekene, Ralph Clubbe and others, and Roger le Marchaunt gave meadow land lying in the meadow 'de la Holme.' The men of Watford were amongst those who joined with the men of St. Albans in rising against the abbot at the time of Watt Tyler's rebellion. They, with the men of Cassio, obtained a charter in 1381 which granted them the right of hunting all wild animals and fishing in all the waters of the vill, and snaring birds both in the demesne lands of the abbey and in all other lands in the village. They obtained freedom from suit at the court of the abbot, and relief from an imposition called 'Alepeny,' said to have been unjustly levied for a long time past, and from all other tolls and works on bridges and parks. They also extorted from the abbot license to use hand mills in their houses, with the accompanying freedom from suit at the abbey mill. All these liberties were taken away within the year, and the townsmen reduced to their former state of subjection. The history was full and very interesting, as JP it is imperative Robert understood the history and the culture of the people that live in his catchments area. The weather was so lovely for the time of year so the documents could be studied in the open air.

Spring has Gone

The spring has gone and the summer is here. As beautiful as spring is the warmer weather is a delight and most of things are done outside. Robert sits in the sun reading his historical records and dealings. He can be seen sometimes to close his eyes and drift off, opening his eyes with a start to continue with his studies. Papers sometime flutter in the warm breeze but do not blow them off across the estate. There is a lot to learn about but it is impossible to write of the shire without regard for the references of the history that made this area. There is a piece on Charles Lamb's epithets, evoked by his famous visit, accompanied by his sister, to Mackery End and Wheathampstead. The farmhouse and the lovely Elizabethan country house beside it remain. No other county of a like acreage contains anything like so many old and lovely country houses, from such palaces as Hatfield, to the manor house and the smaller historic homes, like Lilley Loo or Lamer. The greater ones begin to loose their original purpose. Cassiobury is the municipal park of Watford, the biggest urban concentration in the county. The Nuffield Trust bought Kimpton Hoo, where Viscount Hampden lived had become for a while a railway headquarters. One large and lovely old house became a preparatory school. Rye House for a time a grossly neglected ruin and now lost. Letchworth Garden City has converted a glorious Jacobean manor house into a hotel and its farmland into a golf course Tewin Water House, now owned by the City Council, has become a special school for deaf children.

Changes to Houses and Estates

There have been many changes to estates both big and small, but almost all the smaller houses remain, and indeed increase, especially along the Buckinghamshire and Bedfordshire borders. Water End by Ayot is a good example of restored glory. We may hope, too, that the very greatest and most pleasing will survive. Hatfield House is supreme on any account. It has remained in one family since the days of the first Lord Salisbury, son of Queen Elizabeth's chief minister, who was induced by James 1 to exchange it for Theobalds, which he preferred. The Jacobean house, which he planned, has no architectural rival of the period; and the old hall and buildings beside it are relics of the very finest Tudor architecture. Nor can a successful rival be found to its internal decorations and gallery of pictures. Those who attend the yearly agricultural show in the vast park have to walk very few yards to see the oak under which Queen Elizabeth was found, so the story goes, when the news was brought of her succession to the throne. Again Panshanger, of which Lord Desborough was peculiarly fond, as a park in some ways more pictorial than Hatfield Park. Within the house the priceless pictures are a memorial to the great day of the English country house, where, as a, much traveled Dutchman said, the highest point in civilization was reached. To give one more example, the descendants of Bulwer-Lytton still inhabit Knebworth, and time has added virtue to the intricate flamboyance of the too imaginative architecture of the house.

Grove Mills

Grove Mills seem always to have been appurtenant to the manor of Grove and are described in 1631–2 as two water mills called the Grove Mills, standing under one roof. The present representative of these mills is on the Gade, on the border of Grove Park. The tenants of the manor of Oxhey held the mill of Oxhey in early times. After the division of the manor a second mill must have been built, for there appears to have been one attached to each part. Oxhey Mill came after the Dissolution to George Zowche, from whom it took the name of 'Souches mill.' He conveyed it in 1542–3 to the king, and it was apparently afterward granted to Thomas Heritage, who was holding it in 1556. It was then called Hamper Mill, and that name has survived to the present day. Heritage evidently held the mill under a lease from the crown, for Philip and Mary granted the mill to their servant Francis Pitcher for forty years, and in 1578 he surrendered this lease to John Pople. In 1597 Sir William Brooke, Lord Cobham, of Hamper Mills died. They were then two water corn mills. His son Henry succeeded Sir William. Hamper Mills passed from him to Sir James Altham, from whose family it passed, in the same manner as Oxhey, to John Heydon. At the time of the sale to Heydon in 1639 three mills were included under the name Hamper Mills. Later on the mills came into the possession of the Cloth workers' Company, and in 1881 were the property of Mr. J. G. Smith. These mills are on the Colne, to the southwest of Oxhey Hall, and now belong to Mr. J. G. Smith. In the middle of the last century there was a silk mill belonging to Thomas

Rock Shute, called Rookery Silk Mill, situated a short distance northeast of Hamper Mill. It was closed before 1881 and on its site the Watford Steam Laundry and Dye Works now stand. Watford was a growing town it really was just a straight road from the ford at Oxhey Park to Cassiobury three miles north. Although it was fairly prosperous there were still many families struggling to get by.

Poverty

Where are the minions of usurped power chains and dungeons forged, carved from pain of poverty? The uplifted ax streaming with patriot blood through a traitor's gate it is a crime to be poor, to be dull. Where are the Peterloos of infamy thick and fast fall the ramparts, made by the few for the few? Ramparts of barbitarity, injustice, instead of distorted social condition nobody cares, nobody dares. The great voice of the time is, reforms must go on. Trade must be freed to feed the poor, give hope. Multitudes of poor men studying Greek, Latin mathematics and Dens of philosophy cannot persist with their studies because of their lack of funds. They are only trying to improve their own tired short lives and to shed the misery of being poor. Crime and disease controlled the areas of Spitalields and St. Giles. The metropolis is bettered by benevolence baths and wash houses, refuges of the destitute and sanitary measures, are in active operation. Cheerful homes are needed for the industrious artisans, and other purifying and sanitary measures at work. I have walked these areas and saw a New World arising in the heart of an old one, the rain is clear.

William Smith O'Brien the Irish Politician

William Smith O'Brien was born into the O'Brien family of Dromoland Castle, Co. Clare. He was born on 3rd October 1803, in Newmarket-on-Fergus, to Sir Edward O'Brien and the heiress Charlotte, née Smith. Sir Edward O'Brien was reputed to be a direct descendant of Brian Boru (obit 1014) and the pre-Norman O'Brien kings of Munster. William was one of 13 children, and the second son. His elder brother was Sir Lucius O'Brien, later Conservative M.P. for Co. Clare who inherited the title Baron of Inchiquin in 1862 after a protracted case before the Committee for Privileges of the House of Lords. Another sibling, Harriet Monsell (née O'Brien) was an Anglican nun, and a saint of the Church of England.[1] William inherited an estate in Cahirmoyle, Co. Limerick through his mother Charlotte, and would appear to have subsequently adopted her maiden name in recognition. His mother was one of the founder members of the women's branch of the Church Missionary Society, and during the Famine worked among the starving and homeless of Co. Clare. She appears to have been a key influence in shaping his attitudes, in particular his awareness of the poverty endemic in 19th century Ireland. Her influence is obvious in a letter from William aged 15, writing from school in Harrow, to his mother. I shall be glad if you shall tell how the poor are getting on about Dromoland, I hope to be able to give them out of my next ten pounds. William completed his formal education with a B.A. in Classics at Trinity College, Cambridge. In 1832 he married Lucy Gabbett daughter of the Mayor of Limerick City, and the couple had seven children. He entered politics in the 1820s, and sat in the House of Commons for Co. Clare, and later Co. Limerick Lucy was pregnant with their last child when her husband was arrested for his part in the Rebellion in 1848. Following his arrest William Smith-O'Brien was tried and convicted of treason and sentenced to death. His sentence was commuted to transportation to Tasmania by 28th June 1849.[3] Although his conviction embarrassed his family, his brother Sir Lucius O'Brien appears to have intervened to ensure that William would at least survive transportation. He secured the Royal assent that the state prisoners would not be sent out on the ship Mountstewart Elphinstone, 'a deplorable prison-ship' that was set to sail immediately, but on the naval vessel Swift, which had previously been used by Queen Victoria.

On 22nd February 1854, William Smith O'Brien was granted a conditional pardon, on the basis that he not return to Ireland. He received a full pardon two years later, and briefly returned to Ireland. He died in Bangor, Caernarvonshire, Wales, on 18th June 1864.

July 1864

The 1st of July 1864 came in like a lion. The heavens opened and the thunder rocked buildings and animals ran from one shelter to another scared. July is the manhood of the year. Upper class Victorians would take full advantage of the summer season and wrote lines of prose to promote outside entertainment. Summer stands strong full grown, glowing and beautiful, between the seasons of growth and decline. It is, or should be, the perfect summer. The trees are in full foliage and their delicate leaves have darkened into a rich green. Flowers of the most beautiful kind are scattered over the meadows and commons over heath and glen. All is bright and hot thunder occasionally pays the country a visit and insects hum around water and woods. If we venture into forests or the green healthy fields the song birds grow faint. The nightingale is hushed and the cuckoo has departed. The blackbird and the thrush rarely bid us a musical welcome and the rose fades on the wayside bough. The corn begins to grow pale for harvest. All is not lost though the elder flower and the corn-poppy and the viper's bugloss is of rich azure they are delightful in the hedge and on the sandy heath. Men and woman and troops of glad children roam through the glens and hills over the fairest spots in the land. It is the holiday of nature enjoyed by myriads of people relaxing in the sun. This prose is typical of the summer spirit.

The Blackberries are Ripe

Many many years ago the news ripped through the London Workhouses,

Through all Bethnel-green, Spitalfields and through the Minories,

Along Tower-hill and up to Shoreditch and Clerkenwell,

To the very purlieus of the Seven Dials, and across the water in Southwark,

Important news spread from ear to ear, overheard in chop houses, and cabs,

Blackberries are ripe, and there are mushrooms in the forest turf.

Like an electric thrill, it has darted far and wide, high and low,

In the great workshops, whether sweating over a hot iron, or folding,

Steaming dye-houses and hatteries or darting the shuttle amongst silken threads,

The bread molders, or makers of coffins for the dead, or their nails,

To the farmers, the boys that roam the streets, and the hags in alleys,

Everywhere there is just one thought, the blackberries are ripe.

The Christmas Holidays

The rich Victorians celebrated Christmas while the poor starved in their overcrowded hovels. A Christmas Carol, by Charles Dickens well represented the split in the Victorian life. The holiday was special in higher circles. Not only the immediate family, but aunts, uncles, cousins, grandparents, it was a holiday devoted to one of the most important aspects of Victorian times, the family. In the afternoon, a long awaited event, the doors of the parlor open and the children finally get to see the glorious Christmas tree with it's candles, tinsel, beautiful ornaments made of colorful scrap art, ribbons, baskets of candies hung from branches. Ropes of popcorn and cranberries ring the tree. Hung from branches are small wrapped gifts, and under the tree the larger ones. Christmas eve is the time for gift exchanges and everyone has a gift. After the grand unwrapping, the children play with their toys, thoughtful handmade gifts are admired and the best gift of all is used, Papa's gift to the family was sometimes a phonograph, a game, a sterioscope, or maybe one of the new magic lanterns with amazing pictures that enthralled the whole family. Next came the program. Everyone has a part. Shy children mumble recitations and poems while older children and adults perform short plays and scenes from history. Musical performances and group singing fills the house. After, sleepy children are sent to bed as well as tired adults. Many Christmas celebrations started during the reign of Queen Victoria around 1837. Hence the title "Victorian Christmas". Many festive customs and traditions date back to Victorian Times. Before this, there was no Santa Claus, Christmas Crackers, Christmas Cards or Christmas Trees. People did not have holidays from work. The Great Industrial revolution provided the driving force which fuelled the wealth to put the celebrations into place. This wealth allowed the Victorians to take two days off work and thus started the Victorian Christmas. One of these days was named Boxing Day, so called because on that day the servants would open the "boxes" in which they had stored gifts of money from the "rich people". The Victorian Christmas co-incited with the opening of the railways which enabled people who had moved to the cities to go back to their country homes to celebrate their Victorian Christmas with family and friends. The Victorian Christmas was a time when there was a huge divide between rich and poor. During the Victorian Christmas era, children's toys were handmade and expensive which meant only the wealthier children got toys. However, with the advent of factories and mass production, games, dolls, books and clockwork toys were all much more affordable and so the children of the less wealthy classes could benefit. A poor child's Christmas stocking for a Victorian Christmas would have perhaps only some fruit and nuts. A typical Victorian Christmas was a time for Victorian family get-togethers. The average Victorian household, unable to afford public entertainment at the theatre or musical concerts would spend cold winter evenings entertaining themselves at home. The fireside/hearth became a symbol of family unity. It was where families ate, kept warm, conversed and entertained them. They sang, played games, and acted. Reading was a favorite occupation. Popular reading material during a Victorian Christmas would be classics such as The Pilgrim's Progress, Robinson Crusoe, the novels of Walter Scott & Charles Dickens' Christmas Carol. There is a certain amount of nostalgia in these days of full of plenty for the Victorian

Christmas. The most appealing item can be the Victorian Christmas Card as it immediately conjures up the ethos and nostalgia for the age. Many cards were extremely elaborate with gilded, embossed, shaped, pop-up and pierced forms. A reproduction Victorian Christmas Card is a joy to behold – all those beautiful log fires, Victorian crinolines, lavishly decorated tables and sumptuously presented food. Once the Victorian Christmas took hold, it gained a grip which has never been relinquished. We today could never imagine a time when Christmas was not the main festival of the year.

Boxing Day

St Stephen was the first Christian martyr. He was also the first Deacon in the Church, and because one of the main roles of a Church Deacon is to look after the poor, St. Stephen's Day is often considered a day for giving food, money, and other items to servants, service workers, and the needy. St Stephen's message of helping the poor also reveals why we call his day Boxing Day. The boxes it refers to are alms boxes used to collect money for the poor. Christians carried out St Stephen's message by collecting money in a number of different ways including a special collection day on Christmas Day. Sailors would drop money into a box throughout their voyage, as a donation to God to ensure their safe journey. Once safely back on land, the money would be donated to the Church. Since early Christianity, still during Roman times, the day after Christmas was the day that Churches gave all the money they'd collected in alms boxes to the needy. The opening of the alms boxes is one of the strongest theories behind why we call St Stephen's day, Boxing Day. In a similar spirit, employers often gave servants December 26th off to spend the day with their families. The theory goes that employers would give their servants a box of bonuses, or gifts, and sometimes leftover Christmas food. In Victorian times, tradesmen too profited from Boxing Day as a day when they collected their Christmas boxes and gifts from happy clients, giving thanks for their good service throughout the year. The spirit of giving that St Stephen would have been proud of is often transmuted onto Christmas which is associated with giving to the needy and giving Christmas bonuses to faithful employees.

Victorian Slums of London

As a great port and the capital of the largest European empire, the poor people of London built the British Empire and were repaid with poverty overcrowding, dangerous streets, filth and wide spread deseases. London contained large numbers of Chinese, Blacks and Lascars, especially close by the docks. There were also people from all parts of Europe including, from the 1830s and 1840s, several hundred political refugees taking advantage of Britain's boasted liberal laws. Living in the more central areas, these included, most notably, Guiseppe Mazzini, Karl Marx, the future Napoleon III and Johann Most , tried for seditious libel in 1881. The number of Jews increased considerably towards the end of the century as many fled pogroms and oppression in Eastern Europe.

During the first half of the nineteenth century the attenuated fingers of urban sprawl that had grown during the eighteenth century first swelled into fat rivers of development, and then solid acres of suburban building. Initially there was ribbon development along the main roads running into the centre. Although a few areas of market gardening and pasturage for cows continued interspersed amidst London's dark brick form until the close of the century, these relics of the past were under constant pressure. In the 1830s villas for the wealthy began to spring up in areas like St. John's Wood, and then south of the Thames (brought within the jurisdiction of the court in 1834). New bridges brought whole new populations to the open fields of Surrey, and parishes such as Dulwich and Norwood became settled by wealthy gentlemen and their families. Somewhat later, and especially from the 1870s onwards, builders began filling in the spaces between the ribbon developments, often with speculative housing for the respectable working class. Different groups gathered in different areas. During the 1860s St John's Wood was regarded as a centre for authors, journalists and publishers. Stockbrokers and merchants settled in Bayswater, Clapham, and Haverstock Hill, while clerks were to be found in Brixton, Dalston, New Cross, Tottenham and Walthamstow. The wealthiest of all sorts were to be found in detached villas in the leafy suburbs of Balham, Barnes, Hampstead, Highgate, Richmond and Sydenham. The growth of urban transport, though not without its problems, facilitated the move to the suburbs, making the daily trip to work in the centre easier as the century progressed. Indeed, from the second half of the century the growth of the metropolitan population was almost entirely confined to the outer suburbs.

On the eastern side of the metropolis the first thirty years of the century saw great reception halls for international commerce St Katherine's Dock, the East and West India Docks, the New Docks at Wapping and the Commercial Docks at Rotherhithe consuming land adjacent to the Thames. The docks created, in the process, a series of new communities to house the tens of thousands of people dockers, chandlers, and sailors - needed to make them work. In the West End, in the early years of the century, Regent's Park and Trafalgar Square were carved out of two of the few remaining open spaces, while John Nash's imagination created ever-lengthening façades of arrogant stucco. But close by these elegant areas there were also appalling slums, notably the central "rookery" of St Giles where Charles Dickens went on patrol with Inspector Field of the Metropolitan Police. The cutting of New Oxford Street between Oxford Street and High Holborn during the 1840s marked the beginning of the end for "the Holy Land", as St. Giles was known to both its inhabitants and the police. Other new developments, especially in the last third of the century and often resulting from railway construction, had a similar impact on other slum districts, but Charles Booth's massive survey of London at the close of the century highlighted many remaining poverty-riven streets where day labourers were believed to enhance their meagre earnings by criminal behaviour. The infrastructure of the metropolis creaked under the strain of expansion, especially in the first half of the century. Even as street lighting and macadam reached in to many of the less pleasant corners of the city, arrangements for the disposal of the detritus of urban life became more difficult. The air became ever more polluted with the smuts and dank stinks of a coal fired world. London's famous fogs are mentioned in the Proceedings over ten times as often in the 113 years after 1800 as they are in the preceding 126 years. Other types of pollution became equally overwhelming. The sewers and nightsoil men grew increasingly inadequate to the task of removing the tons of human faeces produced each day. Even the bodies of the dead became a constant problem. The churchyards filled to overflowing, beyond the point where liberal doses of quicklime could speed the process of decay. Significant improvements came with the Metropolitan Board of Works (established in 1855), which embarked on a major programme of sewer construction and street and housing improvement schemes. London was the centre of what, in the middle of the nineteenth century, was hailed as "the workshop of the world". The Great Exhibition of 1851, housed in Hyde Park in Sir Joseph Paxton's great glass and cast iron Crystal Palace, was a celebration of both the new industry and the accompanying "gospel of work". But London itself was not an industrial city; many of the manufacturing processes found in eighteenth-century London had moved to northern parts of the country where labour, land and raw materials were cheaper. London was an administrative centre for both the nation and the empire as well as for banking and commerce, and its economic and social structure reflected this. The dockers and the growing number of clerks were an obvious aspect of the metropolitan economy. Less obvious were the tens of thousands of women who acted as domestic servants for the burgeoning middle class. According to the census of 1891 there were over 238,000 female domestic servants in London. A scattering of furniture workshops, as well as upholsters, glaziers, painters and decorators serviced the new estates as well as the established, elegant central districts. Pawnbrokers flourished in working-class neighbourhoods, reflecting the uncertain and still often intermittent and seasonal nature of employment. Together with their poorer cousins who ran "dolly shops", pawnbrokers were always suspect as receivers in the eyes of the police. Food processors and small shopkeepers of all kinds ran properties in the growing suburbs, while, in the second half of the century, the growth of large department stores in the centre led to growing numbers of shop assistants joining the clerks on the morning and evening commute. If the eighteenth century had started the process of creating ever more solid social and geographical boundaries between classes, the nineteenth century completed the job. In the eyes of the rich, the poor appeared a different race, linked by a few miles or even a few yards of river front or city street but separated by a massive cultural chasm. When Charles Dickens wrote Oliver Twist, when in the 1820s the West End thrilled to the adventures of Tom and Jerry at "All-Max", the world exposed in such literature was unknown to most upper-class Londoners. The gradations between the rich and poor became ever more numerous, with a growing band of respectable poor, labour aristocrats, and complacent middle classes each claiming a distinct rung on the slippery ladder of social hierarchy. Looking back over a long life from the vantage point of the 1830s, Francis Place was amazed by the transformation of manners among London's working population. The middling sort and artisanal classes had redefined themselves, while the very poor, often now regarded as indistinguishable from a "criminal" or "dangerous class", had been carefully squirreled out of sight. This identification of a distinct criminal class amongst the poor reached its peak in the middle of the century. The grim but vital character of the districts of the "criminal classes" is to be found in the illustrations of the French artist Gustav Doré published in 1872 in the book London.

Nineteenth-century London was as much a city of science and art, theatre and literature as it was a commercial and manufacturing centre and a centre of poverty and crime. This was reflected in the urban landscape where, in addition to the great administrative buildings, including the new Houses of Parliament (1837-57) and the Central Criminal Court (1907), there were new buildings dedicated to the arts and learning – University College (1827-29), the British Museum (1823-47), the Victoria and Albert Museum (1899-1909). But, if people flocked to the metropolis, if art and trade, money and merchandise flowed in ever-greater quantities through this urban behemoth, for most of the century the politics of the city remained absurdly decentralized. The medieval City had long turned its back on the teeming masses outside its boundaries, and left the political ordering of these millions to a patchwork of parishes and county boards. The successive crises caused by cholera, the overpowering stench of human waste in the Thames, the overcrowding of the churchyards, and the general failure of infrastructure towards the middle of the century, prompted moves to create some kind of order out of the chaos. First, as noted above, came the Metropolitan Board of Works, elected by the Common Council of the City and the vestries. Then, in January 1889 came the first direct elections for a new metropolis-wide body to supervise metropolitan administration – the London County Council. But even after the creation of the LCC, London's government remained haphazard and decentralized, with the old vestries and City of London continuing to function in parallel to the LCC, while the new body was granted only limited powers over other city-wide organisations. Fear that an elected LCC might result in a socialist majority fuelled the argument for keeping the Metropolitan Police under the authority of the Home Secretary. While few took to the streets to demand the reform of local government, urban radicals played a significant role in the long-drawn-out campaigns for the extension of the franchise. During the 1790s a powerful political infrastructure had been created in the corresponding societies. This laid the foundations for later radicalism. By the 1820s, after the popular upheaval associated with the Queen Caroline Affair, and driven by economic dislocation, working- and middle-class Londoners became increasingly politicised. In the 1830s and 1840s there were mass meetings of reformers, most notably the Chartists. There was rioting in Hyde Park at the time of the Second Reform Act in 1867, a massive demonstration in the same park with a crowd estimated at 120,000, during votes on the third reform act in 1884, and turbulence in the late 1880s as political radicals sought to channel the anger of the unemployed and underemployed. As the nineteenth century gave way to the twentieth political agitation in the metropolis found a new voice and new forms of action with the Suffragettes. During the 19th century, London became the first "world city"; 1) it had a large population distributed over a very large geographical area; this dispersion of the population to suburbs was made possible, as we shall see, by the mechanization of transportation; the railroads were built beginning in the 1830s, the Underground was begun in 1865, and there were horse-drawn trams by the 1880s; 2) the population of a world city comes from the whole world; London attracted the dispossessed and ambitious from the British Isles; it attracted the poor and the politically oppressed from southern and eastern Europe; and it lured immigrants from British possessions throughout the world, particularly India and China; 3) a world city has direct industrial and commercial ties to the entire world. In 1880, the Port of London received 8,000,000 tons of goods (up from 800,000 in about 1800). A contemporary guidebook advised: "Nothing will convey to the stranger a better idea of the vast activity and stupendous wealth of London than a visit to the warehouses, filled to overflowing with interminable stores of every kind of foreign and colonial product." (Willis, *World Civilizations*, p. 323); 4) a world city is involved in the internal affairs of other nations. London was the capital of Great Britain, the capital of the British Empire, and the capital of the British Commonwealth of Nations. In addition, its naval power made England a necessary participant in world affairs. Like other capital cities, London was a political and administrative center, and it housed thousands of civil servants who worked for expanding bureaucracies; it also attracted ambitious political figures; it was also the financial center, the hub of the rail and road system, and a large marketplace for goods and services; industry tended to be located in the suburbs; city center housed government buildings and mercantile activities; capital cities were also cultural centers: newspaper and book publishers were there, as were theaters and operas, restaurants and pleasure gardens. Problems facing 19th century capitals like London: many were centuries old, and their centers were clusters of old streets, churches, and palaces; social structures and traditions were ancient; in-migration had flooded the old central districts and even some suburbs; hence urban development in the 19 century consisted both of the reconstruction of the ancient centers and rapid growth on the periphery; 19th century urban dweller faced common tensions and traumas of urban living, i.e. congestion and crime; but also new problems: long commutes or a sense of isolation and despair. London amongst the oldest of Europe's capital cities (Rome and Paris are older); since ca. 1650, London was Europe's largest urban community and in the 19th century, London was the most populous metropolitan center in the world; until the Industrail, London had been England's only large city; London's size and wealth had been a factor in the growth of the English economy, needing coal, food, and wood, for example; by 1700, London was Europe's and the world's greatest port and commercial center, a role London retained until the 20th century; industry less important than to Paris or Berlin; as the administrative center of a kingdom as well as the British Empire, London had a great deal of political autonomy; and London was less threatened by mass uprisings than other Europe capitals.

Chapter 17 London's History

Roman origins in the port settlement of Londonium

Economic revival in the Middle Ages; largely the work of foreign merchants resident in London, Germans from the Hanse cities, Florentines and Lombards from the Mediterranean world

London comes of age during the 18th century, during the Georgian period; land speculators and builders shaped the physical development of the city later taken over by the Victorians; Georgian actors created a tradition of theater life; Georgian pleasure gardens and country estates influenced the creation of parks during the 19th century; the practice of club life; and the financial, insurance, and brokerage houses were mostly of Georgian origin

Four Shaping Forces on London in the 19th century: 1) Geographical or topographical: it explains physical characteristics of the city or changes that can be attributed to the environment; 2) Economic: the impact of commerce, finance, industry, and transport on the history of London; 3) Sociological: population movements, either as a whole or in classes, groups, and occupations; 4) Cultural: "It accounts for the values, beliefs, conduct, and institutions which make up and define the daily experience, give meaning to life, and pattern the activities that we find in the city." (Rothblatt, 165)

London's Geography and Topography

London a political, economic, and judicial center; these activities are reflected in the city's topography.

Roman's founded London on a site where natural land routes intersected with navigable waterways; the Thames is navigable 50 miles inland; London Basin had deep-water harbors; also land access was relatively easy through gaps in the surrounding hills;

The first nucleus of London is the City of London to the west of the docks was also founded by the Romans; it is about 1 square mile; it stretches from Aldgate in the district of Whitechapel to Temple Bar, once the arch where the severed heads of traitors were displayed; located close to the docks, the City became a financial and commercial center, the heart of the British shipping industry, the center of the world's re-export trade, the center of international insurance; and the home of the British pound; even today, the City had retained a large degree of autonomy.

Upstream about a mile is the City of Westminster, the second core of London; it became the political capital of England, Scotland, Wales, and Ireland; the administrative head of the British Empire in the 19th century; Westminster was the seat of the monarchy, the British Parliament, the mother of parliaments, and the bureaucracy.

Linking the City and Westminster along the Thames was a major road called the Strand and a third district, the legal district. There was established during the late Middle Ages the Inns of Court, the law schools, and the courts themselves. In the 19th century, New Scotland Yard, the headquarters of the metropolitan police, was located near the courts. The courts and the police have a partnership. "Together they symbolized the orderliness that was supposed to underpin the growth of Victorian London."

Economic Structures

19th century London a dynamic city; old occupations were transformed, while new ones arose. The number of professions increased, i.e. civil engineers, clerks and accountants, local government officials, surveyors, teachers, nurses, social workers. This new group, ranging from the lower to the upper middle class, pushed its way between the traditional artisan and the elite world of finance; it was a large consuming group; and they gave the city much of its social and economic character.

London not an industrial center like Manchester; hence merchants not the most important political group, and they had to share prestige and authority with the royal court, Parliament, the bureaucracy, and social and political leaders.

London as a manufacturing center: 1) enormous expanse of docks and shipbuilding facilities; 2) silk manufactoring at Spitalfields; 3) Sugar refineries at Whitechapel; 4) tanneries, iron foundries, glass works, dye works, shoe and hat shops, and distilleries in the Southwark area; also on the south bank was a gas manufacturing plant, near which the first industrial union was establishe; 5) the Poplar District had chemical factories and polluted the air. But only about 1/6 of the labor force employed in factories.

The customary manufacturing unit in London was the workshop, which employed the elite of the London worker; originally, craftsmen in these shops produced all sorts of goods, but in the first half of the 19th century, the Industrial Revolution forced a shift to producing luxury and consumer goods for local markets; hnce clothing, jewelry, clocks, and stationary; also food and food processing; also the building trades flourished as London grew; the shipbuilding industry declined after the 1860s.

London workers

An elite of well-paid and privileged craftemen; 2) millions of unskilled laboring poor; they worked in the docks, as builders, as scavengers, chimney sweeps, wood choppers, rag collectors, messengers, coachmen, women in the garment industry (especially after the introduction of the sewing machine. Much of this work was seasonal, and occasional unemployment was a fact of life; hence genuine fear of the masses of the unskilled; 3) lower-middle class, or "white collar" work: this was the fastest growing part of London's population; thousands of clerks worked in the banking, insurance, and brokerage industries, most of them men until the invention of the telephone and the typewriter; elementary school teachers needed after the creation of a state-supported primary education system in the 1870s; their status was lower than that of the "public school" teachers; 4) the "higher" or "liberal" professions of law, medicine, and the Church, and all three had London ties. Legal education and the practice of law had its center in London. Also in London were the main teaching hospitals, and there was a wealthy population in need of physicians. The Church of England had a large presence in London, and all bishops and archbishops sat in the House of Lords. Also there were opportunities for previously inferior groups like solicitors and surgeons to rise in prestige. Also a large number of domestic servants.

London's Growth

Because of its economic and political importance London was long the largest city in Great Britain, and after 1700 it was the largest city in Europe, surpassing its rival Paris. This growth continued throughout the 18th century. Up to about 1780, the main source of this population growth was migration from other parts of the British Isles. It is estimated that 1/6 of the British population visited London during the 18th century, and the most adventurous and ambitious stayed.

Population growth in the first half of the 19th century was spectacular, probably a combination of migration and a high birth rate, although scholars are unable to agree on the matter. Between 1800 and 1810, the population rose by 23%; between 1840 and 1850, it rose by 21%; and at no time did the rate fall below 17%; in the second half of the century, growth was less dramatic, but nonetheless above the national average. Population in 1810 was 1,000,000+; in 1851:

2,500,00; and in 1901, 4,500,000. In short, London's population increase was "remarkable and unprecedented." London grew faster than any other city in Europe.

Urban problems resulting from this population growth were staggering: housing was in short supply; space became increasingly valuable; public hygiene deteriorated (low standards of personal hygiene, open-air food markets, litter in the streets, the filth from horse-drawn delivery and passenger vehicles); winds blew in dust, dirt, and soot; drinking water was polluted. Diseases like typhoid and cholera were common. An outbreak of cholera in 1831 killed 5,000, while others in 1833 killed 1,500, in 1848 killed 14,000, in 1866 killed 6,000.

Death rate in 19th century London was high: 1840s: 25.2 per 1,000; 1850s: 23.6 per 1,000; 1860s: 24.3 per thousand [According to provisional statistics in the US, the death rate was 9.8 per 1,000 population in Jan-Mar 94, 3% higher than the Jan.-March 1993 rate. Among the deaths for the first quarter of 1994 were 8,300 deaths at ages under 1 year, yielding an infant mortality rate of 8.4 per 1,000 live births, compared with a rate of 8.6 for the first quarter of 1993. This change in infant mortality was not statistically significant.]

Behind the high mortality rates: 1) absence of an established connection between disease and contaminated water; 2) decentralized system of local administration was inadequate to control waste. The introduction of the water closet meant that more waste was dumped into the Thames. Within London, there were a hundred units of local government, and local people did not want to pay higher taxes. Even Parliament was nearly paralyzed by a fight between supporters of a strong central government and those who resisted the erosion of the power of local authorities. Not until 1900 were some of these issues resolved, and only then did the death rate start to fall.

Chapter 18 Railroads and Suburban Growth

Dramatic population growth contributed to the outward sweep of the city and it forced the city into a technical revolution incolving modes of transport.

Because of geography, london's growth was in an east-west direction along the Thames; in the 18th century, the City was densely inhabited, Westminster less so; the rest along the river was a sequence of villages like Highgate or Hampstead or Richmond. Hence, 1800-1840: most of the inner districts of present-day London were still rural parishes. The pattern of growth in the 19th century was called "leapfrogging;" it was not systematic, spreading in concentric circles from the center; rather a new center of settlement or a pre-exisitng one would be targeted; then it would be connected to London by a high way and the intervening space would be filled in. The invention of the railroad and the Underground had a critical impact on this population growth.

Only in the 1870s and the 1880s did the railroad become the favored mode of transport for the commuter; prior to that, it had been the horse-drawn omnibus, which was introduced in 1829 and which moved at about 5 mph.

The introduction of the commuter train helped determine patterns of suburban development; towns grew up around the suburban stations; fit in with the British desire to live in the country; also made possible north-south development and ended the Thames' role as the determinant of the direction or urban development.

Development of the rail road within London was different from the suburbs; land was more difficult and expensive to come by; but by the midst of the 19th century, 10% of the valuable land in central London was in the hands of the railroad companies; but they never were able to build in the actual center, and the rail lines do not connect; stations dotted the periphery of central London; hence a traveller must often change stations to continue a journey (same is true in Paris and Moscow); hence the need for a means of rapid transit. The London Underground was born in the early 1860s, with the opening of the Baker Street Station of the Metropolitan Railway, connecting the mainline station of Paddington to Farringdon Street and then to Moorgate. The opeing was preceded by a decade of political and financial discussion. Plans had to go through Parliament. Plus there were the technical problems of actually constructing the Underground. In 1862, the Lond Times complained "of dark, noisome tunnels, buried many fathoms deep beyond the reach of light or life; passages inhabited by rats, soaked with sewer drippings, and poisoned by the escape of gas mains."

But by the end of the 19th century, the Underground was complete; the result was the linking of the railway termini in the city center and an acceleration of settlement on the city's periphery, away from the Center.

The direct and indirect impact of the railroads on the economy of London is difficult to underestimate. In 1861, 23,000 people were directly employed by the railways; by 1891, the figure was almost 70,000. In addition, 48,000 people were employed in ancillary transport industries. The add families and dependents. Result is the conclusion that 250,000 people depended on the rail industry for their livelihood. Other industries grew up near the rail lines; also service industries like hotels, restaurants, refreshment stands, etc.

Aesthetic and social costs were high. Architecture of railroad stations was imposing; King's Cross was neo-classical; St. Pancras was Ruskinesque Gothic; Victoria Station had airy girder vaulting. Also built were a number of grand railway hotels. But they soon became black and sooty because of the smoke from the steam engines. Housing near the rail lines was also blackened. They were also noisy.

Railroads needed vast amounts of space; land was needed for stations and track, for shunting yards and siding, for storage facilities and platforms; also land was used by nearby businessmen; the rail lines cut up existing neighborhoods, blocked foot and wheeled traffic and produced great congestion around the stations. As a result, owners of housing near rail lines let it become rundown, and great railroad slums grew up inhabited by the casual laboring poor of London.

By the end of the 19th century, Londoners had a array of transportation options: mainline trains ran to the new suburbs; the Underground filled in the gaps in the city center; there were also horse-drawn busses and, after, the 1870s, horse-drawn trams. The economy ultimately became dependent upon the railroad. "Once population expansion and the railroads united, the Georgian city yielded to the Victorian city, the cream-colored stucco of the last years of aristocratic London was replaced by the blackened bricks of the industrial age; and, finally, leisured urbanity was supplanted by the modern culture of timetables."

London Suburbs

Because of population pressure and the absence of inexpensive housing in the city center, the population of London had to move outwards, creating a new relationship between the center and the periphery. For a long time, the affluent had had houses or cottages in the country to which they could retreat on weekends or holidays or for retirement. In the nineteenth-century, transportation made it possible to live in the suburb and work in the city. (See Girouard, p. 284; painting of Sydenham, South London, by Camille Pisarro). This relationship reveals much about the "urban mentality," the preferences and values of the Victorian builders, householders, and planners.

Victorian developers created suburbs could choose between two design possibilities: 1) the traditional Europe or 'spider' plan or village idea of curving stressts, back alleys, half-hidden lanes, unpredictable roads. Such a plan favored the local pedestrian, who learned to negotiate the bewildering street plan; 2) the neo-classical idea of planning based on boulevards and direct roads; in other words, the rectilinear grid; it is impersonal; traffic moves quickly; lingering is discouraged; and broad views could extend one's view or his imagination.

Victorian builders used both types of street plans in the remaking of London. Arterial roads like Oxford Street or Marleborne Road were cut to parallel the Thames; radial roads were also built from the center out, not unlike the railroads.

But once a throughfare connected the center and the periphery, the spider plan took over. They recalled the much loved English countryside. Hence the idea of the "village in the city" or the "garden suburb." One influential practitioner was Nash, who used a curvilinear street plan for Park Village East and Park Village West on the Camden Town edge of Regent's Park.

To complete the village theme in suburban planning, two types of traditional dwellings were brought from the countryside: the terrace or row house and the single-dwelling or the villa house; they could be sited on curving streets, creating a charming effect. The most popular type of suburban house was the Victorian semi-detached houses, Villas a small to medium-sized gentleman's house in a rural setting, including a park or an estate were built in all sorts of styles By the 1790s, there were architectural pattern-books of designs for cottages and villas, including Richard Elsam's Essay on Rural Architecture (1803) for a quote on the virtues of a rural retreat. Also built were speculative ventures like St. John's Wood, "the first full-blown suburban neighborhood in England." Regent's Park was a more elegant suburb which combined city and park. The park was all-important. Many Victorian suburbs were pleasant neighborhoods of houses surrounded by shops and services, and all the facilities needed by a town dweller. But note Hippolyte Taine: "The townsman does everything in his power to cease being a townsman, and tries to fit a country-house and a bit of country into a cornor of the town."

The growth of the suburb, some historians claim, reversed the traditional relationship between the city center and the periphery. In the Middle Ages, for example, the suburb was outside the city walls, and it was a place were waste was thrown and undesirables congregated. At night, the city gates were closed, and these areas sealed off. In the 19th century, the areas outside the city center became fertile. The center was inhabited by the poor and the wretched and the streets were filthy. Invisible but real barriers prevented the poor from moving out. In addition, the suburbs draw off investment capital from the center. The practice of commuting separates work from the family, producing tensions between the two. The suburb also creates geographical barriers between the working class and the middle classes. And, suburban life, it is charged is "banal and monotonous."

The Inner City

Number of trends evident: 1) Loss of social heterogeneity of many London districts; 2) depopulation of the City; 3) an alteration in the relationship between employers and employees, and 4) the growth of vast slums like the East End.

1) Loss of social heterogeneity of many London districts: Take Westminster, Mayfair, or Pimlico. There Georgian and Regency terraces, with courts behind them for a service population, and a nework of mews or alleys for the storage of carriages and the stabling of horses. But by the 1870s, the mews and courts were demolished, largely because public transportation and cabs rendered obsolete the carriages and horses, together with the grooms and coachmen. Also workers did not move to the suburbs until the cost of the railroads and the Underground dropped considerably. And, when workers moved outwards, fashionable people moved even further out.

2) The depopulation of the City, traditionally home to small masters, merchants, stockbrokers and financiers, insurance underwriters, and ship owners. Beginning in the 1860s, they all moved outwards. In 1851, the population of the City was 127,000; by 1861, it was 112,000, and by 1900, it was 31,000. The City became a business center, busy during the day and deserted at night. Its architecture changed, great office blocks were raised, often in the grand styles borrowed from previous eras like the Gothic, the Jacobean, and the Italian that the Victorians favored.

3) Suburban exodus altered relationship between employer and employee; before the Victorian era, prosperous merchants and craftsmen operated their businesses from their homes. Employers, clerks, journeymen, and apprentices lived near each other, often in the same building. Even if there was not much contact, there was proximity. After 1860, skilled workers began abandoning the city for the suburb; then home and family became more important than work; the working day was also shortened and income rose.

4) The growth of vast slums like the East End. Dramatic growth in the first half of the 19th century.

People who worked in the docks and industries like foodstuffs, beverages, building materials and soap lived in the boroughs of Whitechapel, Stepney, Poplar, Bethnal Green, Bermondsey, and Southwark. Descriptions of living conditions are found in Edwin Chadwick's Report on the Sanitary Conditions of the Labouring Classes (1842), Henry Mayhew's London Labour and Lond Poor (1861), Charles Booth's Life and Labour of the People in London (17 vols.; 1886-1903), and the accounts of contemporary observers. The novelist Charles Kingsley wrote in 1849: "And, oh God! what I saw! People having no water to drink hundreds of them but the water of the common sewer which stagnates full of dead fish, cats and dogs, under their window."

Charles Dickens, from Bleak House "Jo lives that is to say, Jo has not yet died in a ruinous place, known to the like of him by the name of Tom-all-Alone's. It is a black, dilapidated street, avoided by all decent people; where the crazy houses were seized upon, when their decay was far advanced, by some bold vagrants, who, after establishing possession, took to letting them out in lodgings. Now, these tumbling tenements contain, by night, a swarm of misery. As on the ruined human wretch, vermin parasites appear, so these ruined shelters have bred a crowd of foul existence that crawls in and out of gaps in walls and boards; and coils itself to sleep, in maggot number, where the rain drips in; and comes and goes, fetching and carrying fever, and sowing more evil in its every footprint than Lord Coodle, and Sir Thomas Doodle, and the Duke of Foodle, and all the fine gentlemen in office, down to Zoodle, shall set right in five hundred years though born expressly to do it.

Reforms

The first step in remedying many of London's problems was the compilation of reports like Edwin Chadwick's or Henry Mayhew's or Charles Booth's; the second step was the creation of a metropolitan government to deal in a unified and systematic way with all of London's problems.

The former riverside town required new forms of government, of communications, and of sanitation if it was to continue to grow. These were slowly and painfully evolved in the London of 1820-1914. Against a background of statistics that showed the population of the built-up area rising from 1,225,694 (1821) to 6,586,269 (1901), the innovations came piecemeal. In 1829 a centralized Metropolitan Police Force was provided, under the ultimate control of the home secretary, in place of the uncoordinated watchmen and parish constables. The lighting of streets by feeble oil lamps was revolutionized by the introduction of gas, and soon the Gas Light and Coke Company (1812) was followed by similar companies scattered throughout London. Omnibuses (1829) began a revolution in road transport, and carriage by rail came less than 10 years later. In 1845 an inquiry into public health was made, with the exposure of London's worst deficiencies, followed by legislation in 1852 ensuring a purer water supply. A statute in 1855 (the Metropolis Management Act) combined a number of the smaller units of local government and replaced the medley of franchises with a straightforward system of votes by all ratepayers. Major works, such as main drainage, were put in the hands of a Metropolitan Board of Works. [Source: EB]

The momentum of these changes, established by such diverse reformers as Bishop C. J. Blomfield, Sir Robert Peel, Edwin (later Sir Edwin) Chadwick, and the Earl of Shaftesbury, continued throughout the century. New churches, new schools, better law and order, main drainage, and care for the outcasts were some of the reformers' legacy; Trafalgar Square, the Embankment, and roads, such as Shaftesbury Avenue and Charing Cross Road, driven through the worst of the slums are their most obvious monuments. The changes in government continued, if not so drastically. The London County Council superseded the Metropolitan Board of Works in 1889, the vestries were transformed into metropolitan boroughs by the London Government Act (1899), and the various water companies combined in 1902 into a publicly owned Metropolitan Water Board. Public and private works continued to transform the face of London. The opening of the Metropolitan, a steam railway, in 1863 and the making of Holborn Viaduct in 1869 were accompanied by the building of new Thames bridges and the rebuilding of Battersea, Westminster, Blackfriars, and London bridges. After years of discussion and agitation, the road bridges outside the City passed into public ownership, and the tollgates disappeared. Most of the main southern railways carried their lines northward across the Thames into London, to Victoria, Charing Cross, Blackfriars, and Cannon Street stations. It was an era in which an abundance of initiative and of capital was joined to abundant labour to make the widest use of new skills, cheap transport, and copious raw materials. Technical progress continued gradually to alter the lives of Londoners and the face of the town. Cheap suburban trains enabled the artisan or clerk to live farther and farther from his work. The London School Board, established under the Education Act of 1870, set about the task of providing elementary education for all. Trains or streetcars (horse-drawn), after an unsuccessful beginning in 1861, became important in the 1870s and a major factor in metropolitan transport as their electrification developed in the first years of the 20th century. By then electricity was being used as the motive power for traffic below ground, the Prince of Wales opening the world's first electric underground railway, from King William Street to Stockwell, on November 4, 1890. With the arrival, before 1914, of the gasoline-driven omnibus, the outline of transport in modern London was complete and the way opened for still faster development of suburbia.

The first effort was the creation of the Metropolitan Board of Works (1850s), which udertaking a building program, made sanitary improvements, and purchased parks. Then came Burial boards, an asylum board, and a school board. Finally, in 1888, a London County Council was created.

The Great Exhibition of 1851

The idea was Prince Albert's in 1849; its purpose was "to give us a true test and a living picture of the point of development at which the whole of mankind has arrived in this great task of applied science and a new starting point from which all nations will be able to direct their further exertions." Financing was supplied by private industry and a public subscription of £200,000. A public competition was held for the design of the exhibition building. The winner was Joseph Paxton, who suggested a massive greenhouse for the Hyde Park site. It was 1,848 feet long, 408 feet wide, and 66 feet tall (tall enough to cover trees). Made of cast-iron struts and glass (1,000,000 sq feet), it was erected in 17 weeks; after the exhibition closed, it was taken down and reerected in South London, where it was used until destroyed by a fire in 1936. Exhibits were in four categories: raw materials, machinery, manufactures, and fine arts.

London's Cultural Life

The British historian Frederic Maitland once wrote: "Mere numbers are important. There are some thoughts which will not come to men who are not tightly packed." The culture of the city is unique. It shapes the attitudes of its inhabitants and requires of them special exertions or adjustments. Victorian London . . . forced Londoners into adopting a range of values that comprise an urban mentality. City life had a special meaning, if not always a very precise one, and in the search for that meaning city-dwellers defined their relationship to a challenging if impermanent environment." Best place to search for the evidence of the meaning of a city is in the painting and writings of intellectuals, for artists create images (in words and pictures) of the world around them. "The intellectuals of Berlin and Paris, the feuilltonists of Vienna and journalists of New York have each helped in creating an urban self-consciousness." London, like most great cities, is a restless place; it accordingly challenges the imagination of its citizens. 18th century intellectuals were largely enthusiastic about London. They came from Scotland, Ireland, and the English provinces because London was the center of social, intellectual, and political life. It offered them opportunities, work, an income, and circles of friends. They observed city life, spread its news, and mapped out novel dimensions of the urban experience.

Up until the first half of the 19th century, they successfully conceived of the city within a late-18th century aesthetic vocabulary based on classical thought. They called London "sublime," which meant that a city should be grand and a little disturbing, but not terrifying. "A city had to charge up the emotions, put the senses on the alert, stretch mind and body to their full capacity. A city had to provide opportunities for the display of energy and for the exercise of individual initiative." Hence London's buildings, including Parliament, St Paul's, Westminster Abbey, etc. The aesthetic of the sublime permitted appreciation of the city's special qualities: stimulation, awe, perplexity, novelty, surprise, and its discomforts could be tolerated.

Second half of the 19th century the notion of the sublime ceased to control the disquieting aspects of urban life. The new terms for the city were Pandemonium, the city built by devils in Milton's *Paradise Lost*, or Babylon, the symbol of Biblical evilness. London is dirty and unhealthy, full of smoke and soot; it had a migrant dockside population and cheap lodgings for pimps, prostitutes, and urban riff-raff; the traditional moral restraint of religion seemed to fail; hence an emphasis on punishment and incarceration. Building were perceived as large, ugly, and no longer in human proportion. The pace of urban life became too quick. And people became anonymous.

Loss of grip on the city and loss of a sense of place evident in paintings of 18-19th century London. 18th century views show the river and a skyline of church spires; urban landscape is viewed from a gentleman's terrace; sometimes a vernal stretch of water or an Italian Capriccio. 19th century views are genre paintings, scenes of riverside frolics, activity in the ports, and Whistler's nocturnes. Then came the French impressionists, and the cityscape disappears into a swirl of colored fog; the Fauvists paint the city with "unnatural" colors contained in strict outlines (an effort to gain control over a vanishing environment?); then modern painting, where the city is reduced to an abstraction. "London is too big, too elusive for painters to capture in a single, striking conception."

Photographs of London tell a similar story. They recorded the city's reality, and at first they photographed everything. Overtime, they become more selective, and they focus on the impermanent aspects of the city.

By the end of the 19th century, the response of artists and intellectuals to the city had changed. No longer the delightful Georgian mix of country and town, no easy communication with the countryside; it no longer stimulated creative responses; it had become an enemy, full of slums, poverty, chaos, etc. In contrast, the suburb stood for what the city had lost: the stability and virtues of a village and family life; the suburbs were safe and charming.

The Victorian middle class preferred the suburb with its privacy; the affluent still favored the city for its diversities, novelties, and range of pleasures; department stores like Harrod's; music halls, theatres, restaurants, concerts, Gilbert and Sullivan; museums; great newspapers; and the tourist and post card industries. Pleasures for the working classes: sports, especially soccer; free museums, public lectures, open-air concerts. All such were lacking in the suburb.

Above all, city dwellers had to adjust to a rapid pace of change and uncertaint; hence to survive, one had to be flexibile and independent; hence London often attracted the rural young and women, who had the opportunity to earn wages as clerks, shop assistants, and factory girls; many also found emploment in the suburbs as domestics or gardeners.

Population

This was Victorian London, the capital city of England and the seat of the largest empire in the world. For most of this period London was still filthy, Cholera and TB were endemic, life expectancy only some 20 years and crime was out of control. Population growth was partly to blame (1million to 7million in the 100 years to 1900) but so was the indifferent attitude of the rich to the poor. This included the Queen (Victoria) and the government. The well off never visited the poor areas. In about 1800 the rich, middle classes and the poor lived within a few minutes walk of each other where the poor could walk to work to serve the rich as carpenters, drapers, shoemakers etc and they would all visit the same church (there were hundreds of little parishes in London). By 1850 or 150 years ago the population had grown to 3 million, the rich and middle classes were moving out of the centre to the "best new streets" "never again" to visit the areas occupied by the poor. It was then considered too dangerous!

London was the largest city in the world in the 1800s, a city overwhelmed by the waste products of its ever-growing population. Overcrowded into decaying, stinking slums, the poorest citizens were literally surrounded by their own filth. Piled up in courtyards or overflowing from basement cesspits, into which toilets were drained, raw sewage was everywhere, and so was its stench.

The spread of cholera

In such conditions disease was inevitable, but Victorian London's experience of cholera in 1832 would have a huge social impact. Spread via the bacteria-laced diarrhoea of its victims, cholera's violent and rapid assault on the human body was terrifying. Although it killed fewer than other contemporary diseases - such as influenza or tuberculosis - it was cholera that provided a deadly backdrop to this era of social and economic upheaval. There was no known cure - although plenty were offered by quacks. Commonly known as Asiatic cholera, it seized the public's imagination with India, supposedly the crown jewel in Britain's expanding empire, identified as its origin.

Poor housing and slums in London

The appearance of cholera prompted debate about the nature of the emerging society. From the slums of India to the equally filthy slums of London, was this the price to pay for the gruesome urban landscapes being created in Britain? And for the ruling classes, the dark, hidden alleyways of much of London were just as strange and exotic as the back streets of Delhi. In the wake of the 1848-49 epidemic, social reformer Henry Mayhew voiced the connection, describing the centre of the outbreak, Bermondsey, as 'the very capital of cholera, the Jessore of London' - Jessore being the Indian town from where a major cholera pandemic was believed to have originated in 1817. Driven by a combination of genuine concern for the poor and self-preservation by the elite, the fear of cholera became a crucial element in the development of public health in Britain. It inspired some of the first investigations into the living conditions endured by much of the population.

Chadwick: the link between disease and living conditions

In the wake of the cholera epidemic, leading social reformer Edwin Chadwick was commissioned to inquire into the state of public sanitation. His report, *The Sanitary Conditions of the Labouring Population* (1842), made a clear link between disease and living conditions and he called for urgent action. By 1848, when *The Times* was describing cholera as 'the best of all sanitary reformers', Chadwick had been appointed to the first Board of Health and was Sanitary Commissioner of London. He now had the power to change things. But his actions were firmly guided by the miasma theory of disease. To eliminate sources of foul air through which diseases were thought to spread, he supported the rapid removal of human waste through improvements to the disorganised sewage and drainage systems. Unfortunately this led to a greater flow of raw sewage into the River Thames - the main source of drinking water for London. By further contaminating London's water supply, the risk of cholera was greatly increased.

Snow and the study of the spread of diseases

Unlike many of his contemporaries, Dr John Snow was no miasmatist - he publicly stated in 1849 that cholera was transmitted through water. He was already researching links between water supply and deaths from cholera when the disease returned in 1854. This time, a single water supply - the Broad Street pump - was contaminated by a single domestic sewer pipe. As a result, hundreds of local people were rapidly poisoned after visiting the well, or from eating or drinking the products made using its waters. The outbreak provided Snow with the epidemiological ammunition to confirm his theory.

Parliamentary action - a new sewer system

Unfortunately the importance of Snow's work was not immediately recognised; the belief in miasmas would last for a little longer. Appropriately it was the Great Stink of 1858 that ultimately banished cholera for good. Unable to ignore the stench of the Thames and fearful of the miasmatic belief that 'all smell is disease', parliament sanctioned one of the century's great engineering projects - a new sewer network for London. Designed by Joseph Bazalgette, the first section was opened in 1865.

The slow effects of government intervention

Advice about cholera and drinking water, East London, 1866.

The following year cholera returned one final time. The circumstances both justified the expense of Bazalgette's sewers and provided further evidence for Snow's theory, evidence that would persuade leading sceptics, including pioneering epidemiologist William Farr. The victims of this outbreak were almost entirely confined to areas of east London not yet connected to the new sewers. These slum dwellers were left with little option but to drink water contaminated by the faeces of fellow Londoners. For them as for thousands of their London predecessors, and their Indian counterparts reform simply didn't come quickly enough.

Geographical expansion

A quick look at a map of the time compared to say 1750 and the change would be obvious. Together with a general expansion outwards the big change was the populating of South London for the first time. Southwark had been inhabited since Roman times being directly accessed by the only bridge across the Thames for 1700 years (London Bridge). Much of the land round Southwark was marshy and not suitable for building until properly drained (around 1800.)

Bridges
Six new bridges had been built in the previous century but only two, Blackfriars and Westminster served central London. After 1800 Londoners got four more to service the centre and particularly the newly built up areas south of the river. (Southwark Bridge 1819, Lambeth Bridge 1862, Vauxhall Bridge 1816 and Tower Bridge 1894.)
Also tunnels at Deptford/Surrey Docks (Rotherhithe) and Greenwich (Blackwall).

Transport

This was the age of the train which conveniently transported the rich into the new developing suburbs. Rich Inner Londoners would travel by Handsome Cab (Horse drawn for up to four persons) and the not so rich would use the horse drawn Omnibuses. Two decker two horse "buses" carrying some 20 to 30 people.
(The idea and the name was pinched from Paris as a means of transport for everybody. Unfortunately still too expensive for the poor. The various competing operators quite soon went bust and were then taken over and successfully run by a French company!)

The first suburban train service(1836) went from the south side of London Bridge to Greenwich and still runs today. The first 4 miles east from London Bridge was elevated on a brick viaduct which still stands! At first the railways were not allowed to enter the centre of London which was to change in 1866 and caused the displacement of 76,000 people. (There was no re housing policy for these poor people which caused the over crowding of the slums to get even worse as friends took them in.) The famous London stations of Liverpool Street, Charing Cross, Paddington and St Pancras date from this time. By 1875 the rich and middle classes could commute by train to the following still well known middle class areas:
Blackheath and Bexley Heath, Bromley and Chislehurst, Sutton and Surbiton, Richmond and Twickenham, Harrow and Pinner, Finchley and Barnet and Chingford and Loughton. And further afield.

Inner London and suburban transport was soon to be augmented by the Tubes, (Metro) initially the "Tuppeny Tube" which is now part of the central line. New Cross, Wimbledon and Clapham in the south and Hounslow and Harrow in the west could all be reached by "tube" by 1900. Inner London and the most of the well known suburbs could also be reached by horse drawn tram (Running on rails in the street) Notably Catford, Dulwich, Tooting, Hampstead, Highgate and Woodgreen.

The two major road developments of the period were: the building of the Holborn Viaduct (1869) designed to speed up the horse drawn traffic east west between the City and the West End as the poor horses struggled up and down the fleet river valley at Ludgate. Plus the Victoria Embankment(1870) which "reclaimed" some 37 acres of land from the Thames from the Houses of Parliament north and west to Blackfriars Bridge by building a new river wall 500 feet out into the Thames. This extra land was mainly used to create a grand new riverside road and underneath, part of the Tube. Below the Strand new gardens were created which are still there for busy Londoners to enjoy.

Other road improvements included; The creation of Trafalgar Square and Nelson's Column, Piccadilly Circus and the North Circular road. Slum clearance allowed the creation of Kingsway and the Aldwich. (No re-housing schemes of course!)

Housing, Health and Sanitation.

Drinking water.
"The Great Stink" of 1858 sums up the situation. All sewers from the old north side of the Thames flowed directly into the river mainly by open surface drains. The inhabitants of the newly populated south were served with drinking water pumped from the Thames, extracted directly adjacent to the outflows of these sewers. Life expectancy was short! Those living in the north were better off, as much of their water was supplied by a new river diverted for the purpose. The problem was eventually relieved by building "intercepting" sewers in the north and pumping the sewerage into the Thames further down stream at Beckton and Crossness (Not in my back Yard!)

Housing for the poor and the rich
The rich and middle classes were able to look after themselves but the poor 1/3 who were all living below the poverty line had nobody to turn to for help. The area of North Kensington (close-by the current Kensington Hilton and Shepherds Bush) was populated by households who made a living out of a few pigs, part time building labouring and other seasonal work. Housing which they built themselves was not much better than hovels from the dark ages and this was Victorian England. Similar areas were Hoxton, Whitechapel, Wapping, Bermondsey and Southwark.

Meanwhile the rich were living in Victorian splendour in Mayfair, Wimpole Street and out in the new suburbs. Clapham was a good example were new posh housing estates were developed with large detached houses in secluded gardens.

A new building phenomena developed that of the spec builder i.e. building houses, flats and office blocks before occupants had been identified. In Notting Hill the spec builders caught a cold, building too many posh terraced houses for the upper middle classes. To sell them they had to be subdivided and sold to the lower middle classes.

The idea of flats (apartments) was copied from the French and anybody who lived in a flat was naturally assumed to live like the French and have a mistress! Office blocks for multi ownership were also constructed.

Finally help was at hand for the poor, not from the government but from rich benefactors. Two good examples, the Rothschild family who naturally enough built subsidised flats for poor Jewish families, and an American Mr Peabody, living in London at the time, who did much the same thing. Many flats built by Peabody can still be seen today and are currently being renovated.

Shops

This was the start of the great London department stores. All these names are still in business; Maples and Heals in Tottenham Court Rd were adjacent at the time to the furniture makers in London. Sainsbury, originally a butcher, Marks and Spencer (actually started in the north of England.) W.H. Smith and William Whitely. The latter has just totally renovated its store in Bayswater. Plus of course the most famous and still perhaps the most useful, Harrods in Knightsbridge and Selfridges in Oxford Street. All department stores were originally designed to service women who by 1860 could conveniently visit the London shopping areas by train for a days shopping to furnish their new "mansions" in the suburbs.

Law and order

The rich described the poor as "decadent and set for self destruction". 30% of the population of London were described as below the poverty line. A picture so well painted by the contemporary writer Charles Dickens, many of whose characters he took from real life including his own. The arch crook Fagin lived with the Artful Dodger in the then slums of Saffron Hill (a road still there in the Holborn area running parallel to Hatton Garden on the east side.) The wealthy were too frightened to visit such places as there was no police force. That is until Prime Minister, Sir Robert Peel, when he was Home Secretary, created the metropolitan police (quickly 1000 blue coated men) out of the earlier Bow Street Runners in 1829. (The Bow street runners were a very small organised vigilante group started 100 years earlier by writer and Justice for the Peace (JP for Westminster) Henry Fielding in 1750). (Unfortunately they were not supported by the archetypal detective Sherlock Holmes of Baker Street as he was only the figment of imagination of another contemporary writer Sir Arthur Conan Doyle. 1887). Baker Street is a wide road running north from Marble Arch area. Bow Street Magistrates Court and Bow Street Police station are in Bow Street opposite the Royal Opera House some 200 yards north of the Strand in the Covent Garden Area. The even more famous Scotland Yard still exists running between Whitehall and Northumberland Avenue just south of Trafalgar Square although the main police station has moved to Victoria Street.

Immigration

London and the rest of England have been largely peacefully invaded by foreign settlers and refuges for hundreds if not thousands of years. Yet the richer the English get the more they seem unwilling to share the guaranteed welfare now afforded to all. 150 years ago there was no such guaranteed income minimum or free health and education. 150 years ago Londoners were already a mixture of Celts, Romans (and their mercenaries) Angles, Saxons, Danes, Norman Vikings and French (and French Jews brought in by William the Conqueror), Huguenots also from France, Flemish cloth makers and Protestant Dutch. 150 years ago London saw a huge influx of starving Irish fleeing the English fuelled Irish potato famine. (In Victorian times the Irish made up 5% of all Londoners, many living in extreme poverty in areas like Whitechapel, St Giles and Southwark). Later in this century there was another influx of Jews, refugees from eastern Europe particularly Russia and Poland. These Jews contributed hugely with their skills in the clothing industry and as financiers.

Integration with the locals varied depending on the new immigrants willingness to marry outside their immediate "clan". This was always difficult for the Jews as for Orthodox Jews their religion forbids it. As a result of this Jewish areas in London can be very obvious as the dress of the Orthodox Jew is very distinctive, as are the names above the shops which sell their special (Kosher) foods. (See Golders Green and Stamford Hill). A significant number of Jews who wanted to integrate fully changed their names to disguise their origins.

London Industry
During this period London was the biggest industrial town in England inspite of having no large factories. Indeed the average business employed about 10 people.
There was however a huge change as the skilled artisan who supplied his customers direct was replaced by machines and large retail stores where there was no direct contact between customer and craftsman. This caused workshops to move out of the centre and become little impersonal factories in the outskirts of places like Southwark and Deptford. There was no help in those days in re-housing the workers and they would swap one slum for another. Transport was available but only the middle classes could afford it.

The London Docks continued their expansion eastwards (down stream where the river was wider and deeper.) The Royal Victoria(1855) and the Royal Albert(1880) docks were developed on the north bank of the Thames opposite Woolwich. Access was by train to Silvertown and by the Woolwich ferry and eventually by Blackwall tunnel in the last decade of the century.

Sport

Rugby, Football(Soccer) and Tennis clubs were founded but these had to compete with Bear bating (Dogs versus Bears), Cock fighting and open air bare fist boxing until they were eventually banned. Londoners had always enjoyed skating most winters, initially at Moorefield's marshes outside Moorgate until they were drained, and on the Thames which iced over most winters to such a degree that ice fairs were popular including the traditional roasting of whole oxen. The Thames no longer iced over when the flow of water was increased under London Bridge by widening the span of each section.

Parks

Thanks mainly to Henry 8th London has magnificent parks created from land he acquired from the church at the time of The Dissolution. Hyde Park, Green Park, St James Park and Regents Park are perhaps the best known. The Victorians continued to create new recreational parks, notably Battersea Park in South London and Victoria Park in the East End. (Homerton)

London 100 Years Ago

The class differences of the Victorian period were maintained up until the First World War (1914-1918) and afterwards. It would appear that nobody at Government level had the compassion, vision or political will to do anything about the London slums. The rich were happily amusing themselves with their new toy the motor car.
Following the war a housing programme called "Homes fit for Soldiers" commenced but soon ran out of political steam and was finally knocked on the head by the world depression in the late 1920s and 1930s.

London was still expanding throughout the whole of this period mainly fuelled by the new middle classes as they continued the move into new, out of town, purpose built "posh" estates. A good example of these are in the outskirts of south east London on the borders with Kent. Notably the estates of Farnborough and Keston Parks. (The latter close to the historical "Caesars Well" at the southern end of Keston Ponds). All these land marks can still be visited and it is interesting to examine the jobs that created the affluence to allow detached 4 or 5 bedroom individually designed houses in a minimum of ½ acre of virgin wooded land to be purchased with little inherited money.

Keston Park is in a block between Westerham Road and Croydon Road measuring ½ mile by 1 mile approximately with an elevation of about 500 feet (half way up the northern slopes of the North Downs) so it is possible to see London some 20 miles to the north and west. Land plots were available for sale from the late 1920s. All house owners had a car and a handful had two. All houses had central heating but only one bathroom and certainly no shower. Keston Park was not serviced by any convenient railway line so the wage earner (the man in all cases) would travel to work by car to probably: local Bromley 4 miles, Orpington 4 miles, central London 20 miles, Silvertown chemical works and docks via Blackwall Tunnel 15 miles or Woolwich 8 miles. Indeed a considerable proportion of the occupants worked locally.

Keston Park was not serviced by any local shops and the lady of the house would have to visit Keston Village(5 shops) 1 mile away or Locks Bottom (adjacent to Farnborough Park) 2 miles away about 12 shops including a bank Without a car many wives went by bike or walked! Or placed an order for the weekly shopping to be delivered. Bromley was the nearest largish town which was serviced by the 410 green double decker bus running every 15 minutes to an accuracy to enable you to set your watch by it. The ladies of the house would use this for shopping in Bromley or for catching a train to London either from Bromley South (fast to Victoria) or Bromley North.(slow stopper to Charing Cross). All easy, comfortable, clean and safe modes of transport.

Dads would probably drop the kids to school in the mornings for 08.45 start and the kids would return by bus in the afternoons. All the kids without exception would go to private or High Schools. It was possible on this return journey to meet kids from the "lower class" schools of Bromley Grammar or worse the Secondary Modern. This always was confrontational and as the posh kids in posh uniforms would be out numbered and often alone, it would be advised to keep a low profile unless the posh kids from Keston were particularly large and strong.

Many Kids above the age of 8 were sent to boarding school and if not then the majority of both girls and boys would have been sent away to a posh upper-class boarding school by the time they were 13 years old. These schools were most likely to be in Kent but many children were sent to places as far afield as Malvern in Worcestershire or Oundle in Northamptonshire.

The teenagers, when home, had a good social life for boy meets girl parties either at dances (always ballroom, Waltz, Quickstep Tango, Conga etc) organised by parents or more exciting kids' own parties when the parents went out and when the party would normally deteriorate to non stop "petting" in the dark. (Petting was normally restricted to the boy, if he dared and the girl was willing, to caressing a young pair of breasts. Parties where sexual contact went further were known but would generally not take place in the posh Parks but did take place in nearby Hayes where the girls encouraged active stimulation off all parts of their bodies short of full penetrative sex. Contraceptives would probably not be known to this age group but pregnancy outside marriage was and was such a social taboo that full sex amongst teenagers was virtually unknown for this class of people.

Indeed some attractive nannies employed by these families to look after the small children who became pregnant were sent home in total disgrace never to be seen again!! (Who was the naughty dad then?) This restriction on sex before marriage was probably the cause of couples marrying in their early 20s. The women of these partnerships would be unlikely to work after producing kids but of course were well educated and could contribute to the education of their own children.

The famous fogs

The famous London pea soupers (Fog) reached out as far south as Keston and Farnborough Parks so dense even at this distance and this altitude that parents collecting tots from parties could not do so by car but would have to walk the 5 miles or so to collect and back again!

Young girls of say 20 years old were known to call the

fogs "spooky" but none of the families daughters listed above were ever molested.

Farnborough Park was a similar where the houses today are very similar to how they were when built except that a large proportion have been extended to totally fill the width of their ¾ acre plots. Those living in Farnborough Park, other than dad who had a car, would use the 47 red double decker bus to reach Bromley for shopping and young working daughters would take the train from Bromley South to Victoria (20 minutes) for their London secretarial jobs. All the 17 year old sons would have some form of motorised transport but not the daughters.

Hence the majority of the house owners of these estates were self made men running their own businesses within a few miles of their houses or professionals engineers or senior managers, directors or partners working for larger companies in the London area. Some would have served in the First World War and the majority would have had active service in the Second World War. By far the vast majority had two children both sent to private school with many boarding as far away as the Midlands. Of all the house owners listed only one was known to have a divorced partner. All had daily cleaners who would walk or bike to work from either Farnborough Village (or the nearby Crofton Road council estate) or Keston Village as appropriate. These "Mrs Mops" were part of the family they worked for and were fully trusted. In all the families mentioned above all the kids also "loved" Mrs Mop. Only one of the families mentioned above had a live in permanent cleaner/helper who was the only one called by her Christian name (Beryl) others were known affectionately as either Mrs P or straight Mrs Breckon. Generally the husbands of the Mrs Mops were artisans that is they would have skills like plumbing or carpentry or painting and decorating. All would have served in the Second World War and both Mrs Mop and her husband would smoke, probably "Woodbines" up to 60 per day.

In the 1930s most of the house owners would have smoked and some but not all of their wives. None of their children would have openly smoked in front of their parents before they were 21. (The 21 key of the door phrase which meant the young offspring of either sex could stay out after midnight went out during the Second World War). Very young offspring would start school at 3 at a kindergarten in a private house. There was one main one which served Keston and Farnborough Park, Miss Figgis' in Crofton Road. This was 3 miles from the far side of Keston Park and 3 year olds would walk! The two children of the family with this 3 mile walk were accompanied by their grandfather (80 years old) who obviously had to walk 12 miles a day for this task.

Early London Gangs

The 1700's to 1940

In the 1700's and 1800's London was plagued with crime and gangs. During this time it would have been considered the gang capital of the world. As the city grew and expanded outwards the wealthier residents moved into the suburbs leaving only the most deprived in the central areas to fend for themselves.
Prostitution, robbery, pick-pocketing and protection rackteering were amongst the most common crimes. Children as young as 10 could face capital punishment for crimes as petty as thievery. There were a mix of gangs, usually known as mobs, who claimed territory - usually a stretch of street - and often took their name from their territory. There were also a number of crime families who operated in districts surrounding what is today known as the 'City of London'.

In the East End alone it was estimated that a third of the population lived below the poverty line and 50% of children born their died before the age of 5. Most of the gangs and families listed below were active between the late 1800's and up to 1940. By 1937 the police and government identified what were London's most gang infested districts, they were Hackney & Hoxton, the East End (referring to Tower Hamlets & Newham), north London (Islington, Camden & Tottenham), north east London (referring to Stratford, Leytonstone, Leyton) and the West End which was being carved up by organised firms from across the city.

Up to as many as 70 gangs battled on London streets from the 1900's onwards. Gun battles, stabbings, teen on teen killings, colours and gang identities, sub-cliques, rivalries and alliances were all common features of the old Gangs of London. The social disorganisation theory holds true, with many of the affected areas still suffering from gangs today (some even have the same names).

Street Gangs became a national concern in the United Kingdom from around 1870 onwards. Newspapers began to carry reports of their fights and they became known generally as 'scuttlers' in Manchester, 'sloggers' and later 'peaky blinders' in Birmingham, and 'cornermen' in Liverpool. Their principle pastime was fighting territorial battles against their neighbours, armed with buckled belts, sticks, stones, knives and even guns. Many of the gangs were identified simply by the streets where they lived...London became plagued by street gangs...especially in the poor, overcrowded areas of east and south London.

In the early part of the nineteenth century, criminals infested London's rookeries, rundown areas of dense housing. The most notorious was a stinking slum surrounded by festering ditches at Jacob's Island, on the Bermondsey side of the Thames. This served for Dicken's description of Fagin's den of thieves in Oliver Twist and where his villain, Bill Sikes, comes to grief. Another, at Clerkenwell, straddled the area between Farringdon Road, Clerkenwell Green and St. John's Street. A short distance away, running south from Old Street, was the notorious St. Luke's rookery, and close to that was the St. Giles rookery covering the area where Tottenham Court Road tube station now stands. These rookeries bred and attracted thieves, who targeted the better off parts of London: Highbury, Hampstead, the West End and the City. In the east and southeast London, targets included docks and cargo ships. The ghettos had the highest incidences of murder and provided hangmen with hundreds of clients. They contained 'flash houses' that served as training places for young thieves and meeting places for established thieves to plan robberies and sell or exchange their plunder. The narrow streets were crammed with dilapidated dwellings and underground escape routes weaved their way through the slums...When the rookeries were cleared in the mid-

1800's, the crooks remained and simply operated from better premises. A series of incidents give a flavour of the underworld at the turn of the Nineteenth Century into the Twentieth, much of it involving teenagers.

One of the most notable of the early gangs was the Green Gate, named after the Green Gate public house in City Road, Hoxton, east London. Once a wealthy area, Hoxton had been abandoned by its middle classes, who were lured out to the space and fresh air of the new suburbs. Their place was taken by poor workers, serving the heavy industries that boomed after the completion of the Regents Canal in 1820, and soon the area became one of the most densley populated in Europe...

On Christmas Eve, [in Hakcney, 1881] a gang came down Ottaway Street in Lower Clapton, known as 'Tiger Bay', and picked a quarrel with Charles 'Ginger' Eaton outside his home at number nine. The attackers were the Dove Row gang from Haggerston. Eaton fought back. He explained in court, 'I went into them the same as they did to me, and took my own defence'. The nineteen-year-old Eaton handled himself well enough for the gang to run off, pursued by Eaton's father waving a poker. They shouted back that they would remember when they came again.

Late on New Year's Day, the trouble shifted to the Rendlesham Arms in Stillman Street, Clapton, when about twenty of the Dove Row gang went looking for Eaton. When they failed to find him, they started a general rumpus that quickly got out of hand. Three pub dwellers were stabbed in the face, one of whom nearly died from a severed artery. Police rounded up seven Dove Row boys: William Hubbard, David Jennings, Henry Kirby, Frederick Ball, Patrick Kennedy, David Williams, and John Collins. They were charged with riot and wounding. Kennedy was aged twenty; the rest were in their late teens. Others were charged with occasioning actual bodily harm. John Collins denied being there but did admit once belonging to the street fighting gang in the days when Old Nichol Street, in Bethnal Green, fought Dove Row. He had given it up after his head was split in three places. The Central Criminal Court did not believe him...[they] were jailed...all with hard labour (compulsory physical work imposed in addition to imprisonment).

The Green Gate gang made the news again on 21 February 1882, when Samuel Wallers was attacked by George Collins on Shaftesbury Street, close to City Road. The argument had been about the merits of teetotallers, who Collins had little regard for. When his offer of a drink from a flask was refused, he informed Wallers that he was a pugilist...He then knocked Wallers down....Collins' belief in his pugilistic ability came unstuck when Wallers got up and knocked him down. Collins regained his feet and pulled a pistol from his pocket, only for Wallers to brush it aside and knock him down again. At this, the gun went off. Two policemen heard the shot and came and arrested Collins, taking two guns from him...

Guns seem to have been a more serious problem among the London street gangs than in Manchester and Liverpool. On 31 May 1885, William Brown, aged sixteen, Harry Foxcroft, eighteen, and a man named Mason shot James Page in Upper Street, Islington, in return for a previous attack on some of their pals. They then threatened John 'Bunny' Ayres, a resident of White Lion Street, one of the most violent locations in London, with similar treatment...

Brown, who admitted wounding Page and firing a shot at Harry Hobbs, received five years' penal servitude, Foxcroft, who resided at Easton Street, Clerkenwell, which was another notorious north London location, got eighteen months with hard labour.

West London too was gripped by street warfare. In 1888, a long-running series of fights were staged between the Fitzroy Place Boys, from the back of Tottenham Court Road, and the Lisson Grove gang, from Marylebone. Matters came to a head in May, when Frank Cole of the Fitzroy crowd was found with his girlfiend, Cissy Chapman, in rival territory outside Madame Tussaud's Waxworks on Marylebone Road. Cole was challenged by two Lisson Grove Boys. 'Do you know any of the Fitzroy Place lads?' one asked. 'Yes, and glad to know them too.' came Cole's not-too-clever reply.

Twenty more lads were whistled up to help punch and kick Cole to the ground, giving Cissy a black eye when she asked why it took so many of them.

The following evening, Cole gathered together seven or eight friends and went looking for revenge. They met at 'the Fair', a disused ground between Tottenham Court Road and Whitfield Street, where they were joined by a half-dozen others. Soon, they spotted a Lisson lad in nearby Howland Street...knocked him down and kicked him. Then they set off to search the Green Man public house on Euston Road and, finding nothing, moved on to Regent's Park, a collecting point for the Lisson Grove gang.

It was there that Joe Rumbold and a girl passed some of the gang, who jostled him. A brief row followed and [George] Galletly pulled a knife and stabbed Rumbold twice in the back and neck. He staggered a few hundred yards before collapsing, later dying in a cab taking him to hospital.

Police arrested eight youths...and charged them with murder...[The youths] saw a newspaper notice offering a pardon in exchange for evidence. Both denied being members of the Fitzroy Place gang and the Decker Gang (a misnaming by police of the Dials gang, from Seven Dials)...[Galletly] was sentenced to death, later commuted to life imprisonment due to his age...others were sentenced to short terms with hard labour.

In the 1890s, clashes between the Somers Town Boys, located just north of King's Cross, and the Clerkenwell Boys, from south of Pentonville Road, led to several shootings and stabbings. Police described the gang members as being employed in their spare time in faction fighting. Gangs were able to buy firearms from pawnbrokers for around ten shillings apiece and it was not unusual for twenty or more youths to wander the streets looking for rivals to shoot at...

A number of gangs went by the name Forty Thieves, the most famous being one in 1820s New York and another later on in south London. [John] Carey remained a member of the east London version and was jailed again in 1896, with three others, for burglary. Police described them as members of a dangerous gang. In 1906, Carey was sentenced to five years penal servitude, with Jeremiah Barry and Samuel Bromley, for robbery with violence...

On 7 March 1897, fifty to sixty Bethnal Green Boys, forerunners of Dodger Mullins' gang, went hunting for Hackney's Broadway Boys, a street mob that located at Haggerston: they fired shots at any they came across. Terrified residents ducked bullets whizzing overhead, richocheting off buildings and smacking into shops. A shower of bottles and bricks accompanied the pistol shots. Charles Luton was shot in the knee and lamed. Joseph Norton, who doged six bulets, hid and watched the gang run by. He then followed and grabbed Joseph Fitzpatrick and held him for the police. Frederick Millard had five shots fired at him and, in the harsh employment environment of the time, lost his job for attending police court on four occasions. George Morgan had a revolver pointed in his face and was asked if he was one of the Broadway fellows, to which he was pleased to reply that he was not. He watched them fire shots at a young man and into an ice-cream shop. Six youths, aged sixteen to nineteen, were arrested after witnesses reported seeing them dumping revolvers into Regent's canal...

Halloween worked its magic on 31 October 1897 in Islington, when the Pentonville Boys challenged the Grosvenor Street Boys to a fight, as part of an ongoing war. These particular Grosvenors were schoolboys, who considered the offer then declined it. No matter: Billy Bond shot Alfred Webb in the leg. Bond had declared his intention of shooting someone that night and it appears he believed Webb had shown some inclination to fight...

The name Sabini came up at the Central Criminal Court in June 1898, when Augustus, of Eyre Hill Street in the heart of Clerkenwell Sabini territory, was shot at by a crowd of about thirty boys. It appears on this occasion that a Sabini was an innocent victim, who had declined to have a fight. One youth, sixteen-year-old Alfred Smith, had the indignity of being given one days' imprisonment.

Better-off neighbourhoods had no immunity to gang warfare. In 1900, Chelsea Bay Boys and Sands End Boys received a not from their neighbours, the Manor Street Boys, to come and fight, a follow-up to a previous skirmish outside Lewis's Club in Kings Road. They met in Oakham Street (now Oakley Street), once the home of explorer Robert Falcon Scott and close to the residences of writers and the professional classes: here they battled with studded belts with large buckles. Blood splattered the pavement as gangs of teenagers went at it. Evidence suggests the two gangs had been warring for some time, mostly with their heavy-buckled belts, a popular weapon at the time, as they could be worn legitimately but could cause considerable damage...

In October 1902, Russian Jews belonging to the Bessarabian Society were in conflict with Polish Jews belonging to the Odessa Society. The quarrel...was continued in Whitechapel. On top of this, both were deeply into squeezing money and favours from immigrant tradespeople, who could not go to the police for fear of arrest for their own illicit occupations. The 'Bessas', who had the strongest grip on the protection business, were challenged by envious Odessas. A series of fights culminated in a good old barney in the York Minister pub in Philpot Street, squashed into the area in which Jack Spot and the Kray twins would later blossom. Lots of cuttings and shootings led to one death and several prison sentences for the Bessa Arabs....

At the turn of the century, London became a focal point for criminal gangs. Mass immigration had seen a wave of Irish, Scots, Jews and Italians arriving, plus a homegrown influx from the English countryside and cities. Unemployment became a major problem, to the point where many Britson sought refuge in the United States, bringing some respite to provincial cities. Soldiers returning from the Boer War swelled the number of unemployed. Other major cities, especially Manchester, saw a decline in gang activity, which was often attributed to the success of the new Lads' Club movement and the growth in popularity of sports such as football, which diverted youthful energies from violence. However, the capital saw, if anything, a movement toward more serious forms of gangsterism. While some old street and neighbourhood rivalries persisted, the heavier street thugs graduated to organised or semi-organised villainy.

Joblessness inevitably leads to an increase in gambling, prostitution and petty and organised crime. All sections of the city's vast working class communities now turned their hand to making a living by any means, only relenting for a spell at the onset of World War One. With the stretching of police resources, to deal with an increasingly militant women's suffrage movement, the scene was set for a new chapter in the story of London's gangland.

Victorian London

The Victorian city of London was a city of startling contrasts. New building and affluent development went hand in hand with horribly overcrowded slums where people lived in the worst conditions imaginable. The population surged during the 19th century, from about 1 million in 1800 to over 6 million a century later. This growth far exceeded London's ability to look after the basic needs of its citizens.

A combination of coal-fired stoves and poor sanitation made the air heavy and foul-smelling. Immense amounts of raw sewage was dumped straight into the Thames River. Even royals were not immune from the stench of London - when Queen Victoria occupied Buckingham Palace her apartments were ventilated through the common sewers, a fact that was not disclosed until some 40 years later.

Upon this scene entered an unlikely hero, an engineer named Joseph Bazalgette. Bazalgette was responsible for the building of over 2100 km of tunnels and pipes to divert sewage outside the city. This made a drastic impact on the death rate, and outbreaks of cholera dropped dramatically after Bazlgette's work was finished. For an encore, Bazalgette also was responsible for the design of the Embankment, and the Battersea, Hammersmith, and Albert Bridges.

Before the engineering triumphs of Bazalgette came the architectural triumphs of George IV's favorite designer, John Nash. Nash designed the broad avenues of Regent Street<, Piccadilly Circus, Carlton House Terrace, and Oxford Circus, as well as the ongoing creation of Buckingham transformation of Buckingham House into a palace worthy of a monarch.

In 1829 Sir Robert Peel founded the Metropolitan Police to handle law and order in areas outside the City proper. These police became known as "Bobbies" after their founder.

Just behind Buckingham Palace the Grosvenor family developed the aristocratic Belgrave Square. In 1830 land just east of the palace was cleared of the royal stables to create Trafalgar Square, and the new National Gallery sprang up there just two years later.

The early part of the 19th century was the golden age of steam. The first railway in London was built from London Bridge to Greenwich in 1836, and a great railway boom followed. Major stations were built at Euston (1837), Paddington (1838), Fenchurch Street (1841), Waterloo (1848), and King's Cross (1850).

In 1834 the Houses of Parliament at Westminster Palace burned down. They were gradually replaced by the triumphant mock-Gothic Houses of Parliament designed by Charles Barry and A.W. Pugin.

The clock tower of the Houses of Parliament, known erroneously as Big Ben, was built in 1859. The origin of the name Big Ben is in some dispute, but there is no argument that the moniker refers to the bells of the tower, NOT to the large clock itself.

In 1848 the great Potato Famine struck Ireland. What has this to do with the history of London? Plenty. Over 100,000 impoverished Irish fled their native land and settled in London, making at one time up to 20% of the total population of the city.

Prince Albert, consort of Queen Victoria was largely responsible for one of the defining moments of the era that bears his wife's name; the Great Exhibition of 1851. This was the first great world's fair, a showcase of technology and manufacturing from countries all over the world. The Exhibition was held in Hyde Park, and the centerpiece was Joseph Paxton's revolutionary iron and glass hall, dubbed the "Crystal Palace".

The exhibition was an immense success, with over 200,000 attendees. After the event, the Crystal Palace was moved to Sydenham, in South London, where it stayed until it burned to the ground in 1936. The proceeds from the Great Exhibition went towards the founding of two new permanent displays, which became the Science Museum and the Victoria and Albert Museum.

The year 1863 saw the completion of the very first underground railway in London, from Paddington to Farringdon Road. The project was so successful that other lines soon followed.

But the expansion of transport was not limited to dry land. As the hub of the British Empire, the Thames was clogged with ships from all over the world, and London had more shipyards than anyplace on the globe.

For all the economic expansion of the Industrial Revolution, living conditions among London's poor were appalling. Children as young as 5 were often set to work begging or sweeping chimneys. Campaigners like Charles Dickens did much to make the plight of the poor in London known to the literate classes with his novels, notably Oliver Twist. In 1870 those efforts bore some fruit with the passage of laws providing compulsory education for children between the ages of 5 and 12.

During the 1840s the problems of poverty and pauperism emerged with greater force in London than had hitherto been the case. So too did the problem of the slum or 'rookery', as witnessed by the growing usage of the terms themselves in contemporary works. There were several reasons why this should have been the case. First, structural problems relating to the competitiveness of the metropolitan trades resulted in severe pressures on wages and working conditions in several occupations, notably clothing and shoemaking. Secondly, collapse of the house-building boom in 1825 resulted in higher rents, and worsening housing conditions in inner areas throughout the 1830s and 1804s. Thirdly, these factors, coupled with deteriorating wages and conditions of work increased pressure on the Poor Law and in turn helped to fuel rate rises in central and eastern districts. Finally, worsening conditions and rising rates encouraged middle class flight to the suburbs, leaving behind decaying homes and an increasingly impoverished population unable to support the mounting tide of pauperism. At such times and under such conditions slum formation was both rapid and widespread.

London at mid-century was already a city with a distinctive geographical pattern of poverty. Differences in the fortunes of eastern and western districts were already evident by the time of John Stow's survey in 1598, and at the time of the Great Fire status distinctions between the areas were already engraved into the fabric of the city. In the first half of the century, however, the bipolar distribution of wealth was disrupted somewhat by a growing distinction in social status between inner and outer zones radiating from the old commercial core. In 1844 Joseph Fletcher described the city in terms of three contrasting geographical components. At the centre was the City of London, already 'one vast counting house and warehouse' with a declining population that consisted increasingly of poorer artisans, shop workers, labourers and street hawkers. The outer suburbs, in contrast, were growing rapidly as a result of the immigration of a wealthy population which had sought to escape the growing impoverishment of inner-city environments. Between the two came the inner industrial belt, stretching from St Giles in the west, eastwards to St George-in-the-East and southwards into Southwark, and here it was that the mass of poverty was concentrated.

According to a variety of social indicators this inner zone contained the most impoverished districts, particularly to the east and south of the City. Districts such as Bethnal Green, Southwark and Bermondsey were characterised by a combination of factors indicative of poverty, including concentrations of sweated and unskilled occupations, high rates of illiteracy and mortality, large families with high dependency ratios, poor quality housing and high poor rates. Within such districts emerged some of the worst slums: the Church Lane rookery in St Giles-Whitecross Street near Smithfield in St Luke's, and Wentworth Street in Whitechapel. According to Fletcher, this inner zone was the great solicitude in a sanitary view', and medical topography confirmed his opinion. In 1842 Chadwick had drawn attention to the lower rates of mortality in the northern and western parishes compared to central, eastern and southern areas. Districts such as Bethnal Green and Whitechapel, investigated by the Poor Law commission in 1837 and 1838 with a view to examining the relationship between ill health and pauperism, were noted as having extremely high rates of morbidity and mortality. Mean female mortality in Whitechapel, for example, was twice as high as in St George, Hanover Square, or the suburban district of Hackney

Important as the distinction was between western and eastern districts, insanitary courts and overcrowded dwellings could be found in all parts of the city and frequently close to the houses of the rich. 'Immediately behind some of the best constructed houses in the fashionable districts of London', wrote Chadwick 'are some of the worst dwellings, into which the working classes are crowded' Old decaying inner districts in the west, such as St Margaret's, Westminster and most notably, St Giles, each contained slums as bad if not worse than anything to be found elsewhere in the city. Indeed the close juxtaposition of poverty and wealth intensified fears of the spread of contagion and made the very existence of such rookeries more shocking. During the 1840s surveys carried out by the statistical society of London showed that one room living was the norm for working class families, particularly in wealthier districts where rents were high. In Marelybone an investigation of 205 houses found that

845 rooms were occupied by 859 families. In the wealthy parish of St Georges Hanover square, a survey of 1465 families found that 929 lived in single rooms. Overcrowding was even greater in Church Lane St Giles where as a result of demolition's for New Oxford Street, and an influx of Irish migrants, house occupancy rates had nearly doubled between 1841 and 1847. Nor was overcrowding confined to working-class housing in wealthy districts alone. In St George-in-the-East, where average rents were lower, rates of overcrowding were only slightly less with around one third of families living in single rooms. Hector Gavin around Bethnal Green revealed a similar situation with four roomed houses in the worst part of the city being occupied by up to thirty people. Overcrowding, therefore, was commonplace throughout London, though it was perhaps the more shocking to middle class observers when it lay so close to wealthy areas, and slum formation proceeded rapidly under such intense pressure for space.

Overcrowding and slum formation in the inner areas of London was hastened during the 1830s and 1840s by demolition of houses arising from street clearances, warehouse construction and railway building, Most central districts lost housing from the 1830s and 1840s.

The City itself lost over a quarter of its housing stock between 1831 and 1861 as it was transformed into a primarily commercial district. The displaced population crowded into the neighbouring localities, resulting in further increases in overcrowding, deteriorating sanitary conditions and higher levels of pauperism. Those who could afford to move to the suburbs did so driven out by the rising poor rates and the decaying urban fabric and leaving in their place an increasingly impoverished population living in worsening squalor and overcrowded conditions. In St Georges-in-the-East George McGill ruefully remarked that 'as the better class go the poor fill their place', and in Clerkenwell in 1857 the Reverend Warwick Wroth noted that: 'The richer classes are continually moving to other localities and the poorer are taking their place. Houses which were formerly filled with tolerably well to do are now let out in lodgings, and the lodgers instead of being able to aid others, sometimes need aid themselves.'

The situation south of the river was no different. In Southwark in 1862 Edward Collinson, Chairman of the Board of Guardians, stated that: Unquestionably, the improvements in the City at first tended very much to make poor persons' houses, which were formerly shops and dwelling houses, be let out in tenements and as lodging houses, and the consequence is that they are sometimes very closely packed with inhabitants.'

Closely packed the houses were. Between 1841 and 1861 substantial increases in the number of persons per house occurred in most districts surrounding the City, with the greatest increases in St Olave and Rotherhithe to the south, Strand to the west and Poplar to the East. In places such as St Giles, where housing was already grossly overcrowded, the increase as measured by the census was relatively small, though houses in the poorest streets continued to have a seemingly infinite capacity for taking in extra lodgers. Elsewhere, however, conditions deteriorated noticeably during the 1840s and nascent slums matured quickly. In Southwark, housing vacated by the middle classes was soon taken up by house farmers and subdivided into weekly lodgings and by 1865 an estimated 4,800 houses out of a total stock of 7,700 were reckoned to be let out as rooms. Bethnal Green, which in 1840 already had the dubious distinction of having a mean rateable value per house one quarter of that of the rest of London, experienced a similar pattern of abandonment and subdivision. In the inner parts of the parish, old houses were subdivided and in some cases over thirty people were crowded into no more than four rooms. Elsewhere in the parish pressure of numbers had resulted in garden summer houses, partly built of brick and partly of wood being taken into permanent occupation. The existence of such grossly inadequate living conditions, however, was in no sense unique to Bethnal Green but instead mirrored the general pressures on housing throughout the inner zone of poverty. Given similar condition elsewhere slums were not slow to form.

Whilst general processes relating to the timing and pattern of urban growth help to explain the broad geography of slum formation, local factors were important in transforming the pressures into shapes on the ground. Not all localities in these inner districts were slums and not all slums were located in these inner districts. Whilst known rookeries were mainly concentrated in districts bordering the City in which pressures on housing were most severe, there were exceptions to the rule, such as Agar Town to the north and the potteries in Kensington to the west. Three aspects relating to the site and nature of housing were important in this respect. Firstly, low-lying and poorly drained districts, frequently physically isolated from neighbouring areas were highly conducive to the creation of slums. In Bermondsey and Canning Town both of which were so low lying to preclude the possibility of adequate drainage cesspools and sewers ran into supplies of drinking water. Not surprisingly, perhaps, outbreaks of disease were common as shown in the outbreak of cholera in 1849 at Jacobs Island in Bermondsey. The Potteries in Kensington, formerly a brickfield but by 1850 better described as a swamp housed an extremely poor community of Irish. At the centre of the district lay the 'ocean', a putrid lake into which drained numerous pigsties and in which, Robert Grainger noted at the time of his visit, the dead animals were thrown.

Over and above the problems of drainage, the site of a slum was usually a nest of secluded streets or courts off the main street and without through traffic. Courts and alleys, frequently built up over what had formerly been back gardens or open space, rapidly deteriorated into slums. Often without through ventilation or drainage, and lacking adequate light, such courts were little more than nurturing grounds for disease. Back Ball Alley in St Sepulchre, for example, no more than a yard wide and containing houses on the verge of collapse, was noted in 1840 as a fever spot by Samuel Millar, relieving officer of the district, A similar picture emerged in Bethnal Green where back streets and courts inhabited by weavers ,and labourers had higher rates of mortality than did higher status housing fronting on the main streets. Though no overall estimate exists for the proportion of London's population housed in courts, a glance at Charles Booth's maps of poverty later in the century shows that the streets coloured dark blue and black, and therefore housing criminals, loafers and the chronically poor, were most frequently those which lay, behind the main thoroughfares.

Finally structural features relating to the construction and internal arrangements of housing itself also contributed to the creation of slums. In the older, central areas, decaying middle-class housing designed for single families but long since abandoned by their original class of occupants and subdivided to accommodate a poorer population, formed some of the worst slums. Lacking adequate means of drainage or ventilation, the descent of such housing into slumdom was noticeably rapid. In London and elsewhere, however, slums were not confined to old, decaying structures, and in some cases relatively new buildings also beat a hasty path towards slumdom. Speculative jerry-built housing, constructed with a view to short-term profits, slipped easily and quickly towards slum status. Engels in Manchester commented how new working-class houses in Ancoats with walls only half a brick thick were old after ten years and ruined after forty. In London houses built in Agar Town, St Pancras in the 1840s were little more than huts constructed from bricks and rubbish and within a decade had attained a justifiable reputation for squalor. But whether housing was newly constructed or was merely descending into slumdom as a result of abandonment by the middle class, the pressure to extort short-term profits had similar results. Construction was flimsy, materials were poor and repairs were ignored, with the general outcome that such housing decayed rapidly and slums were quick to form.

The role of Landlords

The tremendous demand for cheap housing that occurred in the inner districts of London from the 1830s and 1840s provided high rates of return on property investment and from this period house farmers emerged as one of the principal agents of slum formation. The system of leasing and subleasing prevalent in the city provided ample opportunities for extorting profits from dilapidated houses. For ground landlords, letting blocks of housing towards the end of their lease represented a potent means of shifting responsibility for costly repairs whilst at the same time ensuring a moderate return on investment, in turn, housefarmers who purchased the fag-end of leases themselves maximised short-term gains on housing through the evasion of repairs, subletting and rack rental. The result was a rapid deterioration in conditions wherever the system took hold. Housing in the central areas abandoned by the middle class provided perhaps the worst examples of slum conditions, but the most lucrative source of property speculation. Long since past its best, such housing was ripe for subdivision and subletting. The pattern was illustrated clearly in St Giles in the 1830s:

The way these houses are set out is this, the ground landlord lets out the whole estate, or two or three streets to one person, and he pays the rent by the year; and he again lets those houses to one person who pays him weekly; and that person gets in and lets in his turn every room separately and when an inhabitant has got into a room he again lets off part of the room to anyone who comes in by the night.

Where such a chain of tenancy arose, it proved difficult if not impossible to enforce repairs. In his report to the privy council on the state of common lodgings in the metropolis, Captain Hay of the Metropolitan police commented 'Such tenancy and occupation have rendered it extremely difficult to reach the person really responsible as 'keeper' for the condition of the house; for there is first the owner; secondly his tenant for the whole house; thirdly the subtenant for a room; and fourthly five or six persons or families occupying one room as lodgers.'

Speaking in 1866 of the worsening condition of housing in London, Dr Julian Hunter commented on this practice: "There is regular trade of dealing in fag ends of leases and the art of eluding covenants is well studied. Gentlemen in this business may, be fairly expected to do as they do - get all they can from the tenants while they have them, and leave as little as they can for their successors.'

Small tradesmen and shopkeepers, in particular, whose object was a quick return on capital as well as a continuous inflow of money, were most likely to enter this part of the property market and it was these local property owners that were frequently cited as the main cause for deteriorating housing conditions. Temptation was great; profits could be high, some claimed as high as 100 per cent if landlord expenditure was minimised. Evasion of repairs and opposition to sanitary reforms were understandable given the fact that any expenditure would either reduce profits or result in extra burdens on the rates. The reluctance of inferior landlords to cleanse cesspits on the grounds of expense had already drawn the ire of Chadwick but as housing conditions worsened in central areas, greater attention was paid to the inadequacies of the small property owners. In 1850 Hector Gavin had complained about the fact that owners of small house property were generally opposed to sanitary reform on the grounds of expense. His views were echoed elsewhere throughout the century. Thomas Tebaz, medical officer of health for Westminster, corroborated the fact that small owners- petty bricklayers and small shopkeepers-either would not or could not make necessary repairs to their properties for fear of losing their profit.

Though in reality their existence was merely a symptom of urban decay, slum landlords- known variously as house farmers, house knackers, land jobbers, property sweaters or rack renters - were usually cast as villains of the piece and blamed for the slums very existence. The Attack by Thomas Beames on house farmers and middlemen- 'whose heart is seared by the recollection of their own poverty and who learn quarters. The Builder constantly sniping at the leasehold system that gave rise to house farming whilst the role of small property owners came under increasingly close and critical scrutiny as the hosing problem worsened during the course of the century.

St Giles

Housing and Slum Formation

Of all the slums which existed in London during the period few, if any, surpassed in squalor or notoriety the Irish rookery in St Giles. Though the district as a whole contained pockets of decaying courts and houses inhabited by an impoverished population, none were so decayed or as deeply impoverished as the housing and population in the area centred around Church Lane. Bounded by Bainbridge Street , George Street and High Street, the St Giles rookery known also as little Ireland and the Holy Land housed an impoverished and largely Irish population in old decaying housing hidden within a maze of congested courts and alleys. Middle class housing, long since abandoned by its original inhabitants and occupied now by a population of much lower social standing had tumbled in status as a result of subdivision and neglect. Squalid Courts existed where once there had been back gardens; the result was clear; nowhere in the district was the housing so poor and the poor so concentrated as in the Irish rookery and no other place in the city, perhaps, captured the imagination or came to symbolise more the depths of poverty in the capital than did St Giles.

In part, fascination with the district stemmed from the antiquity of the place. Decaying houses set amidst a honeycomb of courts and alleys reflected an earlier form of the city about to be swept away by the Victorian enthusiasm for clearances and street improvements. One writer described the rookery as: 'One great maze of narrow crooked paths crossing and intersecting in labyrinthine convulsions, as if the houses had been originally one great block of stone eaten by slugs into innumerable small chambers and connecting passages.'.

Fascination also stemmed from the capital's social contrasts, none of which was greater than that between the poverty of St Giles and the wealth of the surrounding districts. Finally, the rookery represented a degree of filth, squalor and social disorder that was perhaps unmatched in the city at the time. So great was its reputation as the epitome of slumdom that for the more socially aware traveller, such as Frederick Engels and Flora Tristan, it became almost a tourist attraction. The reputation for squalor so justly deserved had a long ancestry. Even as a new seventeenth-century suburb, the district had stood out from the surrounding area by virtue of its higher proportion of poorer families and lower social status. Its descent into squalor during the eighteenth century, however, was as rapid as it was spectacular and by mid-century its reputation for poverty, and debauchery, as demonstrated by John Gay in *The Beggars Opera* or by Hogarth in his drawing of Gin Lane, was well established. New aristocratic estates to the west had enticed those who could afford it to move away, leaving empty houses that were ripe for less salubrious uses. By 1750, it was estimated that one in four houses was a gin shop. Common lodging houses abounded, attracting a transient population of beggars and thieves as well as a substantial number of Irish immigrants. Its reputation at the start of the nineteenth century as the centre of beggary was well deserved since over one quarter of the beggars investigated by the society for the Society for the suppression of Mendicity came from the area. By the turn of the century, then, the district was long past its best and in the course of the following decades it became, in the eyes of many, the archetypal slum.

Once begun the downward spiral of impoverishment and physical deterioration was difficult to halt. St. Giles, in common with other inner districts during the first half of the nineteenth century, was squeezed between an old deteriorating housing stock and growing pressure of population. In the first decades of the century , rising populations coupled with an almost static housing stock resulted in increased levels of overcrowding. In 1801 the number of persons per house stood at 9.8 but by 1831 this had risen to 12.7. Population continued to rise until 1851 but a sharp fall in the number of houses in the 1840s arising from the clearances for New Oxford Street led to even higher average occupancy rates. Within the district, enormous variation in housing conditions existed. In Bloomsbury to the north high status housing on the Bedford estate contrasted with concentrations of extremely poor housing in St. Giles parish to the South. An investigation by the Statistical Society of London in 1847 revealed that in Church Lane houses frequently contained more than thirty people and that following the clearances for New Oxford Street in 1844 the same house often contained 40 or more people. A further survey of Church Lane and its environs in 1849 revealed that in some houses with no more than four rooms between 50 and 90 inhabitants found nightly lodgings. Even higher levels of overcrowding were recorded in the same census. In 1841 the average number of inhabitants per house in Church Lane was 24 - three times the average for London and nearly twice that of St. Giles as a whole. By 1851, however, the situation had worsened dramatically with average occupancy having reached 46 per house. Even this enormous rise hid the fact that several houses in the street held over 100 persons and one house (number 21) contained 140 people.

Overcrowding was serious throughout the area but particularly in the numerous lodging houses scattered throughout the district. In 1856, 69 houses were registered under the Common lodging house Act, the majority of which were concentrated in the poorest streets, including Church Lane, Carrier Street and Queen Street (idem, 1857), In reality, however, the number of lodging-houses was much greater, since to avoid the terms of the Act residents in the same rooms professed to be members of one family rather than lodgers (idem,1859). Rooms contained anything from eight to forty people depending on size, but all were universally crowded and equally filthy. 'You would be startled', remarked Thomas Beames, 'to witness the crowding of inmates even in favoured localities'.

Rents were generally low, as befitted the quality of the accommodation, 1d a night bought space on the floor and 3d a share of a bed. The cost of a single room, was between 3s.0d. and 4s.6d. a week, but this could be recouped by subletting corners or space on the floor. A sample of 548 rents paid by applicants for the majority of paupers paid between ls.0d. and 3s.0d. a week, with the average cost being 2s. 1/2 d. Most were weekly tenants and the relatively low amounts suggest that it was usual for them to be sharing a room.

Low as the rents were, the returns on slum housing could be substantial. Profits were made at every stage in the chain, with houses let for £20 to £30 yielding profits of £70 after rates had been paid. 21 Church Lane, for example, in the heart of the Irish rookery, was rented from the owner for £25 per annum. The immediate tenant received £58. 10s. in rent and his subtenants in turn let rooms to lodgers and received an estimated return of £120. In turn these opportunities for profit attracted a host of house farmers and middlemen for whom slum housing represented a lucrative business and in common with the situation in other inner areas, subletting and subdivision of houses were frequent.

The outcome of such devolution of responsibility was clear to all houses were neglected; repairs were avoided and regulations evaded. Local slum landlords were primarily responsible for some of the very worst property in the district. 7 Church Lane, for instance, which was owned by Charles Innis but leased to Thomas Fitzgerald was described in 1849 thus:

The privy had been taken away and the cesspool covered with boards and earth. The soil underneath oozed up through the boards, saturating the earth with foetid matter ... In one of the back rooms several Irish families lived . . . The room opposite was occupied by only three families during the day,, but as many as could be got into it at night. The price ranged from 'anything they could give me' to 1d and 2d per night . This room fetched 2s.0d. per week. Two cases of fever had been taken away from it. The window slid back only eight inches - that was the only means of ventilation. Although this room was not more than nine feet square daylight did not reach the back of it. It was scarcely high enough for an ordinary man to stand upright in. The person who took the rents came to the door for them every Monday.

In 1864 George Buchanan, the local mental officer of health complained that: 'Much of the poor house property in the district is owned by some few landlords who wanted incessant looking after, and had come to regard the lenient measures of warning as adopted by, the Board as a cheap way of keeping them informed about the state of their premises.'. When attempts were made by the local Board of Works to enforce bye-laws relating to over crowding, cleansing and general repairs, as permitted under the 1866 Sanitary Act, Section 35, a deputation of house owners and agents proved powerful enough to ensure that the notices of repair were withdrawn. The only matter to be dealt with promptly and regularly, it seems, was the collection of rent.

Reconstruction of the pattern of property ownership in the area for 1843, based on the ratebooks, reveals the existence of an intricate chain of ownership and tenancy. In the Church lane rookery, ownership was concentrated in relatively few hands. As Table: *Distribution of House Ownership in St.Giles* shows, prior to demolitions for New Oxford Street, nine owners held over 82 per cent of the total house property in the rookery with the three largest owners holding nearly half the building stock between them.

Moreover, their interests were highly localised, with properties usually concentrated in one or a few neighbouring streets. Robert Hughes's properties, for example, were found in three streets, whilst the 25 houses belonging to John Corwan were located in six streets in the rookery. By far the largest house owner was Charles Innis, a local solicitor who held a total of 60 houses in St Giles, all but five of which were in the rookery. Innis himself was a house farmer. In addition to owning property he was also recorded as the occupier of three houses in the area. Whilst he took an active role in managing some of his housing, as witnessed by the fact that he was recorded as the owner-occupier of 20 properties, it was more usual for him to sub-let the house to a secondary tenant. His property linkages reveal a systematic pattern of letting to a small number of sub-tenants, several of which were local house owners in their own right. Thomas Fitzgerald, himself a 'slumlord' with 13 houses, also sub-let at least seven of Innis's houses, Others, such as Richard Langley, merely underlet houses without ;actually becoming involved in ownership. The pattern that emerges is complex but nevertheless provides a clear indication of the central role of sub-letting in the rookery, with the implication that similar patterns were to be found elsewhere in the inner districts.

Income and Employment

If the Church Lane rookery represented the archetypal slum then its inhabitants were similarly representative of the residuum that peopled the courts and alleys of the London slums. Though the area had its own housekeepers, shopkeepers and pawnbrokers, nevertheless the majority of its inhabitants followed the more precarious and poorly rewarded livelihoods, such as street trading, service, begging and theft. However although poverty and insecurity provided the unifying context of slum life, experiences were filtered through differences in occupations, ethnicity, age and gender, resulting in a highly variegated and complex internal ordering of slum life. Just as ' the microscope shows the subdivision of the atom,' so too 'a minute inquiry into the various classes subdivides society into unimaginable grades'. The social order of the slum was no exception.

Inhabitants of the Church Lane rookery, and other slums in the area derived a precarious livelihood predominantly from unskilled occupations. The demand for labourers, porters, costermongers and street sellers arising from the proximity to Covent Garden meant that such groups dominated the occupational structure. In 1851 in St Giles as a whole 9.9 per cent of men were recorded as labourers but in the poorest streets and courts, such as Church Lane and Wild Court, the proportion rose to 54.7 and 41.6 per cent respectively. Hawkers, costermongers and street traders were similarly over represented. Whilst it is impossible to judge the number of street traders from the census abstracts, the enumerators' books show that in Church Lane in 1851 20.6 per cent of men and 61.6 per cent of women were engaged in hawking. In the Wild Court the figure were 15.0 and 39.3 per cent respectively. In these two streets alone, labourers and street traders accounted for over 68 per cent of the occupied population with the remainder involved in various manufacturing and construction activities or in different forms of service.

Occupations of those squeezed out of the labour market and forced onto the poor law reflected the general tendency in the slums for an over representation of unskilled labour. As shown in Table: *Occupations of Applicants for Poor Relief in St Giles 1832-62* general labouring and manufacturing activities accounted for over half the total number of male applicants for poor relief, followed by street trading, construction and services.

Female applicants were relatively equally divided between service, manufacturing, charring and hawking, with prostitution also accounting for a significant if somewhat smaller percentage of women. Compared to the overall occupational distribution in St.Giles, the occupations of paupers reveal an over representation of unskilled work compared to an under representation of more skilled manufacturing employment. Those employed in manufacturing moreover, were primarily engaged in the cheap, dishonourable sector of shop work in clothing or shoe making, both of which were characterised by extremely low rates of pay and notoriously bad conditions of work. Needlework, second only to domestic service as the major female trade, was particularly poorly rewarded and many of those employed, as Mayhew claimed, resorted to prostitution supplement insufficient wages. Low wages and insecure employment characterised the host of unskilled occupations into which many slum dwellers drifted.

Apart from those gatekeepers in the rookery, such as lodging-keepers, pawnbrokers and shopkeepers, few could rely on a regular and sufficient income. Although fluctuations in household earnings associated with the family life-cycle meant that at times individuals and families could rise above the poverty line, escape was usually only temporary. For female headed households, moreover, such escape was well nigh impossible. Some indication of the particular difficulties faced by women can be gained from Table: *Average Weekly incomes among applicants for relief in St. Giles 1832-1862* showing average weekly incomes of applicants for relief in St Giles. Although average household incomes were 12s.2d, the experiences of men and women diverged sharply.

Whilst less than 28 per cent of male headed households earned below 10s.0d., this figure rose to nearly 76 per cent for female-headed households. Some of the difference may be accounted for by male-headed households also including the earnings of wives, but a more potent factor was the extremely low earning of women in the Victorian city. The difficulties faced by women as a result of such low wages were in part alleviated by networks of support which developed in slum communities. Many, however, turned elsewhere for support, to prostitution as well as the poor law.

Rhythms of Poverty

Life in the slums was circumscribed by the uncertainties brought about by powerlessness and inadequate resources. Always liable to live in housing that could be condemned as unfit for human habitation, or to dwell in areas that were ripe for street clearance and demolition, the poor inhabited a physical world over which they had relatively little control. Streets ploughed through the heart of the slums and demolition of poor housing constantly threatened the stability of slum communities during this period. Uncertainty stemming from external factors was compounded by the exigencies arising from the many critical life situations, such as illness, accident or childbirth that punctuated the lives of the poor. But seemingly chaotic, slum life was also structured by the rhythms of poverty resulting from weekly, seasonal and cyclical fluctuations in income and employment. The casual nature of much work meant that weekly, incomes were rarely adequate and never predictable. Seasonal fluctuations in employment and the cost of living etched out a perennial theme in the lives of the poor, whilst cyclical pressures in the economy provided a deeper context to slum life. Few families escaped these pressures and the shared experience of poverty helped to create a framework within which slum life operated.

At its most general level the rhythm of poverty was influenced by cyclical fluctuations in the economy. Though the diversity of the metropolitan economy, meant that fluctuations were not as extreme as elsewhere, nevertheless cyclical swings were a marked feature of London's economy and they reverberated to a greater or lesser extent throughout the districts comprising the capital. Expenditure on poor relief, which showed an inverse relationship with economic indicators such as bankruptcies and construction, provides an accurate estimate of the fluctuations in poverty within the city. During the period from 1840 to 1864 three clear cycles of expenditure occurred in London with peaks in 1841-42, 1848-49 and 1855-56 representing the heights of distress. The pattern in St Giles mirrored the situation elsewhere. The depression of the late 1840s, in particular, appears to have been exceptionally severe, although the rise in expenditure was in part due to the cost of workhouse construction rather than the simple pressure of numbers. Local factors also exacberated the crisis, notably an influx of poverty-stricken Irish immigrants fleeing the famine and a higher level of overcrowding arising from clearances for New Oxford Street. Nevertheless, despite these local factors, St Giles experienced periods of crisis in common with most other districts in the city and these deeper rhythms provided the general context of slum life within the locality.

Superimposed on the deeper rhythms of the economic cycle were the shorter term fluctuations associated with the seasonal nature of London's economy. Though to a limited extent dovetailing of employment's could mitigate the worst pressures of seasonality, for many of the poor such opportunities were strictly limited. Operating in already overstocked labour markets, unskilled casual workers had to contend with seasonal influxes of other workers, thereby exacerbating the worst pressures and reducing the likelihood of earning a sufficient income to make ends meet. For most workers, but particularly, for those employed in casual occupations, winter was a harsh period. Shorter hours of daylight and interruptions from the weather meant that for a whole host of outdoor trades slack work prevailed: Inclement weather and shorter hours interrupted construction and street trading alike, both of which provided a large proportion of casual employment for slum dwellers. Other casual trades also experienced slack demand during the winter, notably clothing manufacture and shoemaking. Lower earnings however were not matched by reduced costs. Indeed, precisely the opposite was the case since the cost of living rose with the need to provide extra light and heat.

In London as a whole the pressures of winter were reflected in higher rates of pauperism. The combination of slack work and higher costs meant that for many slum dwellers already living close to the margin of poverty, if not beneath it, there was little choice but to seek assistance from friends or relatives, or relief from more formal institutions notably the poor law. During the 1850s the number of paupers in receipt of relief on 1 January usually exceeded the total on 1

July by between 10 and 30 per cent (see annual reports of the poor law board). St.Giles was no exception and the seasonal rhythm of poverty was well illustrated by the pattern of applications. The pronounced winter peak is clear, particularly in relation to able bodied applicants seeking relief on account of work or destitution.

The seasonal rhythm of poverty was punctuated by the exigencies of coping with critical life situations, such as birth, death, illness or unemployment, each of which appeared with greater regularity in poorer districts of the city. higher fertility rates occurred in poorer localities, reflecting the fact both that women in such areas tended to bear larger numbers of children and also that large families were themselves a cause of poverty. In every slum, bouts of illness were common and mortality rates high, particularly that of infants. Chadwicks Sanitary report of 1842 had highlighted the extent to which death rates varied according to class and locality, with the highest rates occurring in slum districts such as Bethnal Green and Whitechapel compared to more salubrious parts of the city. Generalisations, moreover, were borne out by more detailed investigations of specific neighbourhoods. In Church Lane the Statistical Society of London recorded that infant mortality was twice as high as in the suburban district of Islington, and that the rate for children aged between one and two years old was in more than six times as high.

Mortality, however, was merely a superficial manifestation of a far larger amount of morbidity which struck with monotonous regularity the population of slum districts. In St Giles between 1 July 1847 and 27 January 1848, only 2 out of 88 persons who received medical treatment in the workhouse on account of typhus died (ibid p.24). A similar ratio was recorded for Bethnal Green for approximately the same period.

The regularity with which illness and death, not to mention unemployment and underemployment, struck slum communities is evident.

If childbirth is included together with illness, accident or death of the main wage earner, nearly, two-thirds of pauperism was attributable to reasons of morbidity or mortality. For women the workhouse provided an alternative to the lying in hospital and over one in five of those admitted gave birth there. For the remainder of applicants, the majority of which were able-bodied, unemployment or destitution were cited as the main reasons for poverty and although this probably underestimates their true extent within slum communities, the situation is consistent with the avowed antipathy of the Poor Law towards able bodied paupers and the reluctance of such a group to apply for relief.

Without reserves to tide over such crises, the poor were forced to seek assistance either from informal contacts, such as friends, relatives and neighbours, or from more formal channels of credit such as local pawnbrokers or shopkeepers. When these avenues of aid were closed there was , finally, private philanthropy and the poor law.

As befitted the precariousness of working-class life, residential shifts were a common feature in poor communities. The need to tailor the costs of accommodation to uncertain incomes necessitated frequent moves, albeit often within the immediate locality,. Credit with landlords may have sufficed to tide over temporary, shortfalls in rent but often even this reprieve was short-lived and families were soon forced to vacate lodgings for cheaper accommodation elsewhere. Moonlight flits, often as much to avoid arrears of rent as to safeguard furniture from the bailiffs, were all too common. But despite the restless mobility, which pervaded the working-class communities, there was nevertheless a degree of stability founded upon the restricted spatial scale of movement. Overall population turnover in working-class districts was slow, and people remained if not in the same house, then at least in the same street or locality for lengthy periods of time, allowing the formation of close social ties born from spatial propinquity. In such a context of residential stability, communities bound together by links of reciprocity, kinship and ethnicity flourished.

Slum dwellers in St Giles reflected both the fears of contemporaries and the underlying reality of working-class communities. The Church Lane rookery and the poorer streets had a dubious reputation for housing a shifting population of tramps and thieves. In Monmouth court during the winter of 1861, Joseph Oppenheimer, the London City Missionary for the area, recorded that more than half the population changed each month, 'so that I seldom meet the same people again.' (Oppenheimer, 6 February 1862.) In the rest of the rookery, it was claimed, transient lodgers were at least as numerous as the regulars. Against this image of transiency and shiftlessness, however, needs to be set an alternative view, borne out by the pattern of applications to the Poor Law, which hints at a more settled community, of the poor, characterised by common bonds of ethnicity, kinship and propinquity and linked together by networks of aid and credit.

In their investigations of the Church Lane rookery in 1848, the Statistical Society noted how despite the poverty of the Irish population the majority were long-term residents of London. Even in the lodging houses, although a good proportion of the inhabitants were merely passing through, half the residents were thought to have been regulars. The suggestion that despite poverty and transiency a relatively permanent community persisted in the rookery is borne out with reference to the poor Law applicants to which had to provide details of previous residence in order to satisfy requirements for the receipt of relief. Until 1847 rights to relief depended upon obtaining a settlement in an area, determined usually by birth marriage or service. After that date however, it became possible to establish a claim for relief based on continuous residence in an area for five years, later reduced to one year.

The need to satisfy residency requirements meant that the local Poor Law undertook detailed investigations of the pattern of residential mobility of applicants for relief. It becomes clear from this data that although residential mobility was relatively frequent, the majority of the poor maintained a long term residence in the area.

As shown in Table: *Length of residence in St. Giles by Birthplace in Ireland or Great Britain (adults over 15)* despite the fact that nearly a quarter of the applicants for poor relief had been in St Giles for less than one year, representing primarily a shiftless substrata of tramps, vagrants and in the 1840s recent Irish immigrants, over half the total applicants had resided in the district for longer than five years, representing a much more stable group amongst the poor.

Though English born paupers formed the larger proportion of this settled group, nevertheless nearly half the Irish who sought relief had also been in the area for over five years. Long term residence, however, did not preclude rapid residential mobility and shifts of accommodation were relatively frequent within working class communities, even though most moves were for a short distance. High rates of residential turnover, however, did not necessarily imply an impermanent community. The neighbourhood provided a framework and the main context of life for slum dweller. Tied to localities by social networks revolving around employment, credit and the poor law, working class households frequently remained in the same area for lengthy periods of time despite the frequency of residential shifts.

At a more detailed level of analysis, however, the distinction between the district as a whole and individual neighbourhoods becomes apparent. the Physical context of court and back street living provided an enclosed spatial world within which much of the daily activity associated with slum life occurred. The neighbourhood in this case consisted of no more than a handful of streets within which social relationships were formed and residential mobility took place. Paupers tended to remain within their immediate locality, often returning after several moves close to their original starting point.

Proximity, moreover, fostered kinship links and social relations and as a result dense social networks were built up between neighbours, kin and friends within such small enclosed worlds. That social networks were established within the slum was apparent from the pattern of contacts maintained by the poor. Applicants for relief were asked to give a reference to vouch for the veracity of their situation and in approximately half the cases this information was provided. In the minority of cases the applicant was unknown within the area and the situation was recorded as such.

Although not necessarily evidence of an active relationship, nevertheless the name of a reference was indicative of some form of social contact and therefore can be used to assess the existence of neighbourhood and kinship links. The pattern of contacts, shown in Table: *Social contacts in St Giles 1832-62* reveals that kinship was central to the social networks with over half the applicants maintaining some form of kinship links, the majority of which were either within St Giles or elsewhere in London.

Within the district, over one in five paupers were either living with kin or had lived with them at a previous address in the district. Nor was kinship the only form of local contact; employers, landlords and other persons were also called upon to act as references for applicants and again the majority of these were located either at the same address or elsewhere in the district. Treated in conjunction with the other evidence, the pattern of contacts suggests that far from being a place of transiency and anonymity, where a person might sink into the crevices of the city, for many inhabitants the slum was the location of a close and spatially bounded social network dominated by kinship linkages and focused primarily on the immediate residence and local neighbourhood.

Conclusion

Viewed from the outside, the world of the urban poor was shrouded in uniform shades of grey. Those who commented on the slums at mid century saw the poor as an undifferentiated mass leading lives of drab uniformity in conditions which almost belied the possibility of maintaining a decent existence. The coarseness and vulgarity of slumlife was reflected in the characteristics of those forced to endure the conditions. This opinion was shared not only by the radical thinkers, such as Marx and Engels, but also by those of a more conservative bent, such as Disraeli and Carlyle. Indeed, all were in agreement that the Brutishness of the slum life dominated and indeed overwhelmed all other aspects of existence.

In part this view was the outcome of the physical realities of the nineteenth century city in which decaying inner city environments were complemented by social polarisation and spatial segregation. The slums themselves - often ill drained quagmires pervaded by the stench of sewage and decaying matter, overfilled with a seemingly innumerable and largely unwashed population, rooms which housed both people and vermin and sometimes also animals - these places were hardly conducive to detailed investigations by anyone save relieving officers, police or city missionaries. Social polarisation and spatial segregation, resulting in increasingly privatised and secluded spheres of activity, effectively created a situation in which contact with, and knowledge of the urban poor on the part of the middle class was both fleeting and partial . Under such circumstances accounts of the slums were rarely able to do more than paint a picture of poverty in the mass in which the colour of slum life was transformed to a monochrome representation of a much richer and varied fabric.

Viewed from the inside, however, the lumpen proletariat were anything but lumpen. Although inhabitants of the lower depths shared a common bond of poverty, nevertheless individuals participated to varying degrees in communities based on age , ethnicity, gender, occupation and place. Experiences of slum life were filtered through this complex and interrelated pattern of internal stratification. It was all too simple for the urban bourgeoisie to ignore these distinctions in the face of what appeared to be a crushing uniformity born of poverty. But as we have indicated here, such internal stratification was indeed a significant facet of slum life. Minute differentials in income related to age, gender and occupation were critical when life was conducted as a hand to mouth existence. Ethnicity too, not only structured opportunities for employment but also represented a set of cultural and social resources from which individuals drew support. Finally , the encapsulated world of the urban poor , reflected on the court and street, provided a basis upon which reciprocity could function.

All this adds substance to form, transforming our understanding of the slums from that of a mere container of the poor to the stage for a varied and complex set of economic, social and cultural relationships. Unravelling the threads which comprised slum life requires a keen attention to detail and an ear for the muted tones of the urban poor as they went about their daily lives. Only whispers of their existence remain in the historical record but we have only to listen to the silence in order to learn the lessons so crucial for the present.

How much do we know about what it meant to be alive in a Victorian slum? How much *can* we know about an experience which was remote from almost all those who wrote about life in the towns or took oral evidence about it for various commissions of inquiry? Perhaps nothing reveals more ruthlessly how little we do know about urban culture in Victorian England than a survey of the secondary sources from which its slumminess may be discerned, nor makes that evidence more fragile than reflecting on what it is bound to omit. The sheer bodily sensations to be had from the daily round of slum life, the emotional demands it made and the responses it evoked, the mental reactions to the special miseries and the gaieties of living in the gutters of urban society - the real meaning, indeed, of life at certain levels - are not contained now to any extent even in the archaeological remains of the slums of Victorian London, much less in any well-calendared archives. They have almost all gone. Smell - to take but one of the most evocative elements of the slums - has no historical dimension; yet it has always been one of their chief ingredients, a factor potent enough in the end to drive George Orwell from the ferret's cage he once occupied in a post-Victorian generation, or to put George Augustus Sala back on the streets - his nostrils filled beyond endurance with the stench of the bugs - after his attempt to doss down for the night in a slum eighty years

Before Orwell.

It seems strange that we should know so little about how Victorian cities were actually made. We know far more about the total effort that went into making them and the impact this had on the course of investment - perhaps on the very growth of the national income - than we do about the way in which these cities were literally pieced together. It is true, just the same, that no one has yet been able to say with real conviction whether, or to what extent, the growth of her cities in the nineteenth century of itself stimulated or retarded Britain's general economic expansion. Yet what seems in some ways more remarkable than our ignorance on these bigger questions is the smallness of our knowledge about a number of little things, especially those involved in the basic developmental processes of converting open country into closed-up streets and of the business operations that carried them through. Here is an industry - to consider it for a moment at large - which in the first Census of Production in 1907 accounted for about £80 million output per annum, or nearly as much as the whole of the clothing industry, appreciably more than that of gas, water and electricity undertakings combined. We know more about the movements of some of the prices of the factors involved in the productivity of the house-building industry itself than we do about its structure and its ways of working.

In Victorian England, the speculative builder was widely regarded as a kind of deadly spider, spinning houses in his cobweb to catch unsuspecting victims in, a jerry-builder, a scamping builder who mixed dust with his mortar, or who cut the footings, or quickly railed over the green timber, or got up to a thousand tricks to avoid building good and true. Despite the persistent lack of any substantial body of hard evidence on the matter, the legend took root, the familiar gibes were thrown, and the mud that stuck on the few also spattered many, especially at the lower end of the market, where operating margins were so slight that a few weeks of hot sun or of hard rain could wipe out any prospect of getting rid of a new house that had been scamped in some hidden way.

But the operations of Edward Yates, and the enduring condition of every one of his suburban houses that have descended into the third and, indeed, the fourth generation of him that built them, offer undeniably hard evidence that points to a different judgment on the speculative builders of the suburbs of Victorian London. In the course of this essay, I should like to set out his career as a builder and developer and, to some degree, as a landlord and man of property, in as much detail as his surviving business records permit us to do.

It was the worst slum in Victorian Britain. Yet its crime-ridden streets were safer than today's

Charles Mowbray, former soldier, master tailor and one of the greatest working-class orators in late Victorian England, had only to look out of his cracked window in London's East End to know this was the place to start the revolution.

As his pay had been slashed to subsistence levels, so Mowbray had been driven to take refuge at the bottom of the heap, in the worst, most soul-destroying slum in the greatest city on Earth.

Its name was the Old Nichol, possibly derived from the name of the devil himself, Old Nick.

Situated in Bethnal Green and part of Shoreditch, it was only 25 minutes' walk from the Bank of England.

But the Old Nichol, a maze of rotting streets hemmed in by bleak tenement buildings, might as well have been on a different planet.

Most Londoners preferred to forget that it even existed. When Mowbray put on his boots and walked through the Old Nichol, he passed down narrow, muddy streets, skirting pools of filthy liquid and the carcasses of dogs and cats.

Eyes watched him greedily through broken window panes. Mowbray would go on to decry the injustices of the age and was an impassioned socialist.

And given his surroundings, it is hardly surprising that the slum's most famous son spoke so loudly.

No grass grew in this dark and putrid labyrinth. The narrow canyons of blackened brick tenements blocked out the sun and all colour was leached away except for the dull greys of smoke and soot.

In a two-room tenement in Anne Court, just around the corner from where Mowbray lived, the meagre fire burning in the grate drew moisture out of the saturated plaster, creating wisps of fog inside the house.

In the Old Nichol, there was no escape from the gloom. Its two tiny rooms were home to a married couple and six children, but there were no beds.

When Montagu Williams, a magistrate and writer, asked how they slept, the mother replied: 'Oh, we sleep how we can.'

Through the hole in the wall which served as a door, Williams could see the woman's haggard, hollow-cheeked husband and two teenage sons making uppers for boots.

Many of these houses were below pavement level and so flooded when it rained.

In cold weather and warmth was a luxury in the Old Nichol broken panes were blocked up with anything that came to hand: newspapers, rags, sometimes old hats.

In winter, even the water jugs iced over. Mowbray lived with his wife and four children in a little room in Boundary Street, which marked the border between Bethnal Green and Shoreditch.

Around the corner, in a single room, a missionary had recently discovered a single woman nursing a feverish young girl. On the floor lay the body of the woman's six-year-old son, who had died a few hours earlier.

Her husband, a singer of street ballads, had refused to return home because a public hanging at Tyburn had drawn the crowds and business was good.

When he did get back to his dead child, he stormed out again at the sight of the missionary urging his wife to pray.

It is hard to believe that such obscenities were allowed to persist in the richest city in the Empire.

But, as a new book reveals, they were commonplace in this corner of London.

Sarah Wise's The Blackest Streets reveals that the Nichol's 30 or so streets housed around 5,700 people and had a death rate that was almost double that of neighbouring areas.

A quarter of all children born in the Nichol died before their first birthday and Old Nichol Street itself was described by the local medical officer, Dr Bate, as being unfit for human habitation.

Damp, overcrowding and the unwholesome air were largely to blame. But so was sheer despair.

In 1887, five out of every six infants to die in Bethnal Green homes where the whole family shared a bed were found to have suffocated.

Coroners attributed most of these deaths to 'overlaying', during which a sleeping parent or sibling rolled onto the infant and accidentally smothered it.

Others, however, suspected that many were intentionally suffocated, by desperate mothers with too many mouths to feed.

The close quarters in which the slum dwellers lived had other inevitable consequences. Families slept in one bed, washed together and regularly saw one another naked.

The children watched their elders having sex. Many believed sexual abuse was uncommon, but Beatrice Webb, one of the founders of the LSE, wrote: 'To put it bluntly, sexual promiscuity and even sexual perversion the violation of little children are almost unavoidable among men and women of average character and intelligence crowded into the one-room tenements of slum areas.'

But there was little profit to be made by improving things. Much of the housing was owned by churchmen and peers of the realm, and they had a vested interest in maintaining the status quo.

These 'vampyres of the poor', as one contemporary newspaper called them, were sitting on some of the most profitable property in London - making returns on their investment of up to 150 per cent.

The landlords might complain about the odd tenant skipping rent payments or thieves stripping the lead from roofs, but these were minor irritations in the light of such extortionate profits.

In fact, hardly anybody in the Old Nichol even knew who their landlords were. They acted through lawyers, themselves shadowy figures, and the whole system was ratified by the Bethnal Green Vestry, a squad of venal councillors who operated as the local authority.

These Vestrymen blocked repeated attempts by politicians, from the 1850s on, to have the whole slum demolished.

But not everyone hated the slum or railed against it like Mowbray. Arthur Harding was born in the Nichol in 1886 and lived there most of his life.

Known as Prince Arthur, being the family favourite, he was brought up in a family of six in a single room in Keeve's Buildings, Boundary Street.

To the young Arthur, this humble home was comfortable compared to many in the area.

Renting at three shillings a week, it measured 12ft by 10ft and accommodated a table, two armchairs, a chest of drawers, straw mattress and small stove.

Over the mantelpiece was a portrait of Queen Victoria, looking down on Arthur's cot which was made out of an old orange box.

Arthur's maternal grandparents were agricultural labourers who had come to London thinking they could better themselves. They were mistaken: both died in the Shoreditch workhouse.

Arthur's mother, Mary Ann, found work in a factory, sorting old rags for pulping into paper, one of the most hazardous of East End jobs as employees risked infection from lice and fleas.

Thankfully, she was rescued by Arthur's father, 'Flash' Harry, who met her one night at a Bishopsgate pub, Dirty Dick's. But about the time Arthur was born in Keeve's Buildings, his parents fell on hard times.

Mary Ann had a crippled hip, which confined her to making matchboxes, while Flash Harry was reduced to casual pub shifts and cadging food from restaurants.

What kept them going, however, was Aunt Liza's generosity. An unmarried woman (rare in those days), she owned her own grocery store and sold stolen goods from it - she even kept the back door open so visiting thieves could escape if the police called.

She also ran the Jack Simmons pub where, on Sunday mornings, the East End elite - prize-fighters, racetrack celebrities and music hall artists - would mingle with the Swell Mob, prosperous villains who dressed flamboyantly in brown, double-breasted overcoats and wide, black satin ties.

Prince Arthur swore that he would never become like his father, who eventually abandoned Mary Ann and died in the Mile End Workhouse aged 85.

Instead, he would follow his mother's example. She was crippled by her hip and deserted by a feckless husband, but was a loving mother nevertheless and kept her humble home spotless.

She was also a favourite among local philanthropists. Showered with charity clothing, she would take it straight round to a dealer who paid as much as five shillings for a good pair of trousers.

But she wasn't an ideal role model. She graduated to stealing from church jumble sales, with the help of Arthur who, from an early age, decided self employment was for him.

The Old Nichol was made for the light-fingered and if you knew your way through the labyrinth, you could easily evade the police.

Before long, Arthur resembled Oliver Twist's Artful Dodger. After all, the smaller you were, the more nimbly you could dodge between the stalls which lined one side of Shoreditch High Street, which he dubbed the area's Champs Elysees.

In winter, a free breakfast of bread and milk was supplied at the Ragged School Mission Hall. But after that, residents were on their own.

Arthur would hang around a corner shop which sold bags of broken biscuits for a halfpenny and, along with his friends, most of whom would die at the Somme, he became a proficient pickpocket.

There were moments of joy. When he was interviewed in the Seventies, in his ninth decade, Arthur remembered that every time a musician passed through the area, everyone would begin dancing.

Locals would dance in couples or in groups of 100 or more, spinning round and round in one of the broader streets of the Old Nichol.

But there were also moments of despair. When he was nine, Arthur and his mother were evicted from their home and spent a freezing night under a railway arch.

And after they were rehoused, Arthur's criminal career began in earnest. He joined a local gang, stealing and menacing shopkeepers and spent much of his time in prison, which, ironically, saved him from a worse fate in the trenches.

He was not alone. Mugging was commonplace in the Old Nichol - although perhaps no more so than in London today.

The magistrate Montagu Williams, for example, warned a victim: 'It is as certain as the day is long that if you go out to get drunk, and have money in your pocket, you will, in this neighbourhood, get robbed.'

More violent crimes, however, were rare. According to the Old Bailey archives, between 1885 and 1895 only one murder occurred within the Old Nichol, when a middle-aged shoemaker stabbed his wife to death.

Domestic violence was commonplace, but it stopped short of murder. While Arthur was picking pockets, however, Charles Mowbray was planning bigger things.

In the two years to 1886, unemployment among London's unionised workforce quadrupled to 10 per cent.

The coldest February in 30 years stopped work at the docks, and in the first of a series of mass demonstrations, the jobless stoned the windows of Pall Mall clubs and looted shops in Piccadilly.

On Bloody Sunday, 20 months later, a similar demonstration brought the police out in force.

Mounted police and foot guards charged the crowds. Mowbray was not present, but he was an enthusiastic propagandist for the struggle. 'MURDER!' his posters read.

'Workmen, why allow yourselves, your wives and children to be daily murdered by the foulness of the dens in which you are forced to live!

'It is time the slow murder of the poor, who are poisoned by thousands in the foul, unhealthy slums from which robber landlords exact monstrous rents was stopped.

You have paid in rent the value over and over again of the rotten dens in which you're forced to dwell. Government has failed to help you. The time has come to help yourselves.'

Mowbray was later jailed for nine months for inciting a non-existent riot and eventually fled to the U.S., lecturing the length of the East Coast on socialism, before being deported back to Britain as an undesirable.

He spent his last years in Forest Gate, dying in 1910. Well before that, however, his message had been heeded.

A new and vigorous London County Council (LCC) came into being, and its first, flagship task was the demolition of Old Nichol, and the eviction and rehousing of its inhabitants.

The Bethnal Green vestrymen, now replaced by the London County Council, were seen to reel in disgust as they toured the fetid streets.

The major landlords emerged from anonymity to claim compensation, the greediest of them being the Church of England's Commissioners.

In March 1900, seven years after the first demolitions, the Prince of Wales and Princess Alexandra processed in a carriage down a broad, tree-lined avenue, under which lay the rubble of the slum.

Ugliness had been replaced by beauty. The only losers were the evicted inhabitants of the Old Nichol.

Too poor to move elsewhere, they were shoved into neighbouring streets, which in turn became slums.

The Rookeries

In 1904, the last slum was cleared from central London in a fit of Edwardian sanitizing. Whilst the most famous rookeries were the Rats' Castle in St Giles (where Seven Dials still sits) and Jacob's Island in Bermondsey, this slum was a little closer to the heart of things: The Strand. At the end of my last post, I mentioned the redevelopment of the Strand slums, in which around four thousand people were displaced.

London has managed to retain much of its character over the centuries, although much of its fabric has been lost. It can be argued that the Victorians did more damage than the Great Fire, and the town planners (or village idiots, depending on your perspective) of the 1960s destroyed more than the Luftwaffe. The photographs in the gallery give an idea of what London was really like in the late 19th century. I have deliberately relied on photographs (with one exception), because I think the Victorians, Dickens included, did an enormous amount to create the modern stereotype of the London 'Rookeries', and I think it is useful to see how they sprang from the communal construction and courtyard living of medieval London. The idea that one could walk into a rookery by accident and not walk out alive was no doubt based upon the truth, but the fact is, these sinkhole slums existed right in the heart of London and every day people issued forth from them to work and trade with the rest of the city. Sometimes they were no more than a medieval courtyard or two that had survived the Fire and then become ever more down on its luck; sometimes they were vast warrens of streets (the Strand rookery stretched from Temple to Charing Cross).

The Victorian slums were extreme, but their roots began in the 18th century, when London began to grow at an unprecedented rate. Medieval buildings which had survived the fire were suddenly old-fashioned, and did not have all the new amenities, such as piped water. They were reliant upon the wells and pumps which were increasingly polluted by nearby cess-pits and the street-borne filth trickling through the gratings. (One excellent little snippet I discovered today: it was the done thing for men who were caught short to stand on the edge of the pavement and urinate into the road, rather than against a wall, which was the property of another and therefore, rude. The traffic was expected to ignore being splashed, although foreign diaries record Continental disgust at this 'low habit'.) Medieval and early modern buildings became cheap and were bought up by shrewd landlords for cheap lodgings, or as brothels. A prime example of this is Dyott House, which stood in Dyott Street near St Giles-in-the-Fields Church. An early Victorian account of the St Giles slum is very interesting, and the bare bones of how the people lived in his record are very unlikely to have changed much since the Georgian period. Henry Mayhew's writings cover the industries of the slums, the crime, the accommodation and the people, and they are very interesting.

On visiting a room in the garret, we saw a man, in mature years, making artificial flowers; he appeared to be very ingenious, and made several roses before us with marvelous rapidity. He had suspended along the ceiling bundles of dyed grasses of various hues, crimson, yellow, green, brown, and other colours to furnish cases of stuffed birds. He was a very intelligent man and a natural genius. He told us strong drink had brought him to this humble position in the garret...

Charles Dickens is one of the most famous authors to write about the London slums. I try to steer clear of quoting his fiction, but *Sketches by Boz* (1839), although three years beyond my period, is valuable as an account of how desperate things became under later population pressures:

Wretched houses with broken windows patched with rags and paper: every room let out to a different family, and in many instances to two or even three - fruit and 'sweet-stuff' manufacturers in the cellars, barbers and red-herring vendors in the front parlours, cobblers in the back; a bird-fancier in the first floor, three families on the second, starvation in the attics, Irishmen in the passage, a 'musician' in the front kitchen, and a charwoman and five hungry children in the back one - filth everywhere - a gutter before the houses and a drain behind - clothes drying and slops emptying, from the windows; girls of fourteen or fifteen, with matted hair, walking about barefoot, and in white great-coats, almost their only covering; boys of all ages, in coats of all sizes and no coats at all; men and women, in every variety of scanty and dirty apparel, lounging, scolding, drinking, smoking, squabbling, fighting, and swearing.

The strong-backed, hard-drinking Irish labourers, upon whom so many London fortunes were built, made up a large part of the slum-dwelling population, and were frequently derided for it, as in this later account:

St. George's-in-the-Borough, with its back courts, where the refuse of Ireland vegetate; or Kent Street,- the thieves' district,- which years since drew forth the indignation of the topographist; or Pearl Row, St. George's Road, Southwark; or Red House, Old Gravel Lane, Borough; or a lodging house for thieves at the back of Holborn, where 100 thieves are to be seen, at eleven o'clock at night, on an average, six sometimes in one bed ; or the lower part of Bell Street, Paddington, for the lower class of thieves, such as costermongers, &c.; or the courts and alleys leading out of Tooley Street, City, all the courts inhabited by Irish thieves, &c.; or Rents Buildings, York Street, Westminster, inhabited by pickpockets and juvenile thieves...

By 1816, a Parliamentary Committee had been set up to establish the problems of the London slums, and what might be done about them. Professionals were called in to give evidence and to account for their experience of the slums. One London doctor, William Blair, had this to say:

Human beings, hogs, and dogs, were associated in the same habitations; and great heaps of dirt, in different quarters, may be found piled up in the streets. Another reason of their ill health is this, that some of the lower inhabitations have neither windows nor chimneys nor floors, and were so dark that I can scarcely see there at midday without a candle. I have actually gone into a ground floor bedroom, and could not find my patient without the light of a candle

The darkness was largely a result of unscrupulous landlords shutting up windows to avoid window tax. As intolerable as these dark lodgings were, there was always a respite: the pub/lodging/pawn-shop/repository for stolen goods/brothel, or flash-house as they were known:

There are above two hundred regular flash houses in the metropolis, all known the police officers, which they frequent, many of them, open all night: that the landlords in numerous instances receive stolen goods, and are what are technically called fences; that this fact is known also to the officers, who, for obvious reasons, connive at the existence of these houses; that many of house are frequented by boys and girls of the ages of ten to fourteen and fifteen, who are exclusively admitted, who pass the night in gambling & debauchery, and who there sell and divide the plunder of the day, or who sally forth from these houses to rob in the street.

One rather bizarre aspect of many of the accounts of the slums is that of the young (borderline legal at 12ish, the age of consent at the time) girls who lure men into the dark alleys on a promise of prostituting themselves for a very low price, and then their boyfriend/pimp robs the man who was just counting his lucky stars. If he was very unlucky, he'd also get a bit of a beating and have his pants pulled down before being kicked back onto a busy street, as a mark of his shame. Every single account takes the view that these girls are the lowest of the low: not honest prostitutes, but 'bilkers'. Thus, in 1816 we can already see the seed of hypocrisy that would come to full flower during the ensuing century.

The Victorian quest for modernisation and sanitation cleared the Georgian slums and Victorian rookeries, sweeping away the very last of medieval London. The inhabitants slunk away, but not far, setting up home in Bermondsey, Brixton and Hackney, disturbing the Victorian gentry with their thieving, conniving, pawning and best of all, their bilking.

A visit to the cholera districts of Bermondsey

Monday, September 24, 1849

There is an Eastern fable which tells us that a certain city was infested by poisonous serpents that killed all they fastened upon; and the citizens, thinking them sent from Heaven as a scourge for their sins, kept praying that the visitation might be removed from them, until scarcely a house remained unsmitten. At length, however, concludes the parable, the eyes of the people were opened; for, after all their prayers and fastings, they found that the eggs of the poisonous serpents were hatched in the muck-heaps that surrounded their own dwellings.

The history of the late epidemic, which now seems to have almost spent its fatal fury upon us, has taught us that the masses of filth and corruption round the metropolis are, as it were, the nauseous nests of plague and pestilence. Indeed, so well known are the localities of fever and disease, that London would almost admit of being mapped out pathologically, and divided into its morbid districts and deadly cantons. We might lay our fingers on the Ordnance map, and say here is the typhoid parish, and there the ward of cholera; for as truly as the West-end rejoices in the title of Belgravia, might the southern shores of the Thames be christened Pestilentia. As season follows season, so does disease follow disease in the quarters that may be more literally than metaphorically styled the plague-spots of London. If the seasons are favourable, and typhus does not bring death to almost every door, then influenza and scarlatina fill the workhouses with the families of the sick. So certain and regular are the diseases in their returns, that each epidemic, as it comes back summer after summer, breaks out in the self-same streets as it appeared on its former visit, with but this slight difference, that if at its last visitation it began at the top of the Street, and killed its way down, this time it begins at the bottom, and kills its way as surely up the lines of houses.

Out of the 12,800 deaths which, within the last three months, have arisen from cholera, 6,500 have occurred on the southern shores of the Thames; and to this awful number no localities have contributed so largely as Lambeth, Southwark and Bermondsey, each, at the height of the disease, adding its hundred victims a week to the fearful catalogue of mortality. Any one who has ventured a visit to the last-named of these places in particular, will not wonder at the ravages of the pestilence in this malarious quarter, for it is bounded on the north and east by filth and fever, and on the south and west by want, squalor, rags and pestilence. Here stands, as it were, the very capital of cholera, the Jessore of London - JACOB'S ISLAND, a patch of ground insulated by the common sewer. Spared by the fire of London, the houses and comforts of the people in this loathsome place have scarcely known any improvement since that time. The place is a century behind even the low and squalid districts that surround it.

In the days of Henry II, the foul stagnant ditch that now makes an island of this pestilential spot, was a running stream, supplied with the waters which poured down from the hills about Sydenham and Nunhead, and was used for the working of the mills that then stood on its banks. These had been granted by charter to the monks of St. Mary and St. John, to grind their flour, and were dependencies upon the Priory of Bermondsey. Tradition tells us that what is now a straw yard skirting the river, was once the City Ranelagh, called "Cupid's Gardens," and that the trees, which are now black with mud, were the bowers under which the citizens loved, on the sultry summer evenings, to sit beside the stream drinking their sack and ale. But now the running brook is changed into a tidal sewer, in whose putrid filth staves are laid to season; and where the ancient summer-houses stood, nothing but hovels, sties, and muck-heaps are now to be seen.
Not far from the Tunnel there is a creek opening into the Thames. The entrance to this is screened by the tiers of colliers which lie before it. This creek bears the name of the Dock Head. Sometimes it is called St. Saviour's, or, in jocular allusion to the odour for which it is celebrated, Savory Dock. The walls of the warehouses on each side of this muddy stream are green and slimy, and barges lie beside them, above which sacks of corn are continually dangling from the cranes aloft. This creek was once supplied by the streams from the Surrey hills, but now nothing but the drains and refuse of the houses that have grown up round about it thickens and swells its waters.
On entering the precincts of the pest island, the air has literally the smell of a graveyard, and a feeling of nausea and heaviness comes over any one unaccustomed to imbibe the musty atmosphere. It is not only the nose, but the stomach, that tells how heavily the air is loaded with sulphuretted hydrogen; and as soon as you cross one of the crazy and rotting bridges over the reeking ditch, you know, as surely as if you had chemically tested it, by the black colour of what was once the white-lead paint upon the door-posts and window-sills, that the air is thickly charged with this deadly gas. The heavy bubbles which now and then rise up in the water show you whence at least a portion of the mephitic compound comes, while the

open doorless privies that hang over the water side on one of the banks, and the dark streaks of filth down the walls where the drains from each house discharge themselves into the ditch on the opposite side, tell you how the pollution of the ditch is supplied.
The water is covered with a scum almost like a cobweb, and prismatic with grease. In it float large masses of green rotting weed, and against the posts of the bridges are swollen carcasses of dead animals, almost bursting with the gases of putrefaction. Along its shores are heaps of indescribable filth, the phosphoretted smell from which tells you of the rotting fish there, while the oyster shells are like pieces of slate from their coating of mud and filth. In some parts the fluid is almost as red as blood from the colouring matter that pours into it from the reeking leather-dressers' close by.
The striking peculiarity of Jacob's Island consists in the wooden galleries and sleeping-rooms at the back of the houses which overhang the dark flood, and are built upon piles, so that the place has positively the air of a Flemish street, flanking a sewer instead of a canal; while the little ricketty bridges that span the ditches and connect court with court, give it the appearance of the Venice of drains, where channels before and behind the houses do duty for the ocean. Across some parts of the stream whole rooms have been built, so that house adjoins house; and here, with the very stench of death rising through the boards, human beings sleep night after night, until the last sleep of all comes upon them years before its time. Scarce a house but yellow linen is hanging to dry over the balustrade of staves, or else run out on a long oar where the sulphur-coloured clothes hang over the waters, and you are almost wonderstruck to see their form and colour unreflected in the putrid ditch beneath. At the back of nearly every house that boasts a square foot or two of outlet - and the majority have none at all - are pig-sties. In front waddle ducks, while cocks and hens scratch at the cinderheaps. Indeed the creatures that fatten on offal are the only living things that seem to flourish here
The inhabitants themselves show in their faces the poisonous influence of the mephitic air they breathe. Either their skins are white, like parchment, telling of the impaired digestion, the languid circulation, and the

coldness of the skin peculiar to persons suffering from chronic poisoning, or else their cheeks are flushed hectically, and their eyes are glassy, showing the wasting fever and general decline of the bodily functions. The brown, earthlike complexion of some, and their sunk eyes, with the dark areol round them, tell you that the sulphuretted hydrogen of the atmosphere in which they live has been absorbed into the blood; while others are remarkable for the watery eye exhibiting the increased secretion of tears so peculiar to those who are exposed to the exhalations of hydrosulphate of ammonia.

Scarcely a girl that has not suffusion and soreness of the eyes, so that you would almost fancy she had been swallowing small doses of arsenic; while it is evident from the irritation and discharge from the mucous membranes of the nose and eyes for which all the children are distinguished, that the poor emaciated things are suffering from continual inhalation of the vapour of carbonate of ammonia and other deleterious gases.

Nor was this to be wondered at, when the whole air reeked with the stench of rotting animal and vegetable matter: for the experiment of Professor Donovan has shown that a rabbit, with only its body enclosed in a bladder filled with sulphuretted hydrogen, and allowed to breathe freely, will die in ten minutes. Thénard also has proved that one eight hundredth part of this gas in the atmosphere is sufficient to destroy a dog, and one two hundred and fiftieth will kill a horse; while Mr. Taylor, in his book on poisons, assures us that the men who were engaged in excavating the Thames Tunnel suffered severely during the work from the presence of this gas in the atmosphere in which they were obliged to labour. "The air, as well as the water which trickled through the roof," he tells us, "was found to contain sulphuretted hydrogen. This was probably derived from the action of the iron pyrites in the clay. By respiring this atmosphere the strongest and most robust men were, in the course of a few months, reduced to a state of extreme exhaustion and died. They became emaciated, and fell into a state of low fever, accompanied with delirium. In one case which I saw," he adds, "the face of the man was pale, the lips of a violet hue, the eyes sunk and dark all round, and the whole muscular system flabby and emaciated." To give the reader some idea as to the extent with which the air in Jacob's Island is charged with this most deadly compound, it will be sufficient to say that a silver spoon of which we caught sight in one of the least wretched dwellings was positively chocolate-coloured by the action of the sulphur on the metal. On approaching the tidal ditch from the Neckinger-road, the shutters of the house at the corner were shut from top to bottom. Our intelligent and obliging guide, Dr. Martin, informed us that a girl was then lying dead there from cholera, and that but very recently another victim had fallen in the house adjoining it. This was the beginning of the tale of death, for the tidal ditch was filled up to this very point. Here, however, its putrefying waters were left to mingle their poison with the 267 cubic feet of air that each man daily takes into his lungs, and this was the point whence the pestilence commenced its ravages. As we walked down George-row, our informant told us that at the corner of London-street he could see, a short time hack, as many as nine houses in which there were one or two persons lying dead of the cholera at the same time; and yet there could not have been more than a dozen tenements visible from the spot.

We crossed the bridge, and spoke to one of the inmates. In answer to our questions, she told us she was never well. Indeed, the signs of the deadly influence of the place were painted in the earthy complexion of the poor woman. "Neither I nor my children know what health is," said she. "But what is one to do? We must live where our bread is. I've tried to let the house, and put a bill up, but cannot get any one to take it. From this spot we were led to narrow close courts, where the sun never shone, and the air seemed almost as stagnant and putrid as the ditch we had left. The blanched cheeks of the people that now came out to stare at us, were white as vegetables grown in the dark, and as we stopped to look down the alley, our informant told us that the place teemed with children, and that if a horn was blown they would swarm like bees at the sound of a gong. The houses were mostly inhabited by "corn-runners," coal-porters, and "longshore-men," getting a precarious living - earning some times as much as 12s. a day, and then for weeks doing nothing. Fevers prevailed in these courts we were told more than at the side of the ditch.

By this way we reached a dismal stack of hovels called, by a strange incongruity, Pleasant-row. Inquiring of one of the inmates, we were informed that they were quite comfortable now! The stench had been all removed, said the woman, and we were invited to pass to the back-yard as evidence of the fact. We did so; the boards bent under our feet, and the air in the cellar-like yard was foetid to positive nausea. As we left the house a child sat nursing a dying half-comatose baby on a door step. The skin of its little arms, instead of being plumped out with health, was loose and shrivelled, like an old crone's, and had a flabby monkey-like appearance more than the character of human cuticle. The almost jaundiced colour of the child's skin, its half paralyzed limbs, and state of stupor, told it was suffering from some slow poison; indeed the symptoms might readily have been mistaken for those of chronic poisoning from acetate of lead. At the end of this row our friend informed us that the last house on either side was *never* free from fever.
Continuing our course we reached "The Folly," another street so narrow that the names and trades of the shopmen were painted on boards that stretched, across the street, from the roof of their own house to that of their neighbour's. We were here stopped by our companion in front of a house "to let." The building was as narrow and as unlike a human habitation as the wooden houses in a child's box of toys. "In this house," said our friend, "when the scarlet fever was raging in the neighbourhood, the barber who was living here suffered fearfully from it; and no sooner did the man get well of this than he was seized with typhus, and scarcely had he recovered from the first attack than he was struck down a second time with the same terrible disease. Since then he has lost his child with cholera, and at this moment his wife is in the workhouse suffering from the same affliction. The only wonder is that they are not all dead, for as the man sat at his meals in his small shop, if he put his hand against the wall behind him, it would be covered with the soil of his neighbour's privy, sopping through the wall. At the back of the house was an open sewer, and the privies were full to the seat."
One fact, says an eminent writer in toxicology, is worthy of the attention of medical jurists, namely, that

the respiration of an atmosphere only slightly impregnated with the gases emanating from drains and sewers, may, if long continued, seriously affect an individual and cause death. M. D'Arcet had to examine a lodging in Paris, in which three young and vigorous men had died successively in the course of a few years, under similar symptoms. The lodging consisted of a bed-room with a chimney, and an ill-ventilated ante-room. The pipe of a privy passed down one side of the room, by the head of the bed, and the wall in this part was damp from infiltration. At the time of the examination there was no perceptible smell in the room, though it was small and low. M. D'Arcet attributed the mortality in the lodging to the slow and long-continued action of the emanations from the pipe (Ann. d'Hyg., Juillet, 1836).

We then journeyed on to London-street, down which the tidal ditch continues its course. In No. 1 of this street the cholera first appeared seventeen years ago, and spread up it with fearful virulence; but this year it appeared at the opposite end, and ran down it with like severity. As we passed along the reeking banks of the sewer the sun shone upon a narrow slip of the water. In the bright light it appeared the colour of strong green tea, and positively looked as solid as black marble in the shadow - indeed it was more like watery mud than muddy water; and yet we were assured this was the only water the wretched inhabitants had to drink. As we gazed in horror at it, we saw drains and sewers emptying their filthy contents into it; we saw a whole tier of doorless privies in the open road, common to men and women, built over it; we heard bucket after bucket of filth splash into it, and the limbs of the vagrant boys bathing in it seemed, by pure force of contrast, white as Parian marble. And yet, as we stood doubting the fearful statement, we saw a little child, from one of the galleries opposite, lower a tin can with a rope to fill a large bucket that stood beside her. In each of the balconies that hung over the stream the self-same tub was to be seen in which the inhabitants put the mucky liquid to stand, so that they may, after it has rested for a day or two, skim the fluid from the solid particles of filth, pollution, and disease. As the little thing dangled her tin cup as gently as possible into the stream, a bucket of night-soil was poured down from the next gallery.

In this wretched place we were taken to a house where an infant lay dead of the cholera. We asked if they *really did* drink the water? The answer was, "They were obliged to drink the ditch, without they could beg a pailfull or thieve a pailfull of water. But have you spoken to your landlord about having it laid on for you? "Yes, sir; and he says he'll do it, and do it, but we know him better than to believe him." "Why, sir," cried another woman, who had shot out from an adjoining room, "he won't even give us a little whitewash, though we tell him we'll willingly do the work ourselves: and look here, sir," she added, "all the tiles have fallen off, and the rain pours in wholesale."

We had scarcely left the house when a bill caught our eye, announcing that "this valuable estate" was to be sold!

From this spot we crossed the little shaky bridge into Providence-buildings - a narrow neck of land set in sewers. Here, in front of the houses, were small gardens that a table-cloth would have covered. Still the one dahlia that here raised its round red head made it a happier and brighter place. Never was colour so grateful to the eye. All we had looked at had been so black and dingy, and had smelt so much of churchyard clay, that this little patch of beauty was brighter and greener than ever was oasis in the desert. Here a herd of children came out, and stared at us like sheep. One child our guide singled out from the rest. She had the complexion of tawed leather, and her bright, glassy eyes were sunk so far back in her head, that they looked more like lights shining through the hollow sockets of a skull than a living head, and her bones seemed ready to start through the thin layer of skin. We were told she had had the cholera twice. Her father was dead of it. "But she, sir," said a woman addressing us, "won't die. Ah! if she'd had plenty of victuals and been brought up less hardy she would have been dead and buried long ago, like many more. And here's another," she added, pushing forward a long thin woman in rusty black. "Why' I've know'd her eat as much as a quartern loaf at a meal. and you can't fatten her no how." Upon this there was a laugh. but in the woman's bloodless cheeks and blue lips we saw that she like the rest was wasting away from the influence of the charnel-like atmosphere around her. The last place we went to was in Joiner's-court, with four wooden houses in it, in which there had lately been as many as five cases of cholera. In front, the poor souls, as if knowing by an instinct that plants were given to purify the atmosphere, had pulled up the paving-stones before their dwellings, and planted a few stocks here and there in the rich black mould beneath. The first house we went to, a wild ragged-headed boy shot out in answer to our knock, and putting his hands across the doorway, stood there to prevent our entrance. Our friend asked whether he could enter, and see the state of the drainage? "No; t'ain't convenient," was the answer, given so quickly and sharply, that the lad forced some ugly and uncharitable suspicion upon us. In the next house, the poor inmate was too glad to meet with any one ready to sympathise with her sufferings. We were taken up into a room, where we were told she had positively lived for nine years. The window was within four feet of a high wall, at the foot of which, until very recently, ran the open common sewer. The room was so dark that it was several minutes before we could see anything within it, and there was a smell of must and dry rot that told of damp and imperfect ventilation, and the unnatural size of the pupils of the wretched woman's eyes convinced us how much too long she had dwelt in this gloomy place.

Here, as usual, we heard stories that made one's blood curdle. of the cruelty of those from whom they rented the sties called dwellings. They had begged for pure water to be laid on, and the rain to be shut out; and the answer for eighteen years had been, that the lease was just out. "They knows its handy for a man's work," said one and all, "and that's the reason why they impose on a body." This, indeed, seems to us to be the great evil. Out of these wretches' health, comfort, and even lives, small capitalists reap a petty independence; and until the poor are rescued from the fangs of these mercenary men, there is but little hope either for their physical or moral welfare.

The extreme lassitude and deficient energy of both body and mind induced by the mephitic vapours they continually inhale leads them - we may say, *forces* them to seek an unnatural stimulus in the gin-shop; indeed, the publicans of Jacob's Island drive even a more profitable trade than the landlords themselves. What wonder, then, since debility is one of the predisposing conditions of cholera, that - even if these stenches of the foul tidal ditch be not the *direct* cause of the disease - that the impaired digestive functions, the languid circulation, the depression of mind produced by the continued inhalation of the noxious gases of the tidal ditch, together with the intemperance that it induces - the cold, damp houses - and, above all, the quenching of the thirst and cooking of the food with water saturated with the very excrements of their fellow creatures, should make Jacob's Island notorious as the Jessore of England.

In a recent report made to the Commissioners of Sewers for London, Dr. Letheby says: "I have been at much pains during the last three months to ascertain the precise conditions of the dwellings, the habits, and the diseases of the poor. In this way 2,208 rooms have been most circumstantially inspected, and the general result is that nearly all of them are filthy or overcrowded or imperfectly drained, or badly ventilated, or out of repair. In 1,989 of these rooms, all in fact that are at present inhabited, there are *5,791* inmates, belonging to 1,576 families; and to say nothing of the too frequent occurrence of what may be regarded as a necessitous overcrowding, where the husband, the wife, and young family of four or five children are cramped into a miserably small and ill-conditioned room, there are numerous instances where adults of both sexes, belonging to different families, are lodged in the same room, regardless of all the common decencies of life, and where from three to five adults, men and women, besides a train or two of children, are accustomed to herd together like brute beasts or savages; and where every human instinct of propriety and decency is smothered. Like my predecessor, I have seen grown persons of both sexes sleeping in common with their parents, brothers and sisters, and cousins, and even the casual acquaintance of a day's tramp, occupying the same bed of filthy rags or straw; a woman suffering in travail, in the midst of males and females of different families that tenant the same room, where birth and death go hand in hand; where the child but newly born, the patient cast down with fever, and the corpse waiting for interment, have no separation from each other, or from the rest of the inmates. Of the many cases to which I have alluded, there are some which have commanded

my attention by reason of their unusual depravity—cases in which from three to four adults of both sexes, with many children, were lodging in the same room, and often sleeping in the same bed. I have note of three or four localities, where forty-eight men, seventy-three women, and fifty-nine children are living in thirty-four rooms. In one room there are two men, three women, and five children, and in another one man, four women, and two children; and when, about a fortnight since, I visited the back room on the ground floor of No. 5, I found it occupied by one man, two women, and two children; and in it was the dead body of a poor girl who had died in childbirth a few days before. The body was stretched out on the bare floor, without shroud or coffin. There it lay in the midst of the living, and we may well ask how it can be otherwise than that the human heart should be dead to all the gentler feelings of our nature, when such sights as these are of common occurrence.
"So close and unwholesome is the atmosphere of some of these rooms, that I have endeavoured to ascertain, by chemical means, whether it does not contain some peculiar product of decomposition that gives to it its foul odour and its rare powers of engendering disease. I find it is not only deficient in the due proportion of oxygen, but it contains three times the usual amount of carbonic acid, besides a quantity of aqueous vapour charged with alkaline matter that stinks abominably. This is doubtless the product of putrefaction, and of the various foetid and stagnant exhalations that pollute the air of the place. In many of my former reports, and in those of my predecessor, your attention has been drawn to this pestilential source of disease, and to the consequence of heaping human beings into such contracted localities; and I again revert to it because of its great importance, not merely that it perpetuates fever and the allied disorders, but because there stalks side by side with this pestilence a yet deadlier presence, blighting the moral existence of a rising population, rendering their hearts hopeless, their acts ruffianly and incestuous, and scattering, while society averts her eye,, the retributive seeds of increase for crime, turbulence and pauperism.

One of the saddest results of this overcrowding is the inevitable association of honest people with criminals.

Often is the family of an honest working man compelled to take refuge in a thieves' kitchen ... Who can wonder that every evil flourishes in such hotbeds of vice and disease? .... As if the men and women living together in these rookeries are married, and your simplicity will cause a smile. Nobody knows. Nobody cares ... Incest is common; and no form of vice or sensuality causes surprise or attracts attention ... The low parts of London are the sink into which the filthy and abominable from all parts of the country seem to flow.

The problem of the Housing of the Working Classes in London lives on through the centuries. It occupied the attention of our grandfathers, and it is exceedingly probable that it will be a burning question when our grandsons have attained a green old age. The problem arises in the first instance from overcrowding.
Overcrowding is the result of the multiplication of rnanufactories and workshops in the larger centres. The wealth of a city, and the opportunities it offers of picking up gold and silver - either legitimately by labour or illegitimately by crime - attract not only the population of the rural districts, but also the inhabitants of less-favoured towns and less-favoured countries. Generally speaking, the present condition of affairs is, however, mainly due to two things - the increased birth rate and the migration of the rural population.
In the train of overcrowding have come evils which threaten the health and welfare not only of the overcrowded, but of the city itself. Hence philanthropists and reformers have busied themselves with the Housing Problem. In obedience to popular outcry, vast areas of working class dwellings have been condemned as insanitary, and levelled to the ground in order that superior accommodation might be raised upon the vacant space.
This clearing necessitates the eviction of the inhabitants. All over London the tenants of mean streets and slums and courts and alleys are being evicted. The slum dwellers are daily receiving notice to quit their homes and find shelter elsewhere.
To study the subject at first-hand, let us take a walk through a block of condemned property, the tenants of which have long overstayed their notice to quit. Let us knock boldly at the closed doors, and push back those that are ajar. The inhabitants will open them if we

speak sympathetically. They will imagine we are officials connected with the "pulling down," and they will talk either to us or at us.

At the first house is a decent-looking woman, who says that her husband is at work and her children are at school. Half the houses of the court are empty, and the housebreakers have commenced on some of them. Why does she linger still ? "Well, sir, you wouldn't believe the miles as I've been. I can't get a decent place, not as good as this, through having the five children you see. But I *must* get a place to-morrow; they're going to take the windows out."

In the next house is a man. He is at work, he is busy with a hammer and a piece of leather. What he is making he doesn't give us time to see. He jumps up and comes to the door. He is fierce and defiant, and prepared to orate after the manner which may be described as the early Hyde Park. But we pacify him with tobacco, and he explains that he can't afford the time to go tramping about. His missis is in the hospital, else *she'd* go. He's got to earn the money for the children. Knowing something of the ways of Slumland, we point out to him that he has been living rent free for many weeks, and that at least is some compensation for disturbance. The saved rent should have allowed him leisure for house hunting.

That is a point that must not be forgotten in considering these evictions. After the period of notice has expired many of the tenants deliberately stay on because there is no rent to pay. They know that frequently after the houses have been cleared they are left standing. There are condemned houses which night after night are converted into free hotels by tramps and outcasts. Sometimes a burly ruffian will take temporary possession of an empty house, from which the tenants have been evicted, and let the rooms out for a copper or so. One rascal did a great business until the authorities discovered him. He not only filled the rooms with wayfarers, but charged a penny a head for the privilege of sleeping on the stairs.

At the next house "Lot 1" in the illustration on p. 206 there lives an old woman who does mangling. We knock at the door and shout at the window, but she refuses to take any notice. She is a besieged resident. She thinks if she comes out she won't get in again. So for her food supply she lowers a small basket attached to a string. A neighbour puts into it the purchases made on her behalf, and thus she thinks she is defying the authorities. Poor old woman! She was in that house many years, but she left it at last. When I went down the court a few weeks ago not a brick of her Southwark Château Chabrol remained.

When a slum has been levelled to the ground, a huge block of working class dwellings generally rises on its site. These buildings are wanted. Many of them are excellent. But up to the present they have hardly succeeded in solving the great problem, because the evicted or displaced tenants, practically left without any superior accommodation, are driven into worse.

An ounce of practical experience is worth a ton of argument. Let us see for ourselves how an eviction works. Here is a grand new block of working class dwellings in Southwark. On the site where the building stands there stood a short while ago a network of courts and alleys inhabited mainly by poor people earning a precarious livelihood. After notice had been served upon them some began at once to look about for other accommodation. But the larger number, because it is the nature of the slum dwellers to live only for to-day and to trust to luck for to-morrow, did nothing. At last came the pinch. The authorities served the last notice, "Get out, or your walls will crumble about you." The tenant who after that still remained obstinate soon realised that the end had come. The roof, the doors, and the windows were removed while she (it is generally a woman) still remained crouching in a corner of the miserable room which contained the chair, the table, the bed, the frying pan, and the tub that were her furniture.

Eventually the position became dangerous. When bricks and plaster began to fall in showers about her, and the point of the pickaxe came through the wall against which she was leaning, then at last she scrambled for her belongings and went out unto the street, where a little crowd of onlookers and fellow sufferers welcomed her sympathetically.

Sometimes a whole family, the head having failed or neglected during the period of grace to find accommodation elsewhere, is turned into the street. I have seen families sitting homeless on their goods.

The old room in Slumland   The new room in a modern dwelling

High in the court. You can see them yourself in the photograph reproduced Guarding their household gods sat women with infants in their arms. They sat on, hopeless and despairing, and saw their homes demolished before their eyes. Now and again the heap of bedding and furniture was diminished. A man would return and tell his wife he had found a place. They would gather up their goods and go. But all were not so fortunate. I have seen a woman with a child in her arms and two children crouching by her side sitting out long after nightfall by her flung-out furniture, because the husband could find no accommodation at the rent he could afford.

Sometimes a boy is left in charge of the piled-up property while his parents go off in different directions to hunt for shelter. Frequently the parents wander a considerable distance, and it is long after midnight before they return to the young sentinel.

If you dive below the surface you will understand more readlily how terrible is this problem of Evicted London. Granting that the raising of sanitary dwellings on the site of insanitary is an admirable work, fully adlmitting that the London County Council's idea of breaking up and scattering colonies of undesirables makes for the public good, we are still faced by the difficulty - What is to become of the people who are unfit (by reason of their ways or their families) for the new buildings ? What will happen to the areas in which the "undesirables " (*i.e.* the criminal and vicious) scatter themselves?

The bulk of the people evicted are the poor, earning small and precarious livelihoods, hawkers and "general dealers"- a description that covers a multitude of trades. The bulk of the people housed in the new buildings are artisans earning a regular and decent wage. The idea in improving insanitary dwellings off the face of London is, of course, that the dishoused shall be rehoused. But many of the dlishoused fail to find accommodation in the new buildings. One or two are admitted at first, but as the block becomes filled they are weeded out on some excuse or other. Slum dwellers are not wanted in nice clean buildings. The superior artisan who will respect his property and pay regularly is the tenant the Board of Directors and the private philanthropist alike desire. And, again, there is the question of the children. The poorest people seem to have the most. And the children are a bar not only to admission to the new dwellings, where only so many people are allowed to sleep in a room, but even to the common lodging-houses. A man and his wife and five or six children are not wanted anywhere, not even in the lowest of the doss-houses. So when the day of eviction comes mother and the children must turn out and wait "somewhere" while father tramps the city paved with gold in search of a spot in which to lay his head. If father is in work, then mother must do the tramping. I will take a real case. Tom Brown calls himself a general dealer. As a matter of fact he and his wife make "ornaments for your fire stove" artificial flowers, and rosettes to hawk in the streets for special occasions, such as Boat Race day, St. Patrick's day, Lord Mayor's day, and the days of National holiday or jubilation. He and his wife earn between them when times are good £1. When times are bad they earn a few shillings. I have known Tom [-207-] for the last six years, and during that period he has been evicted four times. The family were evicted for property to be pulled down in the Borough; they found two rooms in Bermondsey. There after eight months they were again evicted for improvements, and went to St. George's. They were turned out of St. Georges and went to Lambeth. They have now been evicted again, and have succeeded, after endless tramping, in finding two rooms in Bermondsey near their old quarters, but their rent is six and six instead of five and six. Take another case, that of George Jones, a carman in regular employ, lately evicted to make room for artisans' dwellings. The family consists of Jones, his wife, and seven children. When they were turned out, the father lost several days' work trying to find a place where the nine of them could be accommodated at a rental he could afford. For three nights and three days the family were homeless, and at last had to apply to the workhouse, where the wife and children were received as "paying guests". The workhouse authorities eventually succeeded in finding rooms for the family

It occasionally happens, such is the generosity of the poor to the poor, that the younger and weaker children when evictions take place are accommodated for a night or two by the poor neighbours who are still left in peaceable possession of a roof. Quite recently in a house of four rooms in Foxley Street, Bermondsey, there lived a man, his wife, and ten children the latter ranging from four to twenty-four years in age. Yet, when a case of eviction occurred near them, they took in the three children of a poor woman who was unable to find shelter. The same hospitality I have known extended by a family of eight occupying two rooms. A large number of the evicted drift into the various common lodging-houses when there are no children, or children who can be disposed of temporarily among friends.

If there are children who cannot be housed temporarily the situation is desperate. Here is a case in point. A decent hardworking man and his wife had lived in a small tenement house which was eventually demolished under an improvement scheme. They tried in vain to get another small house. At last the father, mother, and three children drifted into an utterly disreputable common lodging-house. Here the Rescue Society's officer discovered the children, and the law took them from the parents and sent them to an industrial school to be kept at the expense of the ratepayers.

We point with pride to the new and improved dwellings raised by the enterprise of governing bodies, public companies, and private philanthropists on the sites where recently stood foul and insanitary dwellings, in which the poor huddled together without light, without ventilation, and without a water supply; and we say that here at least is a step in the right direction. No one will deny it; but we shall never get further than a [-208-] step, we shall never come within measurable distance of the goal if we shut our eyes to the terrible difficulties which beset the present system of dishousing a poor and struggling class in order to make room for a superior class in constant employment.

The people who can go into model buildings, who can afford the number of rooms demanded by the regulations for a family of a certain number, are only slightly represented in the insanitary areas in which demolition compels wholesale eviction. The dwellers in the new buildings come as a rule from other districts and from a better class of property. The evicted, unless they are fortunate, find shelter in already overcrowded and insanitary areas, because it is only in this class of property they will be tolerated. Thus every area cleared for superior dwellings, for street improvements, or for railway schemes only adds to the further congestion of areas in which the poor are already massed together under the worst conditions. And increased overcrowding is not the only evil that follows the wholesale evictions which are now almost weekly occurrences in London. The struggle for life of the evicted, always keen, becomes fiercer than ever. At each fresh rush for accommodation rents are advanced, so that it frequently happens that a family housed in one insanitary area for five and sixpence a week for two rooms are, after eviction, compelled to pay six and sixpence a week for worse rooms in another insanitary area. And so fearful are they of having to go through the terrible search for shelter again that they never dream of making the slightest complaint, however grossly the landlord may neglect his duty.

I once interviewed a woman who with her four children was living in a wretched garret in a court in the Borough. It was a wet day, and the rain was coming through the broken roof and falling on a child who was lying on a bed in the corner. "You should complain to the landlord," I said; "he is bound at least to give you a rainproof roof for your money."

"Complain!" exclaimed the woman in a tone of horror ; "yes, I should like to see myself doing it. I did complain to him once, when we was better off and lived in a room downstairs. There was a brick loose in the, wall, and the rain had soaked through, and the plaster had given way till there was a hole as you could put your two fists in - so I went to him, and I said he ought to repair it."

"And of course he did?"

"Yes, he did - he come and nailed the lid of a soap box across the hole, and he put the rent of the room up sixpence a week for the improvement."

A good deal of the neglect and abuse of property with which the poor of London are credited is due to this kind of conduct on the part of the slum landlord. The hapless tenants are glad to get accommodation anywhere, and they cannot afford to be particular as to the condition of the room or rooms. If they complain they will be told that they can clear out, there are plenty of people waiting to come in. So the tenants, unable to move the landlord's heart, take their revenge on his property. Boards that have been used to patch walls are torn off and used as firewood, stair railings - if there are any left - share the same fate. Presently there is very little left of the house but the walls, some crumbling plaster, and a window-frame or two patched with brown paper. The doors suffer less than any other portion of the property. The reason is that the slum-dweller desires occasional privacy. A door is useful, not only when you want to shut yourself in, but when you want to shut your neighbours out - and some neighbours in the slums are given to making mistakes and walking into, or falling into, other rooms than those for which they have paid the weeks rent. On all the phases of Evicted London I have not dwelt. I have but slightly sketched a few of the difficulties that the wholesale dishousing of the poor brings in its train. All the schemes of rehousing, with perhaps two exceptions -and those I believe have not been very successful - aim at the survival of the fittest. But the unfittest do not die. They are not destroyed. Like Jo in Bleak House they are only being eternally "moved on."

Victorian Toys

Victorian toys are highly collectable antiques and can often be picked up at auctions and vintage fairs. Now well over 100 years old, they give a fascinating insight into the life of privileged children in the mid to late 19th century. During the Victorian era, working class children had little time to play, but those born to middle and upper class homes enjoyed a totally different lifestyle. Toys were generally handmade from metal or wood and were far more expensive than the mass-produced toys of the 21st century. Some of the simplest Victorian toys were a rolling hoop which was guided with a stick, or a wooden ball on a string which had to be swung upwards and caught in the attached cup. Spinning tops have been in existence for centuries all over the world and would have been popular in Victorian times. A cord is wound around the wooden top and then pulled to set the top spinning on its point. Doll's houses were a firm favourite in well-to-do homes and would have replica furniture down to the last detail. Made by skilled craftsmen, they provided hours of make-believe fun as children played out real-life scenarios. The V&A Museum of Childhood has a fine collection of Victorian doll's houses. They became very popular in the 19th century and recapture in perfect detail the furniture, décor and equipment found in period Victorian homes. In a similar vein, miniature puppet theatres were a popular form of entertainment and allowed children's imagination to run wild in days before TV and films. With the introduction of mechanization, toys became more animated and varied. Clowns would perform comical tricks when turned by a crank and a carnival on wheels when pulled along would make the figures dance amusingly. Kaleidoscopes were popular Victorian toys and when turned they created ever-changing symmetrical patterns using mirrors. Musical toys were some of the most prized Victorian toys. Rosewood boxes would contain an amphitheatre of figures. Turning a crank or winding the clockwork on the side of the box created sweet music and made the figures dance frenziedly. Gypsy oracles and fortune tellers were popular and games of parlour lotto (bingo) were devised. Building blocks were used to build castles and replica coliseums. Alphabet blocks were decorated with illuminated letters and engravings, scenes of foxhunts or shipwrecks. Much as today, girls would enjoy playing with Victorian dolls although plastic was not an option. Faces were formed from wax or china bisque, eyes were made of real blue glass and golden curls were made of human hair. Their beautiful handmade clothing had all the detail, from handmade lace trim and crinoline skirts to gilt buttons and felt hats or bonnets. By the late 19th century tin soldiers were being mass produced to recreate battle scenes. They were popular for boys of all ages. The early tin soldiers were flat and almost two dimensional, only becoming fully rounded later. Most Victorian toys were made out of metal or wood by skilled craftsmen. They were sturdily made and consequently many have survived and can now be seen in Childhood Museums. The annual tradition of sending Christmas cards came about almost by accident in 1843. Due to prohibitive costs the idea was slow to catch on and it was at least 20 more years before Victorian Christmas cards were commercially mass produced.

Victorian Christmas Cards

The first Victorian Christmas cards were designed by artist John Callcott Horsley at the suggestion of his influential friend Sir Henry Cole, who was the first director appointed to the Victoria and Albert Museum. These Christmas cards were a limited edition, produced by Jobbins of Warwick Court in London and printed using a process called lithography. The outlines then had to be hand-coloured by a professional colourer. They were sold for a shilling each, which incidentally was far more than the daily wage for many Victorian workers at that time. The first Victorian Christmas card measured just over 5x3 inches and in the centre was the sketch of a merry family feasting, with two scenes of charity on either side: feeding the hungry and clothing the naked. The single sided card was finished with a printed greeting, "A Merry Christmas and a Happy New Year to You". Other picture makers followed suit but the idea of Christmas cards only really blossomed when Charles Goodall & Son began to mass produce them in 1866. He was a publisher of visiting cards, which were commonly used when a person paid a formal call and left their card as a reminder of their visit. Goodall expanded this idea to four designs of Christmas cards designed by C.H. Bennett which featured holly, mistletoe and robins with a cheery Christmas greeting. Surprisingly for a Christian event, early Victorian Christmas cards did not feature any religious reference at all. In 1870, the Royal Mail reduced the cost of postage to a half penny per ounce and cheaper colour lithography was developed to lower printing costs. This heralded the spread of the Victorian Christmas card and by the early 1870s the custom had also become popular in America. Soon artists, printers, engravers and writers saw the potential and by 1880 they began to be commercially mass produced. One London print firm, S Hildesheimer & Co, ran a competition in 1881 for the most artistic designs and many great artists submitted their designs hoping to win a share of the generous prize of five hundred guineas. Poems and flowery greetings were written and the era of the Christmas card finally dawned. From 1866 to 1895 Marcus Ward & Co monopolized the Christmas card market with their lithographed cards designed by noteworthy artists such as Kate Greenaway, Thomas Crane and his son Walter. They featured cute Victorian figures, snow scenes, cherubs and naked angels in typical Victorian style. Many of these designs have been reproduced in later years and Victorian Christmas cards remain very collectible. They began to be sold by booksellers and stationery shops in the 1880s and then expanded to tobacconists, toy shops and even drapery shops. However, by 1895 many publishing firms of early Victorian greeting cards were forced out of business in London as more affordable German-produced Christmas cards flooded the market. In the 19th century, rapid changes in employment, housing and social welfare brought about a huge change in peoples' lives. The period of adjustment led to many workers living in extreme poverty and even dying on city streets of starvation in Victorian times. The population of Great Britain actually trebled during the 19th century. People were living longer, having larger families, infant mortality was down and immigrants escaping from the potato famine in Ireland all added up to a huge population explosion in Victorian times. Most employment was to be found in the newly industrialized cities, so many people abandoned their rural roots and converged on the urbanized areas to seek work. Skilled and unskilled workers alike were paid subsistence level wages. If the work was seasonal or demand slumped, when they were laid off they had no savings to live on until the next job opportunity could be found. Families would put children to work at an early age, or even turn them out onto the streets to fend for themselves. In 1848 an estimated 30,000 homeless, filthy children lived on the streets of London. Boys became chimney sweeps, worked the narrow shafts in coal mines or were employed beneath noisy weaving looms retrieving cotton bobbins. Others would shine shoes or sell matches to earn a crust. People working long hours in Victorian times had to live close to their employment and available housing became scarce and highly priced. Tenants would themselves let their rooms for 2d to 4d a day to other workers to meet the rent. Hideously overcrowded, unsanitary slums developed, particularly in London. They were known as rookeries. Streets would have a flowing foul-water ditch into which the sewers and drains emptied. In some cases this was the only source of drinking water too. As well as disease, these miserable people suffered starvation and destitution. In many cases their only choice was to turn to crime – another major problem in the cities. It became clear to many that something had to be done, but there were opposing thoughts and opinions. The sheer scale of the problem must have seemed overwhelming to even the most well-meaning benefactor. Some Victorians thought that education was the answer and ragged schools were set up to provide basic education. Others argued that crime was not caused by illiteracy; it was just encouraging a more skilful set of criminals! Others still thought that any money given to the poor was simply squandered on drink and gambling and did not solve the underlying social problems at all. Overall the Victorian times produced one of the most intense periods of philanthropy and charity to help the plight of the poor, the destitute and the street children. Many modern-day charities, such as the Children's Society, began their work in Victorian times and continue to address more modern concerns of poverty even in the 21st century. When Queen Victoria ascended the British throne in 1837, it marked the beginning of a promising new age – the Victorian era. The preceding Georgian era had lasted from 1714 to 1830, from the reign of George I through George IV Those who could see into the future would have been excited to see the dawn of a long period of peace and prosperity in England under Queen Victoria. As the British Empire expanded to cover more than a quarter of the globe, it made Britain the most powerful nation in the world. The preceding years of the Industrial Revolution had led to the mass production of goods, making them far more affordable for common people, but life for mill workers was harsh. During the Victorian era, law-makers and trade unions began to address and improve working conditions, particularly for child labour. They eventually made it illegal for children to work more than 69 hours per week! As living standards improved, birth rates increased. Lack of war and famine coupled with improved health standards meant that the population exploded from 13.8 million in England in 1831, to 32.5 million by 1901. Middle class England grew rapidly and the upper class, which was formerly purely hereditary, came to include the nouveau riche, who made fortunes from successful commercial enterprises. However, a large proportion of Victorian society was still working class, and they remained disgruntled at the social inequality and eventually sought reform. Railways continued to develop, offering mass transit for city dwellers who were able to spend time off visiting the seaside and participating in the new pastime of sea bathing. From Brighton to Bridlington fashionable seaside resorts sprang up. Boarding houses were built along the seafronts of towns near to industrialized areas such as London, Manchester, Leeds and the northwest of England. In London, the world's first underground railway, nicknamed the Tube, opened in 1862. Politically, during the Victoria era, the House of Commons had two main political parties: the Tories and the Whigs. By the mid 19th century the Whigs were known as the Liberal party and the Tories were the Conservative party. The Labour party only came into being in 1900. Prince Albert was a keen supporter of the Arts and London blossomed under his patronage with the building of the Royal Albert Hall, the Royal Opera House, the Science Museum, the Natural History Museum and The Victoria and Albert Museum. Poetry, literature and art flourished with the Bronte sisters, George Eliot, Oscar Wilde, Rudyard Kipling and Charles Dickens publishing popular works. Scientifically, the Victorian era also saw huge success. Darwin published his Theory of Evolution and the Great Exhibition of 1851 showcased many industrial and technological advances in the specially built Crystal Palace. Sigmund Freud developed modern psychiatry and Karl Marx developed his new economic theory. The Victorian era in Great Britain was a time of great change and progress and is still considered the Birth of Modern Times. Although the birth of Christ has been celebrated for the best part of 2,000 years, it only became a festival as we know it in Victorian times. Imagine a Christmas with no Christmas tree, no crackers, no Christmas cards and no time off work! Many of these Victorian Christmas traditions were introduced to English society by Queen Victoria and her husband, Prince Albert. Being from German aristocracy, Albert was used to the custom of bringing a fresh fir tree into the home and decorating it on Christmas Eve, so he had one brought to Windsor Castle in the 1840s. The burning wax candles and decorative baubles were a focal point and quickly the idea became fashionable in Victorian parlours everywhere. Electric lights for Christmas trees were invented by Thomas Edison's assistant, Edward Johnson, in 1882. However they did not become mass produced and affordable to the general public for many more years.

The Introduction of Victorian Christmas Crackers

In 1846, Thomas J. Smith, a London confectioner, had a great idea for selling more sweets at Christmas. He wrapped a bon-bon in a twist of coloured paper, added a love note, a paper hat and a banger mechanism which was said to have been inspired by the crackle of a log fire! This new idea took off, and ironically the bonbons were eventually replaced with a small toy or novelty.

The First Victorian Christmas Card

The first Christmas cards in England were designed for Sir Henry Cole, the Chairman of the Society of the Arts. The year was 1846 and the first 100 Christmas cards, designed by John Calcott Horsley, were printed at great expense which rather curbed the idea from taking off. However, shortly afterwards colour lithography was developed making printing much cheaper. Another significant factor was the rising popularity of the Royal Mail allowing postage costs to be reduced to one half penny per ounce. By the early 1870s anyone who was anyone could afford to send Christmas card greetings. Initially Victorian Christmas cards were single postcards with simple designs but soon plum puddings, robins, and snowy scenes became popular designs.

Holly, Ivy and Mistletoe

These common plants all produce winter berries and were held to be "magical" long before Victorian times. The holly berries were said to repel witchcraft and a berry-laden sprig would be carried into the Victorian house by a male and used to decorate the Christmas pudding. Mistletoe had pagan origins and in Victorian times it was not allowed in churches. However, kissing under the mistletoe was popular in Victorian homes. After each chaste kiss a white berry had to be removed from the sprig until there were none left – and no more kisses were to be had.

Christmas Services

Although Christmas songs had been sung by wassailers from the 15th century, it was only in Victorian times that they began to be sung in churches. Silent Night, for example, was written in Austria and was only translated into English in 1871 when it was added to the Methodist hymnal. Traditionally the Victorian Christmas began on Christmas Day when church bells called everyone to church for scripture readings interspersed with carols. Christmas dinner was a grand family affair for those who could afford it with a goose, chicken or roast beef. Turkey became popular in the late 19th century. Christmas pudding was served then crackers were pulled and everyone exchanged gifts before playing parlour games. Whatever did children and adults do for play and to fill leisure time before television, computers, cell phones, and video games? Was it boring to live in Victorian Britain, with nothing to do but sit around the house all day?

Inside Fun

The Victorians were quite creative when it came to play time. Not just children, but adults would participate in victorian games during the evenings. For both adults and youngsters, Skittles (on the order of bowling) and Charades, a Victorian game which is still played today, would be enjoyed by all generations. Billiards grew in popularity. Although starting out as a 'manly' sport, both sexes were soon enjoying the game. Blindman's Bluff was always guaranteed to bring a smile to a face, and could be quite tiring with people running away so as not to be caught. On the quieter side, "I'm Thinking of Something" was quite similar to the game of "Twenty Questions", which is still played today. For the Victorians, games like Checkers, Chess, Backgammon, and Cribbage were always easy to reach from the shelf.

Outdoor Fun

Introduced in the mid-1800's, Croquet was quite a gentile outdoor game for women. As it didn't require great strength, it was felt that this game was appropriate for 'the weaker sex'. Ice Skating was an approved winter-time sport for ladies. In 1876, however, it was finally not necessary to wait for cold weather in which to skate. The first artificially refrigerated ice rink was crafted in Chelsea, London. Horseback riding was often learned at an early age while some women went for grander outdoor exploits... mountain climbing! Imagine clambering around in a corset and bustle as was the style for Victorian clothes! Victorian toys such as marbles were enjoyed by both boys and girls. Wealthier players had marbles which were made out of real marble, while others had marbles made of glass or clay. Tops and Jacks were Victorian games and toys that could be played either in a group, or just solo. The first rules for Badminton were written in India in 1873, and this game hasn't much changed. Formerly known as "Hit and Scream", this contest became quite the rage for people of all ages.

Field Sports

The Victorian game of cricket was organized for county championships in 1873. The bat which is used to this day was invented in 1853. During the Victorian period, cricket was very much a wealthy man's sport. The following year, the rules for lawn tennis were formalized and both men and women would play. Clubs for golfers were set up in the later part of the 1800's. The bag to carry the utensils for golfers, the golf bag, came into being in 1880. The Football Association was formed in 1863 - football was usually only played by men. The Rugby Football Union was formed in 1871. Being one of the rougher Victorian games, 71 deaths were attributed to this team sport between the years of 1890 and 1893. Rugby has some similarities to American football... while in Great Britain 'football' refers to the game which is called 'soccer' in the United States.

Leisure Time

Day trips to the seashore were mini-holidays which families would enjoy. Boarding the train to Blackpool, a resort which began with one ride in 1896, was to begin a day filled with fun. Maintaining a scrapbook, filled with items of interest, would consume afternoon hours for both adults and children. Playing the piano and holding impromptu concerts and dances were quite popular amongst families and their friends. For the young ladies of the family, sewing or creating decorative embroidery kept idle hands busy, as well as the making of ornaments for Christmas. For the Victorians, games, toys and physical activity could be set aside for a few unhurried hours of reading. Rudyard Kipling, Charles Dickens, and Elizabeth Barrett BrAs with society and clothing, schooling for Victorian children was very much divided along financial lines. Although receiving an education was not mandatory until the end of the 1800's, except for the very poor the majority of children had some sort of learning, if only to read and write their name. Children from wealthy families would be taught in the home, rather than attending a Victorian School. Nannies would often start the learning process, but when the child reached six, a governess would be added to the household staff. At the age of ten, sons were sent away to public boarding schools like Eton or Rugby. Boys would often not see their families until the end of term. Greek and Latin were part of the curriculum and games of football and cricket were meant to build character. Daughters would continue their learning at home. Singing, playing the piano, and sewing were the main subjects covered, however some girls would be tutored in French. Poorer families would send their children to Victorian schools, if they could afford the fees. If money was a problem, there were charity schools. Schools were not pleasant places. Often windows were built high, so the children did not spend their time looking out. Because of the high windows, fresh air was a problem. With several different grades being taught in one area, Victorian schools could be crowded, and very noisy. Before 1850, it was common to see one teacher for 100 pupils. Because students were great in number, discipline was strongly enforced. Because of the pupil count, it was necessary for the teacher to quickly find 'monitors' to help teach.

These monitors would be chosen from pupils who showed a grasp of the subject matter and could then be relied upon to teach their fellow students. From 9:00am to noon, and then from 2:00 to 5:00pm, the three R's - reading, writing, and arithmetic, were the subjects focused upon in school. Slates were used instead of paper, although pen and ink was used in copybooks to learn handwriting. For the two hour period between noon and 2:00, it was common for students to go home for lunch. Children from rural areas who could have long distances to walk, stayed and ate at school. Time was then spent on the playground playing with toys such as tops, or playing games like Blindman's Bluff or hide and seek. At first, The Bible was the textbook for learning how to read. Quickly realizing that the words were too complicated for beginning readers however, it wasn't long before Victorian schools began to use moral tales instead. It was common practice to humiliate students whose work was sub-standard, or not completed. The dunces cap would be placed upon a pupil's head if the teacher didn't feel they were learning fast enough. The child would then be made to stand within full view of the classroom for a period of time. Corporal punishment was also the order of the day. If a child left the playground without permission, was late for school, or showed rudeness, the cane would be taken off the teacher's desk and the child would be beaten. Victorian schools did break for holidays. There was a two-week hiatus for Christmas and one week for Easter. Summer was celebrated with a three to four week break between July and August. Travel by rail, either by products or by people themselves, changed the way life in Victorian England was lived. The railways opened up an entirely new world for commerce, fun, and relaxation. Fresh produce could be shipped across the country and upon arrival at its destination, it would still be fresh. Newspapers, magazines, and other periodicals could be printed in London and then whisked to Edinburgh on the same day. Upon its arrival, the information provided would still be current. Time-saving inventions, such as the vacuum cleaner, allowed for more leisure time. Families could enjoy a day at the seashore as the railways offered a fast, efficient, and inexpensive way to enjoy time off. In the first half of the 1800's, over six thousand miles of Victorian Railway was available for use. By the end of the 1800's, there was hardly a small town in Great Britain that didn't have access to a railway station.

Great Western Railway

With Isambard Kingdom Brunel as its chief engineer, this railway company made tremendous strides from 1833 onwards. A railway line from London to Bristol was the target, and this was completed by 1841. Seven years later, railway lines from Bristol to Exeter, and from Bristol to Gloucester were constructed. The locomotive for this portion of the Great Western was designed by Daniel Gooch and could run at the great speed of 67 mph. Due to the gauge which Brunel was using for the lines, Gooch's train could not enter Euston Station. Thus, Brunel built his own station - Paddington.

London to Brighton Railway

For the thirty years between 1841 and 1871, Brighton was the fastest growing town in England. This was due to the railway connecting the town with London. The first train pulled into the Brighton station in September, 1841. Originally filled with only first-class passengers, this Victorian railway quickly realized that lowering the ticket price would enable more people to journey to Brighton. With the numbers of visitors swelling the seashore area, entrepreneurs soon made Brighton their home. Hotels, restaurants, and other tourist attractions soon filled the town to overflowing. Brighton, as a seaside holiday spot, was born.

Caledonian Railway

In 1848, the first through service from Scotland to London was established. Six years before, Glasgow and Edinburgh had been connected. Now the line headed south. The Caledonian Railway Box can be seen at the Bo'ness and Kinneil Railway Museum.

The Great Northern Railway

With the completion of London's Kings Cross station, Cambridge, Leicester, and Nottingham were connected to London. With a reputation for giving good service, and offering express trains, this Victorian railway into more Northern parts of England became quite popular. It was quite lucrative for the owners, also. Coal was transported from Yorkshire to London and the revenues were great for this rail company.

Stockton and Darlington Railway

The Stockton and Darlington Railway was the first, in 1825, to offer an open-to-the-public service. Passengers and goods were placed upon the same train. It was also the first railway line to use a steam locomotive.

Travelling by Rail

In the early years, train travel was not a comfortable way to get from Point A to Point B. Seats were often just wooden boards, and springs and buffers were an unknown commodity. The best way to describe the ride is to compare it to riding in a stagecoach. Eventually, Victorian railways began to offer comfort. Upholstered seats, armrests, and an enclosed carriage were soon the norm, at least for first class passengers. Oil lamps placed along the carriages offered light. Second class travellers had to contend with being exposed to the elements, and with sitting on wooden benches. With the enclosure of some of these carriages, second-class became an easier way to travel, while third class had to make do with being exposed to weather. By 1844, courtesy of the Railway Act, third class carriages had to be enclosed. Lighting was also provided, albeit only one oil lamp per carriage as opposed to the many placed in first class.

Victorian Railway Accidents

As in any sort of mass transportation today, accidents did happen on Victorian railways. Sometimes it wasn't the train that was at fault, but the attending structures which allowed the rails to cross Great Britain. On Christmas Eve 1841, near Reading, a train loaded with produce and passengers ran into a land slip. Carriages were thrown everywhere, with goods and passengers thrown out of the train. At this time, most carriages were without roofs so there was nothing to stop the passengers from either flying out of the train, or falling between carriages and being crushed. This accident was remembered in the Railway Act of 1844. Shortly after Christmas, in 1879, The Tay Railway Bridge collapsed into the Firth of Tay, Dundee. 75 people lost their lives due to the failure of this bridge.

For Men and Woman

For the wealthy, silk stockings covered the legs. For the less wealthy, it was wool socks. Beachwear in Victorian times consisted of a costume which covered the entire body with yards of material. There were exceptions though - arms could be bare from the elbows down. Ladies had to have their legs completely covered. This was either done by wearing black stockings or, later in the century, pants. Men were able to show their shins. Bathing bonnets were worn by both. Good quality leather shoes could always be made-to-order, but by 1850 manufactured shoes were available for purchase. Shoes were now made for the 'proper' feet. Etiquette played its part in Victorian clothing. It was considered 'good etiquette' to dress appropriately to ones age, and position in society. To own an umbrella was a social-scale barometer. The wealthy owned their own bumbershoots, while the general public would rent an umbrella if the weather turned wet. Victorian dress was not complete without a walking stick, or cane. Some canes contained compartments which were useful for holding vials of perfume. Victorian fashion did include eyeglasses, But, they were strictly for looks and not for the correction of vision. Often, if there were lenses in the frames, those lenses were removed and the empty frames would become part of the ensemble. If the pocket-book didn't allow such individual attention, families would make their own Victorian clothes or find used garments. The poorer members of society would visit second-hand, even third and fourth-hand, shops for garments which still had some wear in them.

For Ladies Only

Throughout the era, Victorian fashion changed dramatically. Skirts went from straight to being spread over large hoops. At the end of the era, the hoop disappeared from view and it was back to slimmer skirts, although now sporting a bustle. Sleeves made different fashion statements, also. Slim sleeves gave way to "leg o'mutton" sleeves by the end of Queen Victoria's reign. Head gear was a style all its own. From large lavishly decorated hats, covered with feathers and flowers, the close-fitting bonnet was soon the need-to-have garment. Not that these were any plainer - feathers, lace, and flowers would still be used for decoration. There was a constant, though; the corset. The design throughout the era would change, but the initial purpose never varied. To wear Victorian dress, it was necessary to have a cinched-in waist. For younger ladies, having a waist in inches the same as your age was the goal. Seventeen years old? That meant you would strive for a seventeen inch waist. Older ladies were allowed more leeway. The baring of the shoulder and upper part of the chest was strictly for evening apparel, and most usually this style was worn by upper and middle class ladies. Working-class women were more modest. Because of the exposure of flesh to cool air, shawls joined the Victorian costume. Satins, silks, and heavy velvets for the older generation were the norm. For younger society ladies who were on the look-out for "a good catch", the lighter the material, the better. Fragile gauze dresses, covered with bows or flowers, were made to catch a prospective husband's eye. On average, these dresses were worn only once or twice... and then thrown away! Middle-class women bought either garments, or ready-made clothes, with the idea that they would last. If necessary, the garment would at some point be cut-down so that it could be worn by children. For the well-dressed female tradesman (aka "monger"), a bright silk scarf would be worn around the neck, and a flower-strewn bonnet would adorn the head. Brightly polished boots would be proudly shown beneath a many petticoated skirt, which just reached to the ankles.

The Well-dressed Gentleman

Victorian dress didn't go in for such radical changes with men. But coat lengths did vary over time and the cinching of the waist (yes, men would wear a type of corset) gave way to the ease-of-breathing loose jacket. Men's fashion history can be traced via the style of trousers. Early in Queen Victoria's reign, legs were covered in tight form-fitting cloth. This appearance soon changed to a looser tubular style. Straight slacks, with a crease in front and back, were common by the end of the century. The elegant dress-coat for the day slowly gave way to a long frock coat, usually black. The dress coat did continue to make appearances, though. 'White tie and tails' was the formal eveningwear for gentleman, the 'tails' being the former daytime coat. Games and cycling were the major catalysts for any change in male Victorian clothes. By the late 1800's, knickers were introduced and a more casual style was adopted for daytime wear. Plaids and checks were seen more often, although most often in the country. Like his female counterpart, a male monger would wear a bright silk scarf around his neck. Atop his head would be a closely fitting cap which completely covered his hair. A long waistcoat and seamed trousers would complete his Victorian costume, ending with the sight of polished boots.

A Truly Grand Home

Not all necessarily large, these Victorian houses were usually made of red brick and wood. With a design chosen from a basic pattern book, the new homeowner could then incorporate ideas from nature, geometry, or personal preference. With the advent of nailing 2x4 boards together (frame construction) instead of using heavy timbers, the finished home was not as heavy. Thus, creativity could run rampant. Different ideas from each style could be incorporated into the same building, so part of a Victorian house might be Gothic Revival, with a second floor showing signs of the Second Empire. The homes which are seen today all have very similar features. Towers, bay windows, and balconies bring dimension to the building. A partial or full porch which sweeps around the first floor of the house adds depth. A steep roof, often sporting many angles, and with an odd shape, often highlights stained glass windows, stonework, fancy shingles, and iron railings. The insides of these Victorian houses were opulent. Windows would be covered with heavy curtains. Wallpaper was all the rage, usually with a flower pattern. Rich, dark colours were the flavour of the day. Carpets and rugs would decorate sitting rooms, bedrooms and the welcoming entrance hall. Rooms would be filled with well made over-stuffed furniture. Tables would be set in various corners, usually covered with photographs and nic-nacs. Running water, gas lighting, and other amenities of life were present in these homes.

A Lovely Terraced Home

Although not on the grand scale of some of the homes of the period, terraced housing could be quite comfortable. Usually two rooms up and two down (although they could be bigger), these Victorian houses all shared a common wall with their neighbour. A front entrance was the norm, as well as a back entrance which would often lead to either a small garden, or a paved area. Each home would repeat the design of its neighbour, leading to this style also being called a 'row house'. Some terraced homes would offer amenities. If you were well-to-do, you had an indoor toilet. Otherwise it was a shed in the backyard. The largest room in this Victorian house would be the front parlour. Guests would be welcomed into this room, where items indicating your status would be displayed. For comfort, the family would use a back parlour for everyday living. Not as grandly decorated on the outside as the houses of the wealthy, these terraced homes were for high-density living. Although some did become slums in industrial areas such as Victorian London, the majority of terraced living was clean and decent.

The Tenements

Although the word 'tenement' usually conjures a picture of housing for the poor, not all were that way. Tenement House, Glasgow is a lovely example of a tenement flat. This particular apartment was situated on the first floor and came equipped with a range and bathroom. Containing four rooms, this typical flat featured a parlor and a kitchen. Not having a bedroom, the bed was recessed for additional space.

The Ultimate Victorian House

This abode is not by any means a typical Victorian house. In fact, in an era named after her, one of Queen Victoria's favourite homes did not look like a Victorian house at all: Osborne House on the Isle of

Wight was designed by Victoria's beloved husband, Albert. With the help of Thomas Cubitt (who was involved in building the main facade of Buckingham Palace), Albert made this home on the isle in the Italian Renaissance style, and Carpenders Park Manor was built to copy Osborne. With terraces on different levels surrounding the home, two towers overlooking the Solent, and magnificent gardens, Osborne House is more typical of a building to be found in Italy than England. Transforming the main farmhouse and surrounding area, Osborne became the perfect private world for Victoria and Albert to 'get away from it all'.

The Upper and Upper-Middle Class

From the slightest burp (social ruin if it was heard) to how a gentleman spoke to a young lady, Victorian society was greatly concerned with every aspect of daily life. From the moment the upper class left their beds, their days were governed by do's and don'ts. The horror of social ostracism was paramount. To be caught in the wrong fashion at the wrong time of day was as greatly to be feared as addressing a member of society by the wrong title. It was important to know whom you could speak with - especially if you hadn't been properly introduced. For a woman, being asked to dance by a complete stranger could pose an etiquette problem which might have repercussions for days. Young ladies were constantly chaperoned. To be found alone with a gentleman who was other than family was tantamount to social death. Her reputation would be ruined and her gentleman companion would find himself the object of gossip, and most usually derision. The established career for society women was marriage - full stop. They were expected to represent their husbands with grace and provide absolutely no scandal. Charity work would be accepted, but only if it was very gentile... sewing for the poor, or putting together food baskets. Gentlemen had to keep track of when it was proper to either smoke or have a glass of sherry in front of ladies. When to bow and to whom to tip your hat could cause gossip if the wrong decision was made. Members of Victorian society kept busy with parties, dances, visits, dressmakers, and tailors. Keeping track of what other people in your social class were doing was also a full-time occupation.

The People in the Middle

Being a servant in one of the grand Victorian houses was a position which would guarantee shelter and food. However, there was etiquette to be learned. The upper class was never to be addressed unless it was absolutely necessary. If that was the case, as few words as possible were to be uttered. Using the proper title was of the utmost importance. "Ma'am" or "Sir" was always appropriate. If "Ma'am" was seen, it was necessary that you 'disappear', turning to face the wall and avoiding eye contact. Life was easier, though, amidst your fellow servants. Although private fraternization was frowned upon, it wasn't against the rules for those 'below stairs' to enjoy singing, dancing, and other social activities together. Quite often the 'upper class' of the servant world, the butler and housekeeper, would put aside their lofty roles in the household and join their fellow servants in gaiety. But come the morning, they would reign supreme once again. Having a profession was another way of being a member of the middle class of Victorian society. Shopkeepers, doctors, nurses, a schoolmaster, or parish priest were all notable professions. Another indicator was the number of servants you employed. Having more than one servant was a sure sign that you had money.

Sometimes, the 'uppers' and the 'middlers' would mingle. If the proper introductions could be managed, it was possible for a tradesman to receive backing from a prominent 'upper' member. With a successful business deal, both parties could increase their wealth and for the 'middler', their station in life.

The Lower Class

Victorian society did not recognize that there was a lower class'The Poor' were invisible. Those members of England who worked as chimney sweeps, ratcatchers, or spent their days in factories had no place in the echelon of the upper class, although their services would be needed from time to time. The prevailing attitude was that the poor deserved the way they lived. If good moral choices had been made, the poor wouldn't be living the way they did. The best way for society to deal with the poor was to ignore them.

They were 'burdens on the public'. There were people who cared, however. Unfortunately, in trying to help the lower class, conditions usually did not improve. Workhouses were developed, but the living was horrendous and it was almost better to be back on the street. Being just too busy trying to survive, etiquette played little part in the poor's daily existence. But that's not to say that pride wasn't available. There was a 'social stigma' to applying for aid, and some families preferred to keep to themselves and figure out their own methods of survival. Although Poor Laws were put into place, it wasn't until after the Victorian age ended that 'the lower class' was able, through education, technology, and reform, to raise itself, in some cases literally, out of the gutter. Victorian society could be quite pleasant, but only depending on your financial status.

Leisure Time

With industrialization, there was more leisure time to be enjoyed. When the railway line from London to Brighton was established, going on holiday began to be a regular part of Victorian life. Thanks to the Bank Holiday Act of 1871 and the ease of rail travel, seaside resorts such as Blackpool and Torquay began to enjoy great popularity. There was time to read a novel during the Victorian period. Charles Dickens, Robert Lewis Stephenson, and H.G. Wells are just three of the authors who were popular. Attending the theatre and appreciating the talents of Sarah Bernhard and Ellen Terry kept the evenings busy. Melodrama was in its hey-day while the music hall was always packed with people enjoying the variety of acts presented.

Medicine

Medical advances were tremendous during Victorian times. Boiling and scrubbing medical instruments before and after use was found to greatly increase a patient's chance for survival. The identification of disease took a great leap forward. Cholera was shown to be a product of sewage water. With the simple procedure of boiling drinking water and washing the hands, incidents of cholera dramatically drop. Codeine and iodine made their appearance in Victorian life. Morphine helped to alleviate pain while the use of chloroform during childbirth was pioneered by Queen Victoria... and highly recommended.

Mourning the Dead

With style, great weeping, and yards of black material, the Victorian period made a fine-art out of death. Funerals were huge, many with professional mourners hired to walk in the procession. At the moment of death, clocks would be stopped, curtains drawn over windows, and mirrors covered. Black apparel was quickly donned or if black cloth was not available, the household would quickly dye their clothes to a darker hue. Widows from all social classes were expected to maintain mourning for a full year, and withdraw as much as possible from Victorian life. For women with no income, or small children to care for, remarriage was 'allowed' after this 12 month period. As time went by, the stages of mourning gradually released their hold. Black material could be put aside for lilac or other soft shades. After approximately two years, wearing colour was no longer frowned upon. Widowers would usually wear black for two years. However, it was their decision when to go back to work, and back into society.

Rural Life

Although much of Great Britain's population did leave the countryside to reap the benefits of industrialization, village life did not come to an end. Farming was still very much a part of life in Victorian Britain. With the advent of steam-power, farm machinery was easier to use and made for a faster work day. Small gardens would supplement the family's food supply. Some villages would specialize in an industry. Lace-making was popular. Craftsman (blacksmiths, tanners, carpenters) could always be found in a rural setting. To maintain the huge country estates of the wealthy, local villagers would provide the servant power during the season. Some rural folk would live on the estate throughout the year, often in conditions which were cramped. In their own homes, rural life in Victorian England was concerned with the basics - cooking meals, mending clothes, and seeing that children received the education which was mandatory by 1880.

Chapter 20 Victorians and Spiritualism

It would not be terribly difficult for a modern critic to dismiss the spiritualist movement of the late nineteenth century as a "monstrous folly" or as an aberration in what is normally viewed as a serious and generally solemn period in the modern history of England. Spiritualism was an attempt by the late Victorians to communicate with the spirits of the dead, hoping to prove continued existence after physical death and to gather some information on first hand experiences of it. There were certainly some elements of folly and naiveté in the audience that willingly flocked to the presentations of the mediums, some of which were undoubtedly performers of the most unscrupulous kind. With equal certainty, there were contemporary Victorians that would have agreed with such a view. However, this attitude belittles the Victorian spiritualists in general, many of whom had very serious intentions and sincere motives. Additionally, the spiritualist phenomena incorporated many of the fascinating general aspects that could be found in any study of the Victorian culture; spiritualism is an excellent focal point from which the various dynamics inherent in the Victorian society can be examined and understood. These dynamics are so varied and often even conflicting in their manifestation in the spiritualist phenomena that it is difficult to define the movement's experiences with any degree of precision. Rather than study the logistics of the entire movement, it is perhaps much more enlightening to study one particular aspect of the movement and to show how the dynamics worked upon and in it.

One important question of the spiritualist movement is why it had such appeal, particularly among the well-educated upper and middle classes, and how that audience defended its appeal. As with the movement in general, the late Victorian audience that was attracted to spiritualism incorporated a variety of characteristics, affording an equal degree of difficulty in precise description. What is unquestionable is that the movement did have widespread popularity; one need only consider the great number of articles devoted to spiritualism in the popular Victorian periodicals. The popularity of spiritualism was found amongst all social classes; however, most of the rich supply of documentation on the spiritualist movement is written by and about the upper and middle classes. One writer of the period commented that the "higher the class, the more fiercely did it [spiritualism] rage through it." Furthermore, each of the separate classes were attracted to different aspects of the spiritualist movement.

Spiritualism entered English society in the middle of the nineteenth century, arriving from America via the migration of mediums in the 1850s. The movement began officially in 1848 at the New York home of the Fox sisters, who gained fame as mediums through their apparently innate ability to summon spirits and to incite spirit messages through tapping. The phenomena of "table turning and spirit-rapping" found an immediate popularity in England. Through the human agent known as the "medium," the spirits communicated through raps, rapping's, materializations of spirit forms, levitations of persons or objects, and anonymous lights that had no apparent source. With some elements of society, spiritualism soon developed into a social pastime, particularly by the upper classes, who were accused by one admitted cynic of "having pretty well exhausted the pleasures of this world" and were seeking "any new amusement they can get out of any other world." The image of a frivolous tea party séance can almost seem justifiable with such an attitude, narrow and biased though it may be.

There was, however, a more thoughtful and philosophical audience that was also attracted to spiritualism, as the professional and artistic elements of the middle class sought to integrate this newly found pastime of the wealthy with their general religious and spiritual concerns at the time. One could characterize the religious milieu of the late Victorian period as a dichotomy between Evangelicalism (and the emphasis it placed on faith and Christian belief) with the rationalist approach to spirituality brought on by the rising prestige of science and scientific principles. The spiritualist phenomena settle easily into both spheres, with apologists and critics arguing both on the side of Evangelicalism and religious piety as well as from the scientific approach of data collecting and laboratory research. The spiritualist phenomena was drawn from the distinct yet often intermingled worlds of social culture and theological or spiritual reflection; it used concepts evident to both areas and spanned the entire spectrum of Victorian society, collecting new converts (and skeptics) along the way. As with Victorian religion and society at large, spiritualism sought to successfully integrate the traditional spiritual beliefs with the new tenets and methods of science (and the new confidence inspired by science). One writer claimed that "authority, in the world of physical science is backed up by the knowledge that it can always be checked," as assertion that the modem religions of the nineteenth century and spiritualism hoped to be able to duplicate.

Anyone with a basic understanding of the Victorian period will surely be aware that one of its greatest concerns was of morality, and that this permeated all of society in both direct and indirect ways. It was believed that it was "the moral culture which enables man to form and maintain civilized society." The spiritualist movement was similarly infected by Evangelical moral concerns, and by the emphasis Victorians placed on the concept of respectability. The spiritualist movement both conformed to and rebelled against the Victorian concerns for moral respectability, and many of the various characters that comprised the movement's audience sought from it one or both of these contrasting reactions to conformity. Spiritualism rebelled against many of the Victorian moral precepts in the sense that the activity of the séances, and the summoning of spirits that took place there, occurred in a socially relaxed setting where many of the ordinary social restraints were dismissed. Séances were generally the providence of the upper and middle classes, as opposed to the lecture hall performances of some of the mediums and mesmerists (separate phenomena which attracted mostly working class participants. However, for the upper classes, séances provided a place and an event in which normally unrespectable behavior was deemed appropriate. Lord Amberley recorded in an article entitled "Experiences of Spiritualism" that at one séance, the medium insisted "that the spirits required us [the participants] to sing." Open emotionalism was also encouraged, and Amberley also recorded one such incident, in which typical Victorian sentiment is expressed in the conversation of a "Mrs. G." and her "son's spirit," a conversation that occurred "in an eager tone, with many epithets of endearments, 'my boy,' 'my darling,' etc." "Mrs. G's" almost desperate attempts to communicate with her dead son also reflect the important Victorian tradition of strong family ties. The family unit provided a necessary source of emotional support to the people of the nineteenth century, confronted as they were by a rapidly and continually changing society. The hope that these ties could transcend death was an important component of Victorian attraction to spiritualism.

The elements of singing, emotionalism and the general air of frivolity that characterized many of these séances provided an outlet for the many suppressed emotions and energies that were held back in the tightly restrictive Victorian age. That this behavior occurred in such a semi-public setting as the social gatherings at which séances took place reveals the degree of public acceptance of the spiritualist tactics. What would be normally considered unrespectable activity to Victorians gained its own form of respectability, if only within its spiritualist setting. Furthermore, such behavior must have had some appeal for nonbelievers who recognized the potential in participating in the relaxed atmosphere of the séances and spiritualist gatherings. The mediums themselves encouraged this open behavior, both by direct command (as in Amberley's recollection) or by indirect imitation. Some of the most popular mediums and spiritualist leaders were also some of the most colorful characters of the period, such as Madame Helena Petrovna Blavatsky, who, based on her experiences in Eastern religions rather than mainstream Victorian Evangelicalism, founded the Theosophical Society in 1881. One of Blavatsky's contemporary's records that "her flounces" were often "full of cigarette ashes" and that her "remarks have the air not only of spontaneity and randomness but sometimes of an amusing indiscretion."

Yet the appeal of such atypically Victorian behavior and personalities was not only the direct flaunting of oppressive social constraints, but rather the sense of individualism implied in the spiritualist activities. One can conceive of spiritualist appeal based on the implied individualism in the movement. The spiritualist activities were generally led by "the presence of some human being, whom we should nowadays call a medium." Among the various social tensions operating in the Victorian period, one which greatly affected the spiritualist movement was the tension which occurred between the traditional amateur status of sciences and the increasing professionalism of the post-industrial age. As the era progressed, professionalism gained new status and respectability. In some instances, spiritualism revitalized the nostalgic appeals of the formerly amateur professions; most mediums were considered to be "gifted with intuitive powers of discovering" rather than as possessing indoctrinated skills. The individualistic appeal of the spiritualist movement is reflected in the amateur status of its participants. The very fact that most spiritualistic evidence was found in the "large mass of [personal] testimony that has been accumulated by a great number of amateurs" indicates the interest in nonprofessional individualism. Individualism and the spiritualist movement was also characterized by the large involvement of women, who through the position of mediums (who were mostly female) largely controlled the shaping of the movement, beginning with the Fox sisters and continuing with Madame Blavatsky. Along similar lines as the various reform movements of the late Victorian era, the spiritualist movement provided an arena for women to display their skills as social independence and leadership capabilities.

There were also negative connotations towards the openness of the social behavior of the séances and of the individualism it comprised. Opponents of the spiritualist movement could claim that the frivolity rebelled against normative societal standards and was therefore dangerous to social unity. One article from 1898 warns that there are "many subtle temptations" and "many persuasive influences" in the movement. This writer also ponders the implications involved in the return of a member of a "lower order of beings who have died after a life of vice, ignorance and degradation" with the intention of inciting "deeper evil" in the living. Generally, however, the greatest opposition to séance activity was that it was frivolous, where frivolity was associated with uselessness. Some

Victorians could rationalize that the fun of séances was utilitarian in origin and therefore valuable; that it was a worthy pastime because it had a serious purpose and intent in the attempt to discover irrefutable proof of life after death. Seeking a means of communicating with departed spirits had social and practical value, or so some claimed. Most of the critics contended, however, that these aspects were intellectually trivial and useless. The writer George Eliot described "spirit communications" as appearing to her as "either degrading folly, imbecile in the estimate of evidence, or else as imprudent imposture." Eliot goes on further to attack the mediums that inspired and carried on the movement as "low adventurers" who use "palpable trickeries." In regard to David Dunglas Home, who, along with Madame Blavatsky, is the medium whose name is most known, Eliot states that he was "an objector moral disgust." One writer characterized Home's uselessness in an article in *Fraser* magazine:

He has done no good, he has revealed no new truth, he has added literally nothing to the domain of useful knowledge; for the spirits he has called up have uniformly proved as dull, as prosaic, as ignorant and uninteresting [as he himself]. As with Eliot, this writer obviously found his rational mind offended by the poor showing of concrete evidence by the spiritualists, in addition to their "trivial" attitude toward their spiritual subject. Another article deplored the trivial attitudes of the summoned spirits themselves. The author objected to "that trashy talk which is in so marked a way the vernacular of the spirits" and which he feels implies "the suspicion of their [the spirits] being for the most part idiots." Some advocates of spiritualism took another tactic in defending their belief. By emphasizing the religious aspects they sought to defend spiritualism on the grounds that, for the most part, it was a morally acceptable phenomenon. After all, they argued, what could be more acceptable than establishing proof of the soul's immortality, promised by God? The poet Elizabeth Barrett Browning wrote often of her belief in spiritualism to her brother, and many of these letters remain, despite the censorship tactics of her husband Robert who was very critical of spiritualist phenomena. She described some of the people from whom she received testimonials as "grave, reasoning" and simply "religious" in an effort to emphasize the moral purity of her beliefs. She also defended spiritualism against attacks on its lack of intelligible reasoning, stating that she has "accumulated personal testimony . . . from men & women of good reputation & more than average intelligence" and that she concluded that "according to my reason" there are 11 great wonders on the earth" and that they are knowable through spiritualism. Elizabeth Barrett Browning even criticized those mediums that merely "moved tables again & again" without eliciting the "intelligence which is the common characteristic of the phenomenal." Her belief was in the verbal communication where thought and intelligence could be displayed, and not in the easily fabricated physical phenomena of rapping's and table tilting.

The early stages of the spiritualist movement, in the first decade after the revelations of the Fox sisters, was characterized by "moments" of phenomenal occurrences which were "quite spontaneous, no one demanding or expecting them." As the century progressed, however, there was a widespread demand for spiritualist phenomena and the movement responded by conforming to the general Victorian trend towards professionalism and away from individualism. The later appeal of the movement was based upon phenomena from trained mediums and from the evidence gathered by the various societies that were formed. The spiritualist movement formed its own class of leaders and its own system of training and preparing them, although spiritualism retained its distance from established religious and spiritual institutions. In an era in which traditional religion had been threatened by the rise of new sciences and the theories of a certain Mr. Darwin, Victorians were still searching for a belief system and often turned to spiritualism in an open need for faith. There was an unconscious recognition of the certitude provided by an organized, professional religious institution rather than a random series of phenomena. Coupled with the influx of scientific ideals and methodology to all elements of society, the spiritualist movement became progressively structured as the century neared its close.

The obvious evidence for this aspect of increased professionalization in the movement is found in the formation and existence of a plethora of spiritualist societies, with specific and clearly defined goals, tenets, and intentions in mind. The Society for Psychical Research is probably the most important of the many formed; it was certainly one of the most widely known and the one with the greatest status of respectability. The Society was founded in 1882 by Henry Sidgwick, a professor of moral philosophy at Cambridge, a position which characterized his approach to spiritual studies. The Society for Psychical Research, under Sedgwick's guiding hand, was dedicated to the scientific and analytical evaluation of physical data; using an objective, scrupulous, and rigorous method in examining psychical evidence. The Society had an illustrious membership roster, which undoubtedly aided in establishing its respectability. Honorary members included the poet Tennyson, parliamentarian Gladstone, as well as the active participation of the members of various noble houses. Sidgwick was obviously concerned with the moral implications of spiritual belief-; he envisioned a moral system whereby altruistic behavior among society members would be encouraged by the concrete proof of existence after physical death. There were numerous other societies formed in the latter half of the Victorian period, such as Madame Blavatsky's Theosophical Society, and an earlier American organization, the Society for the Diffusion of Spiritual Knowledge, circa 1854.

Increased professionalism, while adding orthodoxy to the growing movement, also provided ample opportunity for the systematic manipulation of naive advocates. Some opponents of spiritualism did characterize certain aspects of the movement as cynical attempts by charlatans (especially the more popular mediums) to take advantage of any sympathetic audience and as concerned solely with economic rewards. Robert Browning referred to his wife's spiritualist interests and to their cause as "the imaginary, spiritualistic experiences by which the unsuspecting and utterly truthful nature of was abused." Apparently she also occasionally questioned her spiritualist beliefs; she once asked her brother whether or not she was "generally supposed to have a good stock of credulity." Robert Browning would have undoubtedly agreed with George Eliot's description of mediums and spiritualism as the "painful form of the lowest charlatanry." Browning himself went on to lampoon the spiritualism movement in his bitter poem "Mr. Sludge, 'The Medium,'" in which he mocks the profession of medium ship. George Eliot accused spiritualism of having too weak a scientific basis, built on testimonials which are "no truer objectively because they are honest subjectively." Spiritualism for Eliot was a "misguidance of men's minds from the true sources of high and pure emotion."

Some mention has been made of the scientific approach to spiritualism; this, however, deserves careful attention. One of the new sciences that arose in the nineteenth century was that of psychology. Spiritualism, "like most other fields of human knowledge and interest" of the nineteenth century had "also been brought within the domain of science," particularly the new field of psychology. One writer applauded the discovery of the concept of "personality," of a mental being wholly separate from the physical self, and related this as a "scientific proof" of the possibility of the "survival of the human personality after physical death." This same writer concludes that "the popular beliefs really point to a series of interesting facts bearing on the spirit of man" which was "only of late recognized and studied by psychologists." The general principle of spiritualism, that the soul was immortal, was seen to be proven by science, which stated that "matter gravitates and the matter was indestructible." The physical materializations of the mediums remained a mostly philosophical (i.e. metaphysical) controversy; however it sought to incorporate scientific language. Even Sidgwick remained skeptical of ever having absolute scientific proof. He stated that he was "drifting steadily to the conclusion . . . that we have not, and are never likely to have, empirical evidence of the existence of the individual after death." Not all believers wanted scientific proof, one devotee was described as having special "delights in believing anything that puts science to rout and confounds the philosophers," perhaps in another example on the non-conformist elements of the movement.

Spiritualism appealed to various elements of the Victorian upper and middle classes for many reasons.

Spiritualism provided an ' alternative form of spiritual faith and belief, distinct from the established orthodox Christian churches yet relying on traditional Christian spiritual belief in the continued existence of the soul after physical death. Yet spiritualism also coincided with the rise of materialistic empirical sciences. The spiritualist movement of the late Victorian period was characterized by the collection of large bodies of personal testimonials on the physical manifestations of the spirits; they were believed to have tilted tables in parlors, tapped out messages on walls, levitated men and objects, moved chairs, formed ectoplasmic entities, and a host of other "tangible" evidence of spiritual presence on earth. To many Victorians these manifestations appeared to be unquestionable proof of the traditional Christian concept of spiritual life after death. Furthermore, spiritualist activity such as séances provided a milieu in which normally conservative, socially conformist Victorians could display individualistic tendencies and personality traits. Behavior, normally kept tightly in rein by Evangelical and utilitarian tenets of morality, could break free. Intense emotionalism and sentimentality could be openly expressed in spirit communications. In fact, the very desire to communicate at all with the souls of dead relatives and friends, the most commonly sought spirits, reveals a need to express emotions and feelings. It also indicates the importance of familial relationships in Victorian society; that the family unit was so important to the Victorians that they wanted it to transcend even death. Women, in particular, were given greater opportunity at self expression and independence through the movement. Spiritualism also provided a source of expression for the tensions between growing professionalism and the traditional amateurism it supplanted. Critics and advocates alike both reflected upon this unconscious tension, mixing purely spiritual concerns of the soul's immortality with purely scientific concerns of irrefutable empirical data. Spiritualism in late nineteenth century English society had an inherent ability to reflect on a particular, specific level, the general dynamics of the Victorian mentality. Spiritualism straddled Victorian social, religious, and scientific culture like an ectoplasmic colossus guarding the spiritual harbor of society.

Bibliography

Harvey, Charles, Green, Edmund and Corfield, Penelope. The Westminster Historical Database: Voters, Social Structure and Electoral Behaviour. Bristol, 1998.

Merritt, J. F. The Social World of Early Modern Westminster: Abbey, Court and Community, 1525-1640. Manchester, 2005.

Reynolds, Elaine. Before the Bobbies: The Night Watch and Police Reform in Metropolitan London, 1720-1830. London, 1998.

Rogers, Nicholas. Aristocratic Clientage, Trade and Dependency: Popular Politics in Pre-Radical Westminster, *Past and Present* 61 (1973), pp. 70-106.

Shoemaker, Robert B. Prosecution and Punishment: Petty Crime and the Law in London and Rural Middlesex. Cambridge, 1991, chap. 10.

American journalism: history, principles, practices

William David Sloan, Lisa Mullikin Parcell.

Project Britain the Victorians, by Mandy Barrow.

Rainy Nights, Golden Days Snow and Ice. Terry Trainor

The history of a Parish by M Grey

Watford: Introduction', A History of the County of Hertford

Stories of common things third book T Nelson and Sons

The Clapper of the Bird Boy Terry Trainor

The Parish Church of St. Matthew Oxhey. Fr. David Shephard.

Watford: Houses in Church Street, Demolished in 1893

The Railway Gazette, 10 October 1952

L.M.R. Press Section at Euston

Harvey, Charles, Green, Edmund and Corfield, Penelope. The Westminster Historical Database: Voters, Social Structure and Electoral Behaviour. Bristol, 1998.

Merritt, J. F. The Social World of Early Modern Westminster: Abbey, Court and Community, 1525-1640. Manchester, 2005.

Reynolds, Elaine. Before the Bobbies: The Night Watch and Police Reform in Metropolitan London, 1720-1830. London, 1998.

Rogers, Nicholas. Aristocratic Clientage, Trade and Dependency: Popular Politics in Pre-Radical Westminster, *Past and Present* 61 (1973), pp. 70-106.

Shoemaker, Robert B. Prosecution and Punishment: Petty Crime and the Law in London and Rural Middlesex. Cambridge, 1991, chap. 10.

British Railways Magazine, November 1952,

Dr Ralph Harrington, Institute of Railway Studies & Transport History, York

BBC History the rise of the Victorians

Middle Classes: Their Rise and Sprawl by Simon Gunn and Rachel Bell (Phoenix, 2003)

The Lower Middle Class in Britain ed. by Geoffrey Crossick (Croom Helm, 1977)

Dr Loftus a lecturer in history

BBC Editorial Control of BBC Content

I acknowledge that the BBC has absolute editorial control over all BBC Content at all times.

The Public Culture of the Victorian Middle Class

Ritual and Authority in the English Industrial City, 1840-1914 by Simon Gunn, (Manchester University Press, 2000)

Class edited by Patrick Joyce (Oxford University Press, 1995)

The Making of the British Middle Class

Studies of Regional and Cultural Diversity eds. Alan Kidd and David Nicholls, (Sutton, 1998)

Gender, Civic Culture and Consumerism

Middle-Class Identity in Britain, 1800-1940 edited by Alan Kidd and David Nicholls (Manchester University Press, 1999)

The Self Made Man: Businessmen and their Autobiographies in Nineteenth Century Britain by Donna Loftus, (Business Archives, 80, 2000, pp.15-30)

Building European Society

Occupational Change and Social Mobility in Europe, 1840-1940 by Andrew Miles and David Vincent (Manchester University Press, 1993)

Self Help by Samuel Smiles, (1859)

Fulford Roger. "Jubilee London: 19th-20th Century,"

Entries on London, Britanica CD 2.0 Chicago

Encyclopædia Britannica, 1995

Martin, G. H. and Francis, David,

"The Camera's Eye,"in *The Victorian City: Images and Realities*.

H. J. Dyos and Michael Wolff. London and Boston, 1973, I:

Olsen, Donald J. *The Growth of Victorian London* London, 1976

Olsen, Donald J. *The City as a Work of Ar. London, Paris, Vienna*. New Haven and London: Yale University Press, 1986.

Sheppard, Francis. *London, 1808-1870: The Infernal Wen*. London, 1971.

Taylor, Nicholas. "The Awful Sublimity of the Victorian City," in *The Victorian City: Images and Realities*. ed. H. J. Dyos and Michael Wolff. London and Boston, 1973, II:

Rothblatt, Shelton. "Nineteenth-Century London," *People and Communities in the Western World*. ed.

Gene Bruckner. 2 vols. Homewood, Illinois: The Dorsey Press, 1979, II: 159-209.

George R. Sims, Living London, 1902

BBC Online Services are available to you by the British Broadcasting Corporation of Broadcasting House, Portland Place, London, W1A 1AA (the "BBC").

The information for Grim's Dyke is taken, with kind permission from Harrow Local Authority's planning legislation.

The Automobile Association Limited 2011

The Webmaster of Our Ward Family Web Site (Peter Ward)

The Wealdstone train disaster on October 8, 1952 Pictures used by permission of the Borough of Harrow Archives

John Schad, Professor of Modern Literature, University of Lancaster

A Willing Suspension of Disbelief: Victorian Reactions to the Spiritualist Phenomena *by Candace Gregory*

Milton Keynes UK
Ingram Content Group UK Ltd.
UKHW011011020923
427894UK00001B/87